Repurposed Rebels

STUDIES IN SECURITY
AND INTERNATIONAL AFFAIRS

Repurposed Rebels

POSTWAR REBEL NETWORKS
IN LIBERIA

MARIAM BJARNESEN

THE UNIVERSITY OF GEORGIA PRESS
Athens

Portions of chapter 3 appeared previously as "Demobilized or Remobilized?
Lingering Rebel Structures in Post-war Liberia," in *African Conflicts and Informal
Power: Big Men and Networks*, edited by Mats Utas, 101–118 (London: Zed Books,
2012); and portions of chapter 4 appeared previously as "The Winner Takes It All:
Post-war Rebel Networks, Big Man Politics, and the Threat of Violence in the 2011
Liberian Elections," in *Violence in African Elections: Between Democracy and Big
Man Politics*, edited by Mimmi Söderberg Kovacs and Jesper Bjarnesen, 156–175
(London: Zed Books, 2018).

Paperback edition, 2024
© 2020 by the University of Georgia Press
Athens, Georgia 30602
www.ugapress.org
Set in by 10/12.5 Minion Pro Regular by BookComp, Inc.

Most University of Georgia Press titles are
available from popular e-book vendors.

Printed digitally

Library of Congress Cataloging-in-Publication Data

Names: Bjarnesen, Mariam, 1981– author.
Title: Repurposed rebels : postwar rebel networks in Liberia / Mariam Bjarnesen.
Other titles: Studies in security and international affairs.
Description: Athens : The University of Georgia Press, [2020] | Series: Studies in
    security and international affairs | Includes bibliographical references and index.
Identifiers: LCCN 2020004862 | ISBN 9780820357775 (hardback) | ISBN 9780820357782
    (ebook)
Subjects: LCSH: Revolutionaries—Liberia—History—21st century. | Internal
    security—Liberia. | Liberia—History—Civil War, 1999–2003—Peace. | Liberia—
    Politics and government—1980– | Liberia—Social conditions—1980–
Classification: LCC DT636.5 .B55 2020 | DDC 966.6204—dc23
LC record available at https://lccn.loc.gov/2020004862

Paperback ISBN 978-0-8203-6709-5

CONTENTS

ACKNOWLEDGMENTS

There are so many people I am grateful to for both supporting and inspiring my work. But those I wish to thank first are those I cannot mention by name. This book was made possible only by your willingness to share your experiences with me. Thank you for trusting me with your life stories and your hopes and dreams but also with your fears about an uncertain future and sometimes immensely painful memories from times of war. Your life stories are the very foundation of this book. Thank you for entrusting me with them. Even though we have often talked about the struggles in life, we have also laughed a lot together, as you also have showed me the beauty of Liberia, a country I have come to love.

The support and inspiration of devoted colleagues means everything. On that note I wish to express my profound gratitude to Mats Berdal. The research and writing of what later evolved into this book started in London, and I am so very grateful, Mats, for your support, for believing in the project, and for your constructive criticism and patience with me and my work during those years. Another colleague who has always been a great source of inspiration for my research is Mats Utas. Working with you over the years has been such a rewarding and fun experience. Thank you for being there, Mats, both as a colleague and a friend, and for all your wise advice, support, and comments on my texts over the years that now eventually have turned into this very book. I have also greatly benefited from the support of Jan Ångström during this process. Thank you, Jan, for taking time from your busy schedule to read and comment on my drafts and for your sage suggestions for improvements, support, and encouragement. I wish to express a special thanks to my friend and colleague Chris Coulter, for your inspiring research on war and gender, which I have learned a lot from, and for our many long and in-depth discussions on research and fieldwork. I could not have done without them. Furthermore, a special thanks also to David Harris and Sukanya Podder for your guidance and wise suggestions on how to turn this project idea into a book. I am especially grateful to Ilmari Käihkö, for your thorough reading of earlier drafts, your constructive criticism, and your suggestions for improvements. I would also like to thank Mimmi Söderberg Kovacs for excellent comments on an earlier version of the election chapter. The manuscript also benefited greatly from the comments, suggestions, and guidance, on both substance and structure, of the anonymous reviewers. Thank you. During the process of writing this book, I have always felt the warm support and encouragement of colleagues at the Department of Security, Strategy, and Leadership at the Swedish Defence University. For that I'm truly grateful.

There are many people who have been kind and helped me in the field during my research trips over the years, providing everything from contacts to logistical and practical support. I especially wish to thank Hanna Matti, Catarina Fabiansson, and Rukshan Ratnam. Thank you, Rukshan, for hosting me so many times. I hope I have not been too much of a burden. Thank you for being such a good friend to have in Monrovia. Special thanks to Ana Kantor as well, whom I first discovered Liberia with. It is always a pleasure to work and travel with you, Ana. I am so very honored that this book is a part of the Studies in Security and International Affairs series at the University of Georgia Press. Thank you for taking this project on and for believing in it. Thank you also for assigning the excellent Susan Silver as the copyeditor of this book.

Maika and Jonatan, I wish to thank you too, for being part of my life and for just being such wonderful kids. And Jesper Bjarnesen, last but certainly not least, to you I am grateful beyond words for being such an inspiring, knowledgeable, and helpful colleague and, more important, my best friend in life. Thank you for all the hours we have spent discussing the manuscript, for proofreading, and for all your comments and ideas. But most of all, thank you for being there, believing in me, encouraging me, and giving me your never-ending support. I dedicate this book to our beautiful children, Maya, Noah, and Alba.

Mariam Bjarnesen
Stockholm, June 2019

MAIN INFORMANTS

To protect the identities of my informants, I have not used their real names.

Abraham *Based during times of interviews:* Monrovia
Combatant background: NPFL, 1991–1994
Ethnic background: Kpelle
Postwar activities: commander in CDC informal security group
Interviewed: on several occasions in 2013

Alex *Based during times of interviews:* Monrovia
Combatant background: never took part in the war as a combatant
Ethnic background: Krio and Bassa
Postwar activities: vigilante leader in Monrovia; commander in CDC informal security group
Interviewed: on several occasions from 2009 to 2013

Alpha *Based during times of interview:* Bomi County
Combatant background: NPFL, 1990–1997
Ethnic background: Gola
Postwar activities: informal security commander at Guthrie Rubber Plantation / Sime Darby
Interviewed: on several occasions from 2009 to 2012

Jacob *Based during time of interview:* Monrovia
Combatant background: ULIMO, 1991–1993; LPC, 1993–1995; Taylor's presidential guard, 2002–2003
Ethnic background: Krahn
Postwar activities: short-term positions within different private security companies
Interviewed: on several occasions in 2013

Malcolm   *Based during times of interview:* Monrovia
Combatant background: NPFL, 1990–1997; SSU, 1997–1999; ATU, 1999–2003
Ethnic background: Bassa
Postwar activities: commander in CDC informal security group; short-term informal security assignments
Interviewed: on several occasions from 2011 to 2013

Michael   *Based during times of interviews:* Monrovia
Combatant background: AFL, 1992–1993; LPC, 1993–1997; LURD 1999–2003
Ethnic background: Krahn
Postwar activities: commander at Guthrie Rubber Plantation during rebel occupation; senior position in one of the country's security institutions
Interviewed: on several occasions from 2011 to 2013

Simon   *Based during times of interview:* Monrovia
Combatant background: AFL, 1992–1993; ULIMO, 1993–1997; LURD, 1999–2003
Ethnic background: Krahn
Postwar activities: informal security commander at Guthrie Rubber Plantation / Sime Darby
Interviewed: on several occasions from 2009 to 2012

Repurposed Rebels

Liberia

LINGERING HABITS OF WAR

I had assumed he would come alone. We had talked on the phone a few times, but we had never met. Now we had arranged a meeting in central Monrovia. I knew some of his past, though, and I was well aware that nervous rumors about his present activities were swirling. When the war came to an end, Simon, a notorious former rebel general, had taken control of the Guthrie Rubber Plantation.[1] It had been a lucrative business; for three years rebels running the plantation had made a living illegally tapping and selling rubber. But in 2006 the Liberian government resumed control over the plantation, and the rebels left the area. They were said to have been demobilized, and one could assume their networks had been broken. Yet when Simon walked into our meeting that day in mid-October, six years after the war had come to an end, he did not come alone. The ex–rebel general came accompanied by those he called his "boys," a couple of ex-combatants who still addressed him as their commander and who still respected his authority, men Simon wanted around for his personal security. Perhaps there was some truth to that. Perhaps it was a show of force or a useful tool for intimidation, as he was now moving around the plantation area again. If wartime links had been abandoned, rebel identities put aside, and ex-combatants demobilized, it was hard to tell from Simon's entrance. War was long over, but Simon's postwar rebel network appeared far from broken.

On August 18, 2003, the war in Liberia officially came to an end. It had been a devastating war, and the Liberian people and the state had suffered tremendously from the violence and the destruction it had brought. Two civil wars (1989–1996 and 1999–2003) had tormented the small West African nation, and fourteen broken peace agreements had preceded the comprehensive one the warring parties finally signed in 2003, which was to end years of brutal fighting.[2] But the hardship for the Liberian people was far from over. The war-torn republic now stood before immense challenges. The fragile state was to be rebuilt and security established, not the least to avoid the impending danger of a return to war.

Liberia, with major assistance and funding from the international community, has since then undergone a disarmament, demobilization, rehabilitation, and reintegration (DDRR) process of ex-combatants to restore peace and stability, as well as a security-sector reform in attempt to reform the state security institutions, including the institution of the Liberian National Police and the Armed Forces of Liberia.[3] In July 2009, almost six years after the war ended, President Ellen Johnson Sirleaf announced the formal closure of Liberia's DDRR program, noting that the success of the program was a testimony to the return of peace and security.[4] But the road from war and violence to peace and stability is never an easy one. As Paul Richards reminds us, turning back toward peace is difficult, even beyond a peace agreement. It is a rocky path with many pitfalls, where the hidden or silent violence behind conflict has to be addressed if peace is to be sustained.[5] Or, as Carolyn Nordstrom rightly points out, "The habits of war die hard. They can carry beyond the front lines and into the fragile pulse of peace." Peace accords do not hinder the fact that aspects of war can continue to affect the daily life of a society until those elements are dismantled, habit by habit. But as Nordstrom emphasizes, such work is never easy, as aspects of war, such as power, profit, and militarized control, can offer irresistible rewards for some.[6]

In such a light it is, despite the reassuring words of the Liberian president, not surprising that a closer look at the postwar security situation of the country would reveal that insecurity still prevailed in Liberia nearly a decade after the war's official end. Despite efforts to destroy the structures of war, former rebel networks and chains of command remained or had remobilized for new purposes many years after the peace agreement had been signed. The complexity of what could be seen as potential postwar transformation is at the center of this book. The underlying purpose of this study is to examine how and why rebel networks remained relevant and continued to affect the security and political situation in the country after the war. Simon's story and that of his network, along with the stories of other individuals in influential positions in postwar rebel networks, shed light on the dynamics between former combatants, the elite, their communities, and the overall environment of fragile security in which they were active.

The Relevance of Postwar Rebel Networks

To dismantle rebel structures (if they are not turned into political parties, for example) is one of the most important aspects of the transition from war to peace. Combatants are expected not only to lay down their weapons but also to abandon their wartime networks. The general view is that removing ex-combatants from their former fighting units strengthens postconflict security and reduces the risk of renewed warfare. As these networks were once capable of creating chaos and conflict, it is naturally assumed that, if not disbanded, they would remain an acute threat to security and stability.[7] Yet peace agreements and subsequent disarmament, demobilization, and reintegration (DDR) processes do not automatically, or necessarily, destroy rebel networks.[8] In Liberia such structures lingered, and networks of ex-combatants were still active long after the war.

Nevertheless, once a war ends it is natural to assume that rebel networks would no longer be relevant, as their purpose, to conduct warfare against the ruling regime, is no longer relevant. Yet what if there is a logic behind staying mobilized beyond waging war? What if there are incentives, not only for the ex-combatants themselves but also for actors within the elite or among ordinary citizens, to have these networks preserved rather than destroyed, even in a time of peace? What if there is a rationale behind keeping former rebel structures mobilized rather than demobilized, though now activated for purposes other than warfare? If that is the case—that several actors within postwar societies, contrary to the general assumption, do not see the demobilization of former rebel networks as the most optimal solution after a war—would this not force us to rethink the actual chances of success for efforts aimed at destroying such networks? It is with such questions in mind that this book sets out to explore the Liberian case of postwar rebel structures.

Although the overarching argument of the book may be to challenge some mainstream approaches to postwar demobilization, it would be virtually impossible to talk about the end of a civil war and the ensuing situation for the ex-combatants without touching on the issue of DDR, since it is now internationally considered an essential element to postwar peace building and reconstruction. The literature on the challenges of the DDR process, with particular focus on the reintegration of ex-combatants into civilian life, has also provided us with valuable insights into the complexity of such undertakings.[9] DDR is today commonplace in United Nations peacekeeping and other peace operations with the intent to establish long-term peace in countries coming out of war.[10] Yet, despite its almost mandatory usage, the process has never been without problems. The DDR process, especially in the area of social and economic reintegration of former combatants, seldom produces the desired outcomes. In fact, very few DDR programs actually aim to achieve a sustainable reintegration of ex-combatants; instead, focus has been on peace and stabilization in the short term.[11]

The difficulties encountered in creating a stable and secure postwar environment where the former combatants become integrated parts of civil society have also been emphasized. Kathleen Jennings, for example, was among those who early on, with reference to the DDR process in the Liberian case specifically, asked the important question of "reintegration into what?" to shift the focus from individual combatants to the broader social context. The question points to the need to ask what reintegration actually means in a society such as the Liberian one, where it is commonly said that "everybody fought," highlighting whether a reasonably cohesive and functional society existed into which reintegration could occur in the first place.[12] Since then the concept of reintegration in itself also has been further problematized. Richard Bowd and Alpaslan Özerdem have, for instance, pointed out that the DDR process often focuses too squarely on economic reintegration of ex-combatants, leaving a process of much-needed social reintegration behind. Reintegration tends to be measured according to quantitative indicators such as the level of employment or enrollment in training courses. Such approaches neglect issues that are measurable only through qualitative indicators, for example, the need to address ex-combatants' societal relations and issues of the lack of trust between ex-combatants and receiving communities.[13]

Hence much of the literature on postwar ex-combatants has been focused on analyzing and critiquing DDR practice. And if the DDR process continues to be the preferred international approach for strengthening postwar countries, continued critique and nuanced analysis of such practices are absolutely necessary. The research herein acknowledges the complexity attached to such processes, yet it has a different point of departure. In contrast to the bulk of the literature on ex-combatants, I do not focus on the practice of DDR and related reintegration initiatives as such. Instead, I suggest that lingering rebel structures may in fact have less to do with how the DDR process has been carried out than is generally recognized. The practice of DDR, good or bad, may accordingly have little to do with the relevance of postwar rebel networks. The focus of this book is instead on whether there exists a *need* for postwar rebel networks in Liberia today, in particular in the security arena, a need that in this case would make DDR initiatives, no matter how well they are carried out, less relevant than is often assumed.

Leaving the challenges of the reintegration of ex-combatants as part of the overall DDR process aside for now, the broader question of transformation and adaption is more central to the understanding of the ex-combatants examined here.[14] Attention is thereby given to former rebels who, rather than being reintegrated or faced with a failed reintegration process, formed new informal constellations, keeping significant parts of their organizational structures from the war intact. I examine former rebel soldiers' ability to transform and adapt in the aftermath of war to a new but often still-fragile postwar setting. What I am interested in more specifically is to investigate how this can be done in the form of security- (or even insecurity-) providing networks. At the same time I also analyze how organizational structures and skills acquired by the rebels during the wars are not only useful for the ex-combatants themselves but of strategic relevance for a range of actors in peacetime. Such a point of departure leads us to the underlying question of why a need for such networks does in fact exist. This analysis is based on original interview material, mainly with ex-combatants, obtained during my fieldwork in Liberia between 2009 and 2013.

Rebel Transformation and the Informal Reality

To understand how and why rebel networks do not simply vanish in the transition from war to peace, despite postconflict initiatives such as the DDR process, several different aspects of the contemporary postwar situation in Liberia must be considered. To start we need to be aware of the possibility that even though peace agreements have been signed, political arrangements have been agreed on, warring parties have laid down their weapons, and the people have called for peace, the destruction of rebel networks may not be what all concerned actors actually want. In other words, even if the struggle for peace and stability is the common goal for a majority of the involved parties, the dissolution of rebel networks may not be perceived as the most desired way to get there. Therefore, we may need to start by acknowledging hidden or explicit motives of concerned actors, in addition to the ex-combatants themselves, such as the Liberian political or economic elite, formal security institutions, or ordinary Liberian citizens, for why they might wish networks of former combatants to stay connected and active.

Furthermore, to understand why rebel networks can, *and do*, reappear specifically in the shape of informal security networks after wars, the often-neglected informal security context first of all needs to be understood and put into focus. Accordingly, the examples are numerous of how formal security institutions have proven unable, or even unwilling, to provide their citizens with basic security in contemporary Africa. Mistrust in these formal institutions and authorities have made people turn to alternative solutions to cope with their everyday lives and safeguard their basic human security—a situation that also applies to Liberia. The political situation in Liberia, with weak formal security institutions with low capacity and a history of predatory behavior, has created an environment where informal initiatives for security and protection are called on. In such an environment informal security groups have a natural platform. It is under such circumstances that rebel networks, instead of vanishing, can transform to adapt to a life beyond war.

In his research on postwar West African militia networks, William Reno concludes that very weak state administrations have left leaders of wartime rebel factions with considerable space to maneuver their organizational and personal skills and connections from fighting to peacetime pursuits. Reno shows how wartime fighting units can reemerge as commercial organizations or community-based NGOs for example, which demonstrate the ex-fighters' and their leaders' adaptive capacity to survive the end of war and to find new positions by turning wartime bonds to commercial advantage.[15]

Based on my interviews and findings from fieldwork in Liberia, I illustrate how networks consisting predominately of former rebel soldiers are organized and operate in the informal security arena and describe the rationale behind these lingering, but transformed, features of war. By doing so I intend to give further examples of how the adaptive capacity of former rebel soldiers, which Reno refers to, is utilized by various Liberian actors. I show why and how remobilization, or maintenance, of repurposed rebel networks could be consistent with the combined interests of former rebels, key influential actors within the Liberian elite, and formal state institutions, as well as ordinary Liberian citizens, whether this be for political, economic, social, or security reasons. In the next sections of this chapter I also in more detail provide for the definitions and scope of key concepts needed for analyzing postwar rebel transformation in Liberia.

POSTWAR REBEL NETWORKS

This book does not examine the situation of Liberia's ex-combatants in general. The civil wars left Liberia with many men and women who fall within this category, and they are in no sense a homogenous group. They have faced a range of different postwar experiences, depending on factors such as gender, age, family situation, and period spent as a rebel soldier. Such considerations have increasingly been researched and discussed, particularly in relation to the evolvement of DDR practice. For instance, James Pugel's survey study of 590 Liberian ex-combatants with particular focus on the DDRR program's impact on reintegration offers an overarching analysis of Liberian ex-combatants of different prewar backgrounds and war and postwar experiences.[16] I have chosen to focus more specifically on a distinct category of ex-combatants. Here I am interested in ex-combatants for whom the networks established among them and their fellow combatants during the war remain important. I am interested in former rebel soldiers who have actively maintained their links to one another in an organized but not formalized manner. The former combatants examined here have done so not only by keeping in contact but also by relying on one another, and in particular on their former commanders, in the hope of securing a living while using their organizational structures and skills acquired as rebels. I refer to these structures as *postwar rebel networks*.

Furthermore, the decision to focus on this specific category of ex-combatants, instead of the ex-combatant population in Liberia as a whole, is simply because these are the ones we fear most. Organized ex-combatants are believed to be willing to mobilize for renewed violence or even warfare. It is therefore of vital importance that these structures, and their dynamics and reasons for existing, are analyzed and better understood. The subsequent case studies illustrate the mutual dependence that exists between former rebels and former commanders within such networks and why these structures have become important to the individuals attached to them. The case studies explore an "ex-combatant identity," which the individuals within these networks have chosen to, or have felt forced to, preserve, one that other ex-combatants, not attached to postwar rebel networks, may have chosen, or managed, to escape.

I use the term *postwar rebel* networks rather than *ex-combatant* networks, simply because most of the ex-combatants within the structures I have followed have a past as rebel soldiers. Some informants have, during periods of the war, also been army soldiers, though none of them have a purely military background. The term *rebel* may in some contexts be considered controversial, since it can carry a normative negative connotation. Armed groups may want to distance themselves from the term, arguing that they are not opposing a legitimate and functioning government. But in this case the status of the armed opposing groups as rebels has not been specifically contested, neither publicly in Liberia nor by my informants.[17]

As background for analyzing postwar rebel networks, a discussion on the wider concept of *informal networks* and their use in Liberia is required. As a definition I borrow Kate Meagher's description of social networks, in her analysis of African informal economies, as "informally organised arrangements based on social ties." As Meagher notes, a focus on networks allows for an examination of the capacity of social forces to provide a flexible regulatory framework embedded in popular relations of solidarity and trust. Meagher further points out that more insecure economic actors in African societies tend to diversify their social networks in the hope of maximizing access to assistance. This involves the maintenance of existing kinship and community networks, as well as the formation of new networks by joining associations, credit societies, religious groups, and social clubs.[18] In this book the networks examined are understood as constellations individuals are drawn to out of security concerns, whether these are economic, physical, or social security concerns. As Ilda Lourenco-Lindell, in her analysis of informal livelihoods and social networks from an urban West African perspective, has pointed out, the building of networks evolves around daily survival. In African urban settings, daily survival builds extensively on networks of personal relationships through which the poor get access to a living space, a plot to cultivate, credit, and other forms of vital assistance. In difficult environments of constant insufficiency and uncertainty, other kinds of entitlements need to be activated.

Links with others are established to deal with crises, and in this process people generate expectations between one another, develop claims, and create rules to govern relations and behavior.[19]

Accordingly, individuals in all societies and contexts are in need of networks, but, in more challenging environments, the need for such informal arrangements is even greater. People can be tied together by kinship, friendship, ethnicity, gender, geography, shared past experiences, present common daily challenges, and much more. The informal nature of these networks simply implies that they are not formally registered and documented constellations. Instead, they provide flexible frameworks for their individuals, yet not without expectations or even informal rules on how to behave and relate to one another. An important delimitation of the present study is the focus on the postwar rebel networks, which for a Liberian ex-combatant can be one of many informal networks they rely on for economic, physical, or social security concerns.

ETHNICITY IN POSTWAR REBEL NETWORKS

Individuals form informal networks on the basis of a variety of factors. Ethnicity can glue people together and create a collective identification. Yet, when it comes to Africa, and maybe African wars in particular, there is a tendency to overemphasize ethnicity, often at the expense of other important factors, when looking to understand how people are organized. Ethnicity is at risk of being the only thing we see, either when looking at root causes for conflict or when mapping networks people rely on. It might therefore be relevant to specifically bring out the question of ethnicity when discussing different common identities that can bring an informal network together. For example, as pointed out by Einar Braathen, Morten Bøås, and Gjermund Sæther, ethnicity does play a role in most sub-Saharan African conflicts, in the sense that ethnic affiliation often structures the composition of groups in conflict. Still, they point out, it is too simplistic to characterize wars in Africa as tribal. A focus on politics and economics reveals how struggles for power and resources at marginal sites are turned into ethnic conflicts. Conflicting groups and armed factions must be understood in the light of the socioeconomic context in which they operate, and within this context ethnicity is only one among many variables.[20]

In Liberia, ethnicity has played an important role in different ways. Liberians have been oppressed, or been given advantages, along ethnic lines since the very foundation of the Liberian state. During the wars the ethnic divisions were also reflected in the mobilization of armed factions. This of course has had an effect on postwar rebel networks, as these structures reflect the organization arrangements during the wars, and thereby similar ethnic divisions. Yet ethnic identity is but one of people's identifications. Being an ex-combatant may be another. Within postwar rebel networks, individuals have organized themselves around the latter identification. This does not mean that other identities, or other informal networks glued together by other factors of common identification, are unimportant. Different identities do not necessarily compete with one another; they simply might be of different significance depending on the specific context an individual is positioned within at a specific moment. Accordingly, the focus for this study is on the ex-combatant identity within postwar rebel networks, before other shared identities, such as ethnicity.

INFORMAL SECURITY GROUPS

Another important delimitation of the research here is that the focus is not on postwar rebel networks as such, as these constellations could in theory be involved in a variety of activities, as seen, for instance, in Reno's research, previously discussed. Of special interest for this book are postwar rebel networks that have reemerged as *informal security groups*, because of either their ability to act as security providers or their violent potential. From an analytical perspective, a postwar rebel network is thereby an overarching constellation of ex-combatants who have preserved or established links to one another in a patron-client manner, based on wartime structures. The informal security groups examined here are smaller constellations that have emerged within these networks, mobilized for a specific task or during a specific event.

It has not been my purpose to map out the size of these networks by concluding the exact number of ex-combatants attached to them. Currently, there are no studies identifying how many postwar rebel networks exist, or the number of ex-combatants within them, active in contemporary Liberia or during the immediate years following the end of the war. A natural explanation for this is that these networks are not static entities that would be mapped easily. But in addition to postwar rebel networks within the informal security sector and the illegal rubber industry, we do know that such networks have been involved in the exploitation of the country's diamond, timber, and gold resources.[21] But this is rather a qualitative piece of research, whereas I am interested in how these structures function and in the mechanisms and dynamics that tie the ex-combatants together. In the following case studies, however, we discover that postwar rebel networks can be of substantial size. In chapter 3 we find that as many as an estimated five thousand ex-combatants from such a network initially controlled Guthrie Rubber Plantation in 2006. Even if such a large number of organized ex-combatants in informal security groups is an exception, this example illustrates the ability of such networks to generate large groups when the opportunity is given, as they are not formalized static groups but fluid and flexible constellations that continuously change in size and composition.

Not all the individuals active in these groups are ex-combatants. Although the groups I focus on are composed mainly of ex-combatants, it is also interesting to analyze why these networks also attract those who are not ex-combatants, despite the stigma often attached to the "ex-combatant identity." Furthermore, the members of the different informal security groups in focus here are not divided on the basis of former rebel movements. As Danny Hoffman has demonstrated, in Liberia, as in so many other contexts, the factionalism that divided the combatants during the war made little difference to them in the postwar period.[22] As my case studies show, ex-combatants from opposing rebel groups now sometimes live and work together, having in common only their ex-combatant identity regardless of former affiliations.

FORMER COMMANDERS AS POINTS OF ENTRY

In which way, then, are former rebel networks and chains of command important for the emerging informal security groups in postwar Liberia? The roles and positions of former commanders within these emerging groups are an important factor for understanding such constellations. Within each group presented here, I focus on a couple of key former rebel generals who either have the roles as leaders of these informal security groups or possess other influential positions. It is around them that the informal security groups are built. Many of their followers are ex-combatants they commanded during the wars. With the former rebel generals as key nodes in these groups, chains of command can be maintained and reused in the overall postwar rebel networks, and ex-combatants from different factions, or even noncombatants, can easily merge with them. But having been a successful commander during the war does not automatically transform an ex-combatant into a successful leader or mobilizer of a postwar rebel network. Only those who have simultaneously been able to preserve or establish connections to the elite as well as lower-rank ex-combatants have managed to do so.

I follow a few key individuals in postwar rebel networks during specific events or situations. Through their stories we see their networks mobilized as "recycled" rebels in times of regional wars and crisis and as informal security providers for economic motives or political purposes after the war. But we also meet them when there is no specific event that an informal security group could be mobilized for, to fully examine the relevance of postwar rebel networks and ex-combatant identity in contemporary Liberia. The focus on individuals, and former commanders in particular, within these networks is of special importance for my work. I could have chosen a different approach and a different point of entry in search for the relevance of postwar rebel networks. Instead of going into depth with individual trajectories, letting their stories of interactions and mobility after the war illustrate postwar rebel networks, I could, for example, have aimed at mapping the groups from a quantitative approach. One of the reasons for not doing so is because the groups emerging from these networks simply are not static in their nature. Instead, their constitution may change over time or depending on the task they are to execute, which reveals the range of activities groups of ex-combatants can be involved in when it comes to informal security provision. Yet former rebel commanders in particular remain central, and often constant, characters in these networks, which is why special attention is given to such individuals.

As these case studies show, these groups did not only reemerge once after the war for a single purpose and task. These groups constantly adapt, by taking on new tasks and changing their purpose, depending on the current security political situation in Liberia and the motives of actors within the Liberian elite looking to use their services. The case studies show how the leaders within postwar rebel networks (often, but not always, former rebel commanders) can navigate among the elite and individual influential actors to find new roles and tasks for ex-combatants and informal security groups emerging from their networks, highlighting their adaptive capacity. For example, I present postwar rebel networks involved in the provision of local informal security for individuals and communities (such as vigilantism), while showing how members of the same network, owing to the connections of their leader, later could reemerge as informal security providers during the 2011 elections. The case studies show how postwar rebel networks have been involved in informal security provision because of political or commercial interests, but also how they are maintained for social reasons. I suggest that moving from perpetrators to protectors, no matter how contradictory it may sound, might often be a natural progression for ex-combatants, given the opportunity.

Methodological Approach

This book relies on empirical material from fieldwork in Liberia, concentrated mainly in the capital, Monrovia, in Montserrado County and the area and villages around the rubber plantation in Bomi and Grand Cape Mount Counties. Fieldwork for this qualitative analysis was conducted at different periods, normally of one to two months at a time between 2009 and 2013, with a focus on different types of informal security groups that relied mainly on former rebel structures. The most important contribution to this material is original data consisting of in-depth and unstructured interviews that I carried out with Liberian ex-combatants, but the analysis also draws on interviews and private discussions I had with other Liberians without a combatant past, United Nations and humanitarian workers in the country, and more general field observations. In this section I present the empirical material in more detail as well as the research design by discussing the selection of specific case studies and by introducing the main narrators, as well as the methodological challenges that may come with such a fieldwork-based research approach.

CONDUCTING ETHNOGRAPHIC RESEARCH
IN A POSTWAR ENVIRONMENT

As an outsider and observer of the postwar reality in Liberia, being in the field is the most important aspect of my research. Spending time with ex-combatants that have made use of their rebel past in new informal security constellations, discussing their views on security and insecurity and everyday life and work, and hearing their thoughts on their wartime past and hopes and dreams about the future have been the very essence of my fieldwork and the foundation for writing this book. To gain an understanding of the dynamics of the informal security groups emerging from postwar rebel networks I have observed how these individuals and groups are organized; their interaction with key Liberian elite political members and other influential actors; and formal security institutions and ordinary citizens and their strategies, aims, and methods. But researching actors and networks operating in the informal arena is not as straightforward as, for instance, analyzing formal security institutions. These networks and their links to the official state are often kept hidden. Former rebel commanders may still have influence over networks of ex-combatants, and to gain access to these networks through those former commanders may be of strategic importance for the Liberian elite for different reasons. Still, to be seen as encouraging or contributing to the maintenance of wartime structures would not be viewed in a favorable light, especially not in the eyes of the international community, which is spending considerable resources on the DDRR process with an eye to breaking up such structures.[23] Most interactions between key actors within the official state apparatus or Liberian elite and former rebel soldiers or informal security networks would, therefore, take place only in the shadows. Accordingly, studying postwar rebel structures and informal security networks is not something that can be done from afar. Fieldwork and interaction with these actors has been an absolute necessity for me to grasp and capture some of the dynamics of power at play in the informal arena.

While it is not hard to see the value of, and also need for, ethnographic fieldwork when studying ex-combatants and informal security structures, it first of all begs the question of how it is then possible to gain access to these postwar rebel networks. And, yes, there are several potential problems with the qualitative field-research approach I have used in this regard. I am an outsider, a European researcher who, despite partly having a West African background, grew up far from the reality of my informants. I have not experienced war, violence, basic insecurity, and extreme poverty, and I have no firsthand experience of the challenges and struggle for survival that my informants have faced both during and in the aftermath of war. Nevertheless, I am trying to understand and make sense of the postwar reality that my informants are experiencing; I am trying to understand by listening and observing. But such a methodological approach is possible only if my informants are willing to share their experiences with me, despite the fact that I am an outsider.

Ethnographers of war and violence need to be aware of the role rumors play in periods of extreme uncertainty and insecurity. As other sources of information are often not accessible, rumors help people make sense of situations. For similar reasons and in the same manner, rumors can also arise about researchers, Lee Ann Fujii points out. Affected herself during fieldwork in Rwanda, Fujii noted how rumors illustrate the extent to which field research is a two-way street. Not only are the researchers studying their informants; the informants, in turn, are studying them back to figure out whether they could be a potential threat and to establish whose interests researchers really are representing. As Fujii points out, such assessments are critical in violent and fragile settings. Rumors can reveal the source of people's fears about what is at stake if they talk to researchers, and if they believe that researchers are in any way a threat to them, they will be less than forthright in interviews. If people eventually come to believe that researchers are who they say they are, Fujii argues, people are less likely to be distrustful and will have fewer reasons to lie.[24] To avoid rumors that may lead to fears and feelings of uncertainty of me as a researcher among my informants, a vital strategy of mine when conducting field research has always been to be honest and open. My informants need to know who I am, where I come from and work, for which audience I write and publish, what my research is about, and what I intend to do with stories they share with me. My informants should be fully aware of the work I do to decide whether they want to participate or not. I was always careful to ensure that I had my informants' informed consent before conducting any interviews. Such an approach is also vital for security concerns, mainly for my informants, but also for myself.

Having a combatant past can be a sensitive issue in many contexts, a past that many might want to keep a secret because of the risk of stigmatization. This has, however, not been the case with my informants. None of them hide their past as rebels from family, friends, or their communities, despite the risk of stigmatization. Yet, as has been pointed out by Elisabeth Wood, among others, it is important to implement a "do no harm" ethic when conducting empirical research, especially in conflict zones, because of political polarization, the presence of armed actors, the precarious security of most residents, the general unpredictability of events, and the traumatization, from violence, of combatants and civilians alike.[25] I believe that such an approach is vital even in postconflict zones. Besides ensuring that my informants did not run any risks by talking to me as well as making sure that they made their own informed decision to be interviewed, I have therefore chosen to keep the identities of my informants hidden by using pseudonyms instead of their real names or rebel names, to further ensure that I would not in any way put them in danger from my research.

LETTING THOSE WHO ARE STUDIED LEAD THE WAY

As the Liberian war finally came to an end in 2003, more than one hundred thousand combatants were disarmed in the subsequent DDRR process. With such a significant part of the population falling within the category of ex-combatants, Liberia became a very interesting case to study when it comes to postwar rebel networks. But not all Liberians who could be categorized as ex-combatants are studied in this book. My intention is not to construct a representative sample of all Liberian ex-combatants. The main reason for this is that ex-combatants with preserved links to one another are often perceived as one of the most immediate threats to postwar peace and stability. The actual and potential consequences of such lingering wartime structures should therefore be studied carefully.

An important choice for the research here has been to conduct in-depth, unstructured interviews and to present ex-combatant narratives from key informants in more detail than a more quantitative approach would have allowed. My informants' life stories have thereby driven the research in some-times unexpected ways, as their ex-combatant identity has both caused them problems and given them opportunities over the years I have followed them. I have designed my research from the conviction that valuable information can come out of letting in-depth and unstructured interviews open up for the informants' life trajectories to orient the research. The dynamics of the postrebel networks and the opportunities given to them have also directed my selection of case studies. The illegal rebel occupation of Guthrie Rubber Plan-tation, for example, later led to the same network's mobilization for the 2011 elections. Another network's organized activities as vigilantes gave them the opportunity to function as informal security providers in the same elections. The chosen approach has thereby allowed me to follow these networks as op-portunities rose owing to their ex-combatant identity. This provides a unique insight into the postwar realities, including the opportunities and challenges, ex-combatants may face over time.

PRESENTING THE NARRATORS

For this book I have chosen to present seven of my main informants more closely by using parts of their life stories from before, during, and after the war to better understand the networks these individuals are attached to and the postwar reality they operate in. Through interviews and informal conversations, while seeking shade from the hot sun in busy street corners of urban Monrovia, while having lunch together in my informants' neighborhoods, while visiting their homes and meeting their families, or while walking along as they were going about their daily business, I have collected their stories. My notes, transcripts, and observations are what I have used to tell these stories. I have done my best to capture their experiences of life before, during, and after war, as I have tried to understand aspects of the Liberian war and aftermath from their perspective. Yet I have been the one to ask the questions. I have been the one to choose what aspects to present, what not to present, what to emphasize, and what to conclude from the stories they have told me. Ultimately, I have been the one to analyze and interpret their stories in relation to a larger theoretical context. As researchers, we know that this is our job, and we do our best to render the stories of our informants. Still, we need to be aware of the effect of our own involvement. To render and interpret another person's story is a huge responsibility that involves many challenges. It can never be done in an objective way. I have tried to tell my informants' stories as they were given to me. But we all have subjective starting points, and my own personal background and experiences in life of course affect the research I do and how I interpret what I see and hear. Still, despite the challenges of telling the stories of others I believe that it is important to do so. These retold stories can never capture all aspects of my informants' experiences, nor do they represent all Liberian ex-combatants' experiences of war and its aftermath. Nonetheless, I do believe that they contribute to a broader understanding of the experience of the Liberian war and postwar reality for my informants and their networks.

All but one of my informants whom I have chosen to present more closely in this book has a past as a rebel soldier during the Liberian civil wars. The man I refer to as "Alex" (in chapter 4) never took active part as a combatant during the years of war.[26] Still, Alex, as a former vigilante leader, managed to establish himself after the war in the same way as other former rebel commanders within a network of ex-combatants mobilized for informal security assignments. Alex thereby is an important example of how a person without a combatant past in some instances may find it beneficial to attach himself to a postwar rebel network.

Four of my seven main informants have also been soldiers representing the official government during periods of their lives as combatants. This illustrates how the shifting power balance during the course of wars could easily transform a soldier into a rebel and vice versa. "Michael" and "Simon" (whom we meet for the first time in chapter 2) started their combatant paths as soldiers by joining the Armed Forces of Liberia in 1992, mainly to find protection against Charles Taylor's rebel forces.[27] They later became rebels, with Michael joining the rebel group Liberian Peace Council in 1993, while Simon and "Jacob" (chapter 2) chose to join the other main rebel group at the time, the United Liberation Movement of Liberia.[28] Both Michael and Simon came to support the rebel movement Liberians United for Reconciliation and Democracy during the second Liberian civil war, from 1999 onward, Simon as an active combatant and Michael as a recruiter mobilizing for the new rebellion. Jacob was forced to change sides in 2002 and was given official status as a commander, this time during Taylor's presidency. "Malcolm's" (chapter 5) transformation, on the other hand, was the opposite of Michael's and Simon's initial one, as he instead started out as a rebel in 1990 by joining Charles Taylor's National Patriotic Front of Liberia.[29] But following Taylor's election victory in 1997, Malcolm, like many other rebels on Taylor's side, was transferred from Taylor's rebel forces to the new official security unit, the Special Security Unit, after completing six months of training. After an additional training period of nine months, Malcolm came to join Taylor's notorious paramilitary force, the Anti-Terrorist Unit, in 1999. The informant referred to as "Alpha" (chapter 3) never went through the rebel or soldier transformation of the other four men.[30] Alpha instead joined Taylor's forces in 1990 and remained loyal until Taylor took power in 1997. After that Alpha was installed by the Taylor regime as a security commander at the Guthrie Rubber Plantation. In 2003 Alpha went into exile in Ghana as Liberians United for Reconciliation and Democracy forces took over the plantation. "Abraham" (chapter 5), like Alpha, also has a past only as a rebel during his time as a combatant.[31] Abraham joined the National Patriotic Front of Liberia in 1991 and remained with them until 1994. During the second war Abraham, however, never took active part as a combatant.

By following the trajectories of these seven informants with different backgrounds, affiliations during the war, and ways of using their ex-combatant identity today, we see what a life as a Liberian ex-combatant attached to a postwar rebel network can look like. Among my informants there is a variation in background, while all of them are linked to the same or similar postwar structures. For instance, my informants come from opposing sides of the conflicts; altogether they represent four different rebel groups as well as the prewar official forces and those during Taylor's time as a president, but what they now all share is their ex-combatant status (except for Alex) and their attachment to a postwar rebel network, mobilizing for informal security assignments. None of my informants hide their rebel past, and they have all in different ways, with varying degrees of success, made use of their ex-combatant identity. This identity has been a heavier burden for some than for others.

Even in postwar times these informants represented different sides, but then of a purely political conflict. While three of my informants (Michael, Simon, and Alpha) were mobilized as part of a postwar rebel network in different ways to support the incumbent president Ellen Johnson Sirleaf during the 2011 Liberian elections (see chapter 5), three of the remaining seven (Alex, Malcolm, and Abraham) were mobilized in similar ways for the main opposition candidate, Winston Tubman. Here only one side could come out victorious, leaving the ones within the postwar rebel network of the winning candidate Ellen Johnson Sirleaf with clear benefits attached to their ex-combatant status. The losers mobilized for Tubman instead had to face how their ex-combatant identity was made an even heavier burden. Accordingly, by following these specific informants we see examples of when an ex-combatant identity can be both beneficial and burdensome. Among my informants there is a significant difference in how well these men have managed to use their ex-combatant status to find employment and an accepted social position. This makes them interesting from a methodological perspective, as we can compare how, for example, different choices, skills, and political connections make ex-combatants attached to postwar rebel networks more or less successful.

Among my six informants with a combatant past, as many as five have been rebel commanders for periods during the wars. This has been a strategic methodological choice for this study. I have chosen to focus mainly on commanders because of their special position in relation to postwar rebel networks. Former rebel commanders may have the advantage of having secured important connections both to elite actors and foot soldiers during times of war that can prove useful afterward. A different approach, based on ex-combatant narratives from the perspective of mainly foot soldiers, would of course also provide us with valuable information on ex-combatants within postwar rebel networks. Yet I wanted to capture the unique positions former commanders can have within these networks, both as gatekeepers to, and mobilizers of, such networks and the special dynamics generated from these actors. By focusing on their stories specifically we have a better chance of understanding what postwar rebel networks look like, how they function, and how actors at different societal levels benefit.

All of my main informants are men. Considering the fact that many combatants during the war were women and girls, this might seem odd. But among the postwar rebel networks I have conducted research on, very few women have been visible. I discuss in more detail why this is so and what this could be an indicator of in chapter 6.

FURTHER ETHICAL CONSIDERATIONS AND SECURITY CONCERNS

The issue of trust has been crucial for my interactions with my informants. My informants need to at least know that no harm will come to them from talking to me. But feeling comfortable with talking about sensitive issues or not feeling intimidated by the researcher or the process of being interviewed are often not enough. Deeper trust may also need to be established. Julie Norman discusses the concept of trust while doing research in conflict zones. She finds that emotional and relational trust often are important in carrying out narrative research. Formal paperwork and explanations of research design may in some contexts turn participants skeptical. Slowly building relational trust or having someone vouching for the researcher instead can be preferable. Norman also finds that stories often are told gradually, over multiple meetings, as the researcher spends time in the informants' communities while establishing personal relationships with them.[32] Over the years many of my informants had gotten to know me, and I believe that they therefore found it easier to trust me, allowing me an insight into their everyday lives and activities and access to their wider networks. Even though I never had the opportunity to spend longer periods in the field, my repeated interactions with my informants over the years have strengthened the reliability of the information I have been given. I have had the possibility to compare information given to me at different points, but, even more important, I believe that my informants found it more worthwhile to interact with me given that I had followed them for a longer period. Although I was still an outsider, it made me less of a stranger.

My interactions with some of these networks over the years also made it possible for me to reflect on developments over time and on how important political events, such as the presidential elections of 2011, affected the dynamics of their activities and interactions. It has also given me the opportunity to examine what happens to the postwar rebel networks and the ex-combatants within them when there are no important political events or security assignments. It has allowed me to follow and interview my informants in times that have been good as well as bad. I believe that the continuity of my field research over a number of years is an important contribution when it comes to understanding not only postwar rebel networks and the reality for ex-combatants but also the wider context of security and political instability in a postwar country several years after peace was declared.

Moreover, in an attempt to find answers to how and why postwar rebel networks could be relevant to the Liberian political or economic elite, I have tried to understand and follow my informants' links to key influential actors. Additional ethical issues need to be regarded in this type of research. Actors within the Liberian elite and the official state structures may consider collaboration with former rebel commanders and their networks to be of strategic importance, yet there would be strong incentives for the elite not to display these informal interactions in front of the international community, which is spending considerable resources on demobilization and reintegration of ex-combatants. But in Liberia the links between the formal elite and informal networks are nothing but an open secret. Of course, this is nothing the

Liberian government would talk publicly about or give an account of in front of the international community. Yet cooperation with informal power structures is an essential part of the political culture in Liberia, a fact that, at least to ordinary Liberians, is far from secret. This, I would argue, implies that the information shared by my informants within postwar rebel structures is not considered a threat toward actors in power in Liberia. Nevertheless, making sure that I protect my informants from any possible harm connected to their being linked to actors within the Liberian elite is an additional reason I have chosen not to reveal their names in this book.

Coming back to the importance of being honest and open toward informants about the work one does as a researcher, I have always considered this to be an important part of my own safety in the field as well. As Fujii discusses, dealing with rumors is an unavoidable part of doing research, and one should always keep in mind that informants are often equally interested in gaining information about the person interviewing them.[33] I noticed early on that my informants were always well informed about my work and about whom I had talked to in the field—not only because of the information I had been careful to give them regarding who I was and what the purpose of my research was but also because they were good at informing one another of my work and whereabouts in Liberia. One incident illustrating this was the first time I met with the informant I call Jacob. I had never met him before but had heard of him from another informant who had given me his number so that I could contact him. When we first met I started, as I always do, by introducing myself and my research, but Jacob did not seem that interested and interrupted me several times. "Yes, yes, I know all this!" Jacob told me, a bit annoyed. He told me that he obviously knew who I was and what I was doing in Liberia for a long time. Jacob said that he remembered the first time I came to the Guthrie Rubber Plantation several years earlier, a place where I knew Jacob not had been active. He could account for whom I had met and what my research had been about. Jacob continued and referred to people I had met and interviews that I had held over the years, and, even though I knew that my informants were always well informed about my business, I was still a bit surprised at the level of detail that Jacob could provide. This, however, made a great start of our relationship. I felt early on that Jacob never feared talking to me or had reason to be suspicious in any way. The fact that he initially knew more about me than I about him perhaps contributed to the relaxed atmosphere I always felt when we met. Above all, I believe that the trust I have gained among my informants over the years is strongly related to the fact that I have always been careful to inform people about the purpose of my field research and that they therefore have had less need to be mistrustful of my intentions.

Ethnographic fieldwork is to large extent about listening. Nordstrom has pointed out that it may seem surprising that anyone conducting research in a violent context or among traumatized people can elicit personal information of any kind. It is often presumed that war provokes antipathy toward all outsiders and that people therefore will guard their silence because they fear how the researchers might use the information they collect. As Nordstrom also states, these arguments are in many ways valid, yet they are balanced by a need to talk and communicate experiences related to violence. Words serve to give voice to the unspeakable and make it somewhat more controllable. As many of her informants expressed, "We are glad you finally came to ask us our story; up until now, everyone has come to tell us what our story is." Nordstrom draws the important conclusion that it is in the act of listening that we can begin to understand the existence of those who speak.[34] Even though my research was not carried out in a war zone, I believe that the lessons drawn by Nordstrom are equally relevant to conducting research in postwar Liberia, as my informants have been, and still are, affected by the war they actively took part in. Many experiences are not shared with an outsider; still, I have found that many of my informants have a will to share experiences both from the time of war and their present everyday reality. And there are important lessons to be learned from their stories.

CONDUCTING INTERVIEWS AND SEARCHING FOR THE "TRUTH"

With the act of listening, the concept of interviewing has been central for my work. Unstructured interviewing, as my fieldwork to a large extent is composed of, has been defined as going on all the time and at any location—while sitting in people's homes, walking along a road, hanging out in bars, or waiting for a bus. Unstructured interviews are based on a clear plan that the interviewer keeps in mind, but they are at the same time characterized by a minimum of control over people's responses. The idea of such interviews is to get people to open up and to let them express themselves and their experiences on their own terms and at their own pace. Such ethnographic interviewing is best used when there is ample time, as during long-term fieldwork, and when informants can be interviewed on many separate occasions. I have always felt that unstructured or informal interviews—herein understood as a nonstructured conversation taking place in an everyday situation such as while sharing a taxi, having lunch, taking a walk in the neighborhood, preparing food, or resting in the shade for a while—have been most suitable for me as a researcher and for this specific topic and context. As argued by H. Russell Bernard, among others, nothing can beat unstructured interviewing to learn about the lived experiences of fellow human beings: what it is like to survive war or how to get through each day when a child is dying or how it feels to be forced to flee your country. In such cases structured or semistructured interviews can feel somewhat unnatural, Bernard points out, and highly

structured interviewing can even get in the way of your ability to communicate freely with key informants. Unstructured interviews can instead be more
suitable for studying sensitive issues and are particularly useful in the context
of armed conflict.[35] It is of course also a matter of taste, the personality of the
researcher, and an assessment of the situation at hand that makes us choose
what research methods to use in the field.

Conducting fieldwork and even interviewing, when done in this way, is
never one-way communication, where I listen and observe while my informants simply answer questions and provide me with information. It is instead
a constant interaction, where my informants naturally want to know who they
have in front of them. As I have taken part of their lived experiences and life
stories, they have often wanted to hear about mine. They have wanted to know
who my parents are and where they come from. They have enjoyed listening to
the story of how my father, as a young man, crossed the border into Liberia in
the 1960s and how he worked as a teacher in Kakata to make a living and then
made his way to Monrovia and lived on Newport Street for some time while
dreaming of one day reaching Europe. They have laughed with recognition
and called him a "hustler" like themselves, a brave man with big dreams and
little means. They have wanted to know about my upbringing in Sweden, what
I have studied and how I live. As they have shared parts of their life stories with
me, they have also heard about mine. And why should they not? They have invited me to their homes and introduced me to their families. I have seen where
they work and been invited to spend time with them and their friends when
they just hang around. I have been invited to church and listened to one of my
informants' choir concerts. I have been mocked for refusing to participate in
the big weight-lifting competition that I attended at the beach, which some
of my informants had organized. They have scolded me for traveling alone
up-country, and they have laughed at me for waiting half a day on the floor
of a crowded Eco-Bank near West Point to have an interview with one of my
informants who, unfortunately for him, was also stuck there on the floor. They
have talked to me when life has been good to them and also when they have
felt miserable and angry at society and the world. They have shared important
pieces of themselves and their everyday life with me, so why should they not
also know something about me? For me fieldwork has mostly been about trying to understand the lives of my informants and the structures they are part
of by listening, asking, and observing. But it has unavoidably also been about
sharing a piece of who I am with them. Fieldwork is constant interaction, and
I believe that it was only through this exchange that fruitful information could
come about from my research in Liberia.

But, as Antonius Robben points out in his assessment of fieldwork and
interviews among victims and perpetrators of violence, we need to establish
a good rapport with our informants to be able to grasp the world from their

perspective while we at the same time maintain a degree of detachment as observers to enhance our analytical insights. Researching war and violence can make it easy to be led astray from an intended course. As Robben notes, informants can have great personal and political stakes in making the ethnographer adopt their interpretations.[36] As researchers, we should always be aware that this is not always a straightforward task and that it is a difficult balance between empathy and detachment when fieldwork is being conducted. Yet it should not keep us from trying to relate to our informants or from retelling their stories. Nevertheless, related to the question of the risks of being led astray, a concern that consequently is raised when it comes to ethnographic fieldwork and the conduct of interviews, is whether one can ensure that informants are telling the "truth" when being interviewed. As Fujii has pointed out, most researchers use well-known techniques, such as triangulating different sources, to discover lies to get closer to the truth. In my case this was done mainly by comparing information given to me in private by different informants and by always double-checking details such as dates, numbers, and events with different sources, including other informants, official documents, and reports as well as other research within the same field. Since I also met my informants several times over the years, I had the opportunity to ask the same questions and compare answers by the same source at different occasions. But, as Fujii notes, not all stories lend themselves to the determination of truth. For example, one cannot put people's beliefs about how the world works through a truth test. Similarly, Fujii argues, the value of people's narrations about their experiences of violence—what they saw, did, felt, or heard—does not necessarily lie in their factual accuracy or objective truths but in the meaning that the narrator gives particular events and moments. The stories place the narrator in a larger context, and thereby even fabrications, embellishments, and interventions become revealing.[37]

As I let the narratives of my informants drive this book forward from chapter to chapter, I've considered this. I believe that all my informants' stories are important, even if some of the information proved to be incorrect, because they reveal a lot, not only about the individuals themselves and their perceptions and motives but also about the wider context and the reality they see and face every day. As Chris Coulter writes on the issue of telling the stories of her informants' experiences of war and postwar life, she refers to the experiences that emerge in their narratives. The picture Coulter presents of her informants' lives in a war-torn society is thereby the result of a negotiation between her informants and their memories, but ultimately between her informants and herself, with them as narrators and her as listener and producer of text and analysis.[38] As such, the presented experiences of my informants in this book should also be understood. Despite our own subjectivity, and that of our informants, as well as the risks of misinterpretations, we should not refrain from telling the stories we have been told. It is rather a question of being aware of this subjectivity and the limitations it may bring.

THE IMPORTANCE OF IN-DEPTH INDIVIDUAL STORIES

Each case study presented in this book is an attempt to contribute to the understanding of postwar rebel networks and to the ability of ex-combatants to transform, adapt, and make use of the present postwar security and political situation. My methodological starting point for examining these sustained rebel structures is the former rebels within the informal security groups themselves. They are also the most central characters in my research. Their views, reasons, motives, and rationales for taking part in postwar rebel networks are important aspects I seek to understand. For each case study I have relied on mainly a few key informants. I have tried to follow them closely during my time in the field, and during each period of fieldwork I have interviewed them repeatedly. One informant has often led me to another, which has allowed me to follow important links and thereby better understand how postwar rebel networks are composed and how the individual members relate to one another. This snowball, or chain-sampling, method is not likely to lead to a representative sample. That I am very well aware of. But it can be highly useful in dealing with sensitive issues or informal networks. With such a method access can be gained in areas otherwise closed to outsiders and among informants who, without the facilitation of previous informants, would most likely be reluctant to participate in such studies. My informants have shown me a glimpse of their everyday life by letting me spend time with them where they work, are active, or even live. In informal discussions rather than structured interviews, I have tried to capture their experiences, which my case studies build on. I have also discussed my research questions with people closely connected to my key informants and observed the internal interaction and dynamics within these networks for an even more nuanced picture of these ex-combatants' postwar reality.

It has been a strategic choice to focus mainly on a few key individuals. But such an approach has its limitations. More quantitatively oriented studies, where a large population of ex-combatants are interviewed, instead have the advantage of drawing more general conclusions and, depending on approach, the possibility to provide valuable statistics and reveal trends in ex-combatants' postwar life situations, attitudes, and so on. On the other hand, the strength of the type of qualitative research conducted in this study is, to my mind, that it has allowed me to engage with my informants' life stories on a deeper level than if I had chosen to focus on a larger population of ex-combatants within postwar rebel networks.

Furthermore, in using quantitative approaches and focusing on a large population, there is a risk that we do not see the individuals within the statistics. The ex-combatants can become just another anonymous, dehumanized postwar category. In other words, the ex-combatants become nothing more than *ex-combatants*, instead of individuals with the ex-combatant identity as one of their many identities and social roles. In this book I wanted to give my informants' narratives enough space to diminish the risk of reducing them to this single identity. Additionally, we can benefit from more in-depth interviews to also understand the more structural problems connected to insecurity and instability that a country such as Liberia faces, while at the same time better understand the more general mechanisms contributing to the continued relevance of postwar rebel networks.

Most of us would agree that individual stories, as those told by the ex-combatants in this book, are important, as they contribute to a more textured understanding of what war is and what it means for individual human beings, even at a personal level, as they take us further and beyond war as a mere battle between political actors in a national or international context. But what is often forgotten is that such individual stories are much more than that. In fact, these individual incidences that such stories bear witness to have strategic implications that could change our understanding of war. They are important pieces of the puzzle in explaining not only the course of war but also the outcome of war altogether. Jacob's story illustrates this phenomenon. Here Jacob, an imprisoned combatant under Charles Taylor's presidency during the second Liberian civil war, is confronted by Taylor himself. Jacob is released under the precondition that he joins Taylor's forces as a commander of one of his units. Why Taylor is reaching out to an individual combatant who seemingly is without any power, as he at this point has been imprisoned for treason for years, we can only speculate. But the important part of the story is that he does. The president of Liberia, and the most important representative of one of the parties of war, personally reaches out to an individual rebel soldier on the enemy side. Accordingly, Taylor, for whatever reasons, finds an imprisoned enemy rebel soldier to be of strategic importance. Here I would argue that Taylor realized that this man, like so many other combatants, had strategic relevance even as an individual, as he is part of larger networks, networks that can, and do, affect the course of war. By reaching out to (or manipulating) individuals, their extended networks might also be affected. If we, in political science, international relations, war studies, or military strategy, forget to search for these individual stories in our research, we fail to see important mechanisms affecting the course and outcome of war. We fail to see how actors, even at the very highest political levels, are connected to individual combatants on the ground, and we ultimately end up with an incomplete understanding of war. This is also true for understanding postwar and peacetime logics in a society such as the Liberian one. As the case studies show, individuals, and in this case often ex-combatants, seemingly far removed from the center of political power, are intimately connected to official actors of power, creating a mutual dependence with political implications that we should not underestimate.

GENDER MATTERS IN METHODOLOGY

There is one question I have repeatedly been asked over the years when it comes to my research on ex-combatants, a question that can be expressed differently but that always ends up having the same meaning: but how does it affect your work that you are a woman? The question has at times been related to whether my informants, who most often are men, feel comfortable talking to a woman about their personal experiences of war, violence, or security. On other occasions the question has simply been related to whether these men feel comfortable talking to a woman in the first place. But regardless of whether the question relates to conversations about violence or daily life, the point of the matter is the same: whether my gender can have implications for their answers or even their willingness to give honest accounts of their experiences. In my mind the most interesting point about this issue is why I get these questions, while my male colleagues generally do not. We all know that gender matters. Still, there are few discussions on what implications we could expect to encounter when male researchers are interviewing or conducting studies with male informants in the field of war and violence. Most researchers in this field are men, as are most informants. But the gender of the researchers tends to be invisible or even treated as insignificant, unless they in fact are women. For this reason we cannot know for sure what implications the gender of the researcher has on the research produced when it comes to, in this case, the specific matter of ex-combatants in Liberia. Accordingly, I obviously cannot know for certain how my research would have been different if I were a man, just as my male colleagues cannot know for sure the implications had they been women. I can therefore only speculate on the significance of my gender when it comes to the result of my research.

But since I so often have been asked the question, I, unlike most men in the same situation, I suspect, have been forced to think about these issues. And I have never seen the fact that I am a woman as an obstacle in anything, from gaining access to my informants to their willingness to share their stories and experiences with me and trusting me. If anything, I have considered my gender to be an advantage, not despite prevalent gender norms but maybe because of them. Gender norms shape the way we understand the world and what we interpret to be typical or even appropriate female or male roles and behavior. Since men, historically and today, have had the prerogative to interpret and articulate how we are to understand the world, they naturally also have had more training in articulating their own stories and experiences. Women, on the other hand, have been expected to listen. Accordingly, from a gender perspective, male informants may find it quite natural not only to articulate their own experiences but also to do so in front of a female listener, maybe even more so than in front of a male listener. Since I have also had the opportunity to interview many female ex-combatants in the past, I at least have an advantage in comparing the challenges in gaining access to women's stories versus men's, and I have found significant differences.[39] Because of gender norms of appropriate female behavior, female ex-combatants may not be as willing to talk about their own experiences of using violence, for instance, but gender norms may also prevent women from expressing their stories, especially to strangers, which researchers often are, in general. Women have been taught not to take as much space and to guard their stories more carefully. Consequently, gender matters and should not be disregarded in methodological considerations, even if we cannot know for sure how gender norms affect the outcome of research in general or in this specific case.

Outline of the Book

In this book we follow my informants' paths from rebel soldiers to ex-combatants attached to postwar rebel networks mobilizing for different informal security assignments. The main focus is naturally on these ex-combatants' activities and lives after the war. I have therefore focused on a few specific events to illustrate how postwar rebel networks function and operate, as well as described interests contributing to and calling for them to remain mobilized. The cases come in chronological order, revealing how these networks have remained relevant despite the years passing since the end of war. Chapter 1, however, provides the theoretical framework for this book, where I elaborate on the concept of postwar rebel networks and vigilantism. This chapter gives some insight into the informal exercise of power and provision of security, with a specific West African focus.

This, then, is a book on postwar rebel networks and the forces and mechanisms allowing, and calling for, ex-combatants to preserve and maintain their wartime links to one another. Naturally, the main emphasis herein is on *postwar* Liberia and the years following the declaration of peace in 2003. Yet the case studies of this book commence elsewhere. The first example of how postwar rebel networks can be used differs from the following case studies in that I here show how such a network was used for renewed warfare and how rebels were recycled in the West African region following the end of the first Liberian civil war. In chapter 2 we are taken back in time to the emergence of the Liberian civil war in 1989 and continue through the turbulent and violent years that followed in the whole Mano River region until the end of war. Through the stories of three young Liberian men in particular we witness how war and crisis could transform lives, in this case from sons of Armed Forces of Liberia soldiers, to soldiers, rebels, commanders, regional warriors, and eventually ex-combatants. This chapter substantially differs from the preceding case studies, because as these subsequent examples illustrate, postwar rebel networks and ex-combatants are mostly *not* used in their capacity as combatants or with any obvious attempt to start new warfare. On the contrary, in this chapter, we discover how rebels were "recycled" (or recycled themselves) specifically because of their combat experiences and preserved networks for regional warfare. Michael's, Simon's, and Jacob's stories are at the very center of this chapter, allowing us to understand the importance of postwar rebel networks for its individual members but also for the regional elite, as war and crisis ranged not only in Liberia but also in Sierra Leone and Guinea. Through these young Liberian men's trajectories, in this chapter we move across West African borders and discover how the mobility of rebels and their networks, in addition to the antagonism, or loyalty, between the ruling political actors in the region, entangled the conflicts to such a degree that it was impossible to say where one conflict ended and the other one began or whether the different conflicts in fact just were one great Mano River war with distinct battlefields.

The case study devoted to the Guthrie Rubber Plantation (or Sime Darby, as it later came to be known), where ex-combatants and postwar rebel networks have been present since 2003, presented in chapter 3, shows how political and commercial interests as well as security concerns and disappointment in the DDRR process have contributed to the maintenance of wartime structures at this location. The choice of the Guthrie Rubber Plantation is important for a variety of reasons. This case initially shows how a postwar rebel network could use its wartime organizational structure to take over and control such a large and financially important location as this plantation was. This case reveals not only how this network operated in the field but also how it was connected to the highest political and financial elite of Liberia, enabling its continued activities for years. Furthermore, this case also illustrates how former rebels can be transformed into security providers under the right circumstances.

The developments at the plantation, from the time of war until the present, show how postwar rebel networks have been of strategic importance to the ruling political elite, but also how former key rebel commanders strategically have been able to preserve and use their influence gained during the war. Once again, particularly from the narratives of individual ex-combatants—in this chapter Michael, Simon, and Alpha—we discover how a postwar rebel network can be used and how an informal security group can emerge. Furthermore, this chapter also offers a discussion of negative but also potentially positive aspects of having postwar rebel networks involved in informal security provision. This case study also illuminates how formal and informal security provisions are intimately interlinked in a postconflict country such as Liberia and considers the consequences of these overlaps and interconnections.

The third case study, in chapter 4, gives examples of how the 2011 elections in Liberia affected the dynamics of postwar rebel networks as informal security providers. The 2011 Liberian elections were chosen as a case study partly to illustrate how postwar rebel networks had remained relevant even as long as eight years after the end of war. Showing how the main political candidates for the presidential elections mobilized postwar rebel networks for political support and informal security provision illustrates that the elite still sees them as a force to be reckoned with. By also showing the advantages ex-combatants on the winning side gained compared to the disadvantages faced by the ex-combatants on the losing side, in this chapter I clarify the importance of being connected to the right network after the war.

For this case study I followed ex-combatants in support of the candidates who, ultimately, were the most important candidates in the 2011 Liberian elections—the incumbent president Ellen Johnson Sirleaf from the Unity Party and Winston Tubman, presidential candidate from the Congress of Democratic Change—before, during, and after the elections. The Liberian presidential elections work to illustrate both how the political elite used networks of ex-combatants for different purposes, including to provide informal security and to mobilize votes, and how the ex-combatants themselves made use of this political event. This chapter also gives examples of how postwar rebel networks have continued to adapt over time, taking on different tasks depending on opportunity and circumstance. This adaptation is evident, as the key mobilizer of the network supporting Ellen Johnson Sirleaf during the 2011 elections had previously been one of the most important figures among the informal security providers at the Guthrie Rubber Plantation, while the leader of the network supporting Winston Tubman had also been active as a vigilante leader, controlling an informal security group of many ex-combatants from a postwar rebel network prior to the elections. As in previous chapters, narratives of individuals in postwar rebel networks—in this case Michael and Alex—are used to further illustrate the dynamics keeping these networks active.

The final case study, presented in chapter 5, focuses on the complexity of the "ex-combatant identity." In this book we follow ex-combatants who have survived peace by clinging to their wartime links and postwar rebel networks and thereby also their ex-combatant identity. The chapter looks at the lives of ex-combatants within postwar rebel networks when there are no important political events or security assignments or when ordinary Liberians cannot afford to keep them mobilized as vigilantes for community protection. The choice of focus for this chapter is based partly on an interest in what happens to the ex-combatant identity under such circumstances and accordingly to the relevance of postwar rebel networks. I explore what it means for an individual ex-combatant, on the one hand, to be in need of an ex-combatant identity for work and societal security and, on the other, not being able to escape it, and perceptions of what such an identity implies.

Being recognized as an ex-combatant is far from unproblematic. Former rebels tend to be portrayed in research reports and media accounts and by actors in postconflict societies at large as indiscriminately violent and dangerous. Ex-combatants have more often than not been perceived as the real threats to lasting peace. Against this backdrop this chapter explores what it thereby means in practice to be identified, and to identify oneself, with this category, given such negative perceptions. We follow Abraham, Jacob, and Michael to discover what a life with an ex-combatant identity and a postwar rebel network implies. Does the identity as an ex-combatant partly fade? Or does this identity, as well as postwar rebel networks, become even more relevant under such circumstances? Such questions asked in this chapter aim at coming closer to an understanding of what former rebels, and postwar rebel networks, are and do in contemporary Liberia.

Furthermore, another important question is posed in this chapter: where are the women? Many women served as combatants in the Liberian civil war, and it is striking how women have remained absent or invisible in the postwar rebel networks examined here. Based on theories of gender and war, the chapter analyzes whether an ex-combatant identity as such, because of the negative perceptions associated with it, may have different consequences for women than for men. In other words, the analyses explore whether women in general, unlike many men with a combatant background, have more to lose than to gain by being identified as an ex-combatant or by actively using this identity or the networks attached to it.

In the concluding chapter, key findings are summarized and further discussed. The chapter is divided into three separate themes, each presenting an overarching complex of problems examined in this book. The "reintegration paradox" is the first theme I discuss. The demobilization of former rebel groups is much more than a technical procedure and much more complicated than is often assumed. In practice rebel networks can easily remain mobilized long after their initial rebel group has been dissolved, while individual members of these postwar rebel networks may in fact be much more reintegrated into civil society than is often understood. Yet this may demand that we look at the meaning of reintegration in a more comprehensive way than we traditionally have. This theme also provides a discussion of the "demobilization dilemma" that arises from this paradox. Findings are summarized in relation to a wider discussion of why failures or successes to demobilize ex-combatants have had less to do with whether the actual execution of DDR has been good or bad. Instead, the fundamental question is concerned with whether there exists a will, or even a need, for postwar rebel networks to remain active and mobilized, even when there are no wars to be fought.

In the second theme, called "postwar rebel networks in Liberia and beyond," I take a point of departure in Liberian postwar rebel networks but discuss them in a broader perspective, looking at similar networks in a wider African context. Within this theme I argue that postwar rebel networks have not been acknowledged to the extent that they should be. I suggest that this is because such networks are seldom examined unless they are involved in renewed warfare. With the case studies reaching beyond ex-combatants as recycled regional warriors, I explain why their findings should contribute to a more nuanced and complex understanding of postwar rebel networks in Liberia and beyond. This theme also provides a summarizing discussion on key questions relating to the existence of postwar rebel networks. Are they simply the real, and most acute, threat to peace they often are described to be, or are the perils of lingering rebel structures a much more complex issue?

Through the third and final theme of the concluding chapter, we engage in a deeper discussion of the abilities to transform ex-combatants and networks. Here I summarize the discussion of why the move from warrior to security provider is one that the ex-combatants may find natural to make in a postconflict country such as Liberia, where instability and insecurity are still an everyday reality for many citizens. In this context the importance of the ex-combatant identity reemerges. In a concluding and summarizing discussion, I further examine what this identity means for former rebels in postwar rebel networks. I return to the discussion of whether one can escape such an identity and whether an escape is even desirable. This leads me to the question of how it can be possible that a life with an ex-combatant identity can be compatible with that of a postwar informal security provider—or, in other words, how and to what extent the perception of an ex-combatant can be transformed from that of a perpetrator to that of a protector.

CHAPTER 1

Informal Security Provision

THE ROLE OF POSTWAR REBEL NETWORKS

This chapter aims to provide insight into the importance of the informal realm, beyond formal state institutions, for an understanding of how security in large part is provided for in Liberia. The reason for such an entrance into the phenomenon of postwar rebel networks has already been introduced in the previous chapter. The argument is that in the context of weak state structures and the absence of reliable formal security institutions, which postconflict settings often are characterized by, there can be a place for informal security actors to operate. Under such conditions different actors can unofficially be called on, or take it on themselves, to fill a security-providing function in societies. Emerging from war, former rebel networks can be among such actors. And, under certain circumstances, they can, instead of being dissolved, adapt to such an environment, hence with new purposes and tasks.

But to understand how and why such transformation comes about, we need to know more about where and who Liberians turn to for everyday protection. A range of both informal and formal security providers that ordinary citizens rely on can be discovered by acknowledging informal systems of power, institutions, and actors operating within these structures. In so doing, the concept and mechanisms of vigilantism (in the form of local informal security provision) must be taken into account. Theories of vigilantism are given considerable stress here because the activities the postwar rebel networks are engaged in often follow the same logic as vigilante practice. Understanding vigilantism—how such practice is possible and why it is often called on—is therefore an important part of understanding how postwar rebel networks function in the informal security arena as well as their connections to formal power structures.

The approach adopted in this book is that the informal and formal security structures of Liberia must not be understood as each other's antithesis but rather as an intertwined, interacting web of official and unofficial links, shaping Liberia's contemporary security context. Within this context different forms of vigilantism, often carried out by ex-combatants from postwar rebel networks, can be an important aspect of everyday security provision. The insecurity and violence that has perpetuated itself in postconflict Liberia, despite processes to reform the formal security institutions, are discussed in the attempt to find explanations on a structural level for why informal security providers are important. This analysis provides insight into how political and other influential actors, by using their positions within the formal power structures, can use individuals and networks operating in the informal arena.

After a brief description of the Liberian civil war and of the rebel soldiers' path from belligerents to ex-combatants, postwar rebel networks, and informal security groups emerging from such platforms, are covered. This analysis suggests explanations for, and insights into, why and how these wartime structures can be used in new informal security settings, attempting to find answers on both the structural and the individual level.

The Complexity of Security Provision in a Postwar Context

When analyzing security and insecurity in Liberia, we must understand how power is exercised within this arena and, consequently, what actors hold authority over security provision. From a state-centered perspective, formal security institutions would be the natural focus for such analysis. In Liberia, however, as in many other African countries and elsewhere, such an approach would leave us with a very insufficient picture of the complex power structures controlling and influencing contemporary security policy. In other words, the state is far from the sole provider of security in Liberia, or elsewhere for that matter. As has been observed by Rita Abrahamsen and Michael Williams, security today is increasingly in the hand of private actors, and on the African continent this privatization includes a range of everyday security actors such as private guarding companies, risk consultants, neighborhood watch groups, and vigilante groups. State sovereignty has traditionally been identified with its monopoly of the legitimate means of violence. But a too-narrow view on this monopoly risks excluding the manner in which security privatization has become part of new forms of governance and authority. Yet, even though the state often carefully guards the monopoly of the means of violence, it is at the same time often the instigator of private security. This implies that private security actors cannot be understood as merely situated entirely outside, or in opposition, of the state. Instead, Abrahamsen and Williams argue, the multiplicity of private security actors are better understood as part of complex structures and networks of security, giving rise to new forms of security governance.[1] Paul Higate similarly notes, in his analysis of private security in Africa, that it is today rather difficult to avoid the influence of private security, as it is deeply embedded in everyday security landscapes. It is not simply that the state appears to have little to do with security in temporary times because of increased outsourcing. Private security has rather gained an unstoppable momentum in its reconfiguration of the state's public institutions. Privately delivered services are rarely, if ever, taken back into government ownership, Higate argues.[2] Nonstate initiatives, when it comes to security provision, accordingly cannot be ignored. In the following section, the main focus is thereby on actors and institutions in the informal arena. Nevertheless, these actors and institutions are still closely linked to formal structures and institutions as well as to official power and decisions affecting security provision in Liberia.

As a starting point for examining these aspects of contemporary Liberia, I turn to the literature on African politics beyond a state-centered perspective, acknowledging that understanding politics in Africa is to understand how Africans experience and live politics in their daily lives rather than formal politics.[3] I explore literature that emphasizes the importance of understanding public authority, power, and decision making outside the frame of formal state institutions. When examining security and security provision, I adopt the same kind of approach, taking a point of departure in the literature by exploring institutions and actors who have resorted unofficially to "policing" functions. Research with particular focus on Africa and states facing high levels of postconflict violence are central, alongside theories of vigilantism. Furthermore, while discussing the reform of Liberia's formal security institutions, I explore literature on the informal power held by so-called Big Men (regional strongmen), both within or with links to these institutions, and the relevance of their networks. This finally leads me into examining the situation of ex-combatants, their potential role in postwar rebel networks, and informal security groups linked to key political or other influential actors or institutions within the official state system.

THE LIMITATIONS OF STATE-CENTRIC APPROACHES

The limitations of a state-centric approach when it comes to understanding how power is exercised in Africa have gradually received increased attention in recent years. Kevin Dunn, in his analysis of how the concept of the state in Africa has been treated in international relations theory, has called attention to this phenomenon. As Dunn argues, the reason the state is central to political systems elsewhere is because of its hegemonic position in society. But in Africa the state has never achieved hegemonic domination over society. A state-centric focus is thereby bound to miss important elements and actors significant to African politics. Nonstate actors such as international financial institutions, Big Men, international business actors, and nonstate military corporations are important players on the African scene, which a strict state-centric perspective easily would disregard. But, Dunn stresses, he is not arguing for the irrelevance of the state; instead, the state remains an important force in both African domestic politics and international relations, but state-centric approaches have serious limitations for effectively understanding events in Africa. What is occurring in Africa is not the absence of politics, as has often been argued, but the practice of politics in complex and original ways. Models based on Western arrogance need to be rejected so that alternative forms of sociopolitical organizations can be examined.[4]

If one looks at politics and international politics in Africa with a state-centric focus, as for instance Christopher Clapham does in his research on state survival in Africa, one should remember, as Clapham has pointed out, that the less solid the state, the greater the need to look beyond it for an understanding of how the society it claims to govern fits into the international system.[5] Along the same line of thinking, Patrick Chabal and Jean-Pascal Daloz, as early as the late 1990s, demonstrated the importance of acknowledging the realm of the informal when trying to understand African politics. Their analysis was based on the claim that the "real" business of politics in Africa is often taking place elsewhere than where observers have placed their focus of analysis. Additionally, within the political context in Africa, what is actually happening is more often than not informal or personalized in nature.[6]

To answer the question of how and why rebel networks remain relevant and continue to affect the security political situation in postwar Liberia, I start from this perspective, by emphasizing the importance of the informal power bases within African politics. Yet it is not only the informal context beyond the state structures that is important for understanding how politics is carried out and how power is exercised on the African continent. I agree with Dunn when he argues that the state remains an important force in an African context, and I therefore suggest that the dynamic *between* the formal state and the informal realms needs to be emphasized. Understanding the rationale behind the often hidden links tying the official representatives of power to informal actors or networks is even more important when examining posed questions.

As Chabal and Daloz point out, elites are usually linked to the rest of the population through the business of politics along informal vertical channels of patron-client networks and other structures. There is no institutionalized civil society in Africa separated from the governmental structures, since this is only possible where a strong and strongly differentiated state exists. Accordingly, Chabal and Daloz suggest that the understanding of politics in Africa is rather a matter of identifying the complexities of what they call the "shadow boxing" that takes place between state and society the way that political actors, both within the formal and informal spheres, link up to sustain the networks that are the basis for politics in Africa.[7] As stated by Christian

Lund, in what he calls "twilight institutions" in Africa, there is no shortage of institutions attempting to exercise public authority. But, as Lund points out, public authority does not always fall within the exclusive realm of government institutions. Traditional institutions claiming public authority, such as chieftaincy, often with government recognition, exist alongside government institutions. Associations and organizations, which at first sight do not appear to be political, may also exercise political power and public authority. Public authority thereby becomes the consolidated result of the exercise of power by a range of institutions. These institutions often operate in the twilight between state and society, between public and private.[8]

In the subsequent case studies of this book, while exploring the significance of postwar rebel networks, I adopt these perspectives. The networks I aim to examine are not official in character, as the warring parties signed the comprehensive peace agreement years ago. Consequently, their potential links to the political and economic elite cannot be official either. I am therefore not interested in formal governance in Liberia as such and accordingly do not rely on the literature analyzing formal African state structures, politics, or governance. My focus here is instead the informal governance of Liberia, allowing political power and public authority to exist outside the official state structures.

SECURITY PROVISION BEYOND FORMAL GOVERNANCE

When it comes to the exercise of power in the field of security in an African context, my approach for this book is that authority must also be understood from the perspective of informal governance. As shown in the work of Reno on warlord politics and African states, the distinction between collective and private authority can occasionally be blurred. Inhabitants of a collapsed (bureaucratic) state may, for example, enjoy security owing to the presence of an armed organization operating in an area to attain mineral resources. But the critical difference, Reno argues, between this type of organization and a conventional state, even if it is weak, lies in the circumstance that the inhabitants do not enjoy security by right of their membership in a state. Security in this case is instead reliant on the venture's profitability and to what degree the security provision satisfies the interests of the provider. Local security may therefore cease unless inhabitants take it on themselves to shoulder the responsibility for providing it themselves.[9]

The provision of security thereby, as illustrated by Reno's example, becomes something much more complex than if was it merely a collective good provided for by the state and its formal institutions. Furthermore, as Adedeji Ebo states in his analysis of security governance in West Africa, given the alienated nature and structure of the state in this region, other actors have naturally emerged to contest and engage the state in the governance of security. The typical West African state has hardly been a success in the Weberian sense and has often itself been a major source of insecurity for its citizens. Its monopoly of the means of force has been artificial and limited. A viable understanding of security governance in West Africa must necessarily extend beyond both statutory security institutions and the increasingly visible private security contractors. Ebo argues that researchers and policy makers have placed disproportionate emphasis on commercial security actors, which has tended to divert research interest and policy focus away from other nonstate actors who play significant roles in security governance in West Africa.[10] As Peter Albrecht points out, even though nonstate actors are rarely considered in the debate on commercial security, which tends to be the main focus when it comes to security governance, they deal with an estimated 80 to 90 percent of local disputes in the Global South. As such, they do not primarily guard but actively make order and are thereby integral to it.[11] Along the same lines of thinking, Bruce Baker presents arguments concerning the issue of security provision in Africa. He states that a focus on government agencies often directs attention away from the multiple choices of protection from crime and abuse that Africans rely on in their daily lives. Instead there are advantages in focusing on the consumers of governance through a "multi-choice" approach, which examines a whole range of security providers that citizens face for their different security requirements. In contemporary Africa a whole array of formal and informal groups exercise policing functions as either an ancillary or primary role. Among the informal or autonomous citizen groups exercising policing functions, anticrime groups, religious police, ethnic militias, or vigilantes are common. With different means of coercion, these groups can and do perform tasks assigned to the public police force. Law enforcement thereby becomes a broader activity than simply what "the Police" do, Baker states.[12]

The arguments on security provision presented here are central for the approach in this book. Liberian citizens' need for security provision goes beyond what formal security institutions are able, or willing, to provide. As Ebo has pointed out, the starting point for understanding security in West Africa is the recognition that the state at no point has had a monopoly of legitimate force. Just as West African states have operated dichotomized regimes of formal and informal economies, the security sector has also manifested both formal and informal tracks. In fact, statutory security institutions have been focused primarily on security functions to secure the state and its institutions themselves, while the main parts of the populations have relied instead on parallel, less formalized security structures.[13] For that reason we need to further engage with how informal security provision functions and the reasons for its importance. In the following section I therefore start by examining the violence ordinary citizens often face in postwar environments, seeking to understand the challenges, and the creativity people resort to for meeting these challenges and safeguarding their everyday protection.

LIVING WITH EVERYDAY VIOLENCE AND SEEKING PROTECTION

Violence, or the threat of violence, shapes the everyday lives of many African citizens. And when it comes to postconflict contexts, security needs are often massive. As Mats Berdal points out in his research on postwar violence, societies transitioning from war to peace often harbor high and persistent levels of violence following the formal end of conflict. The link between postwar violence, on the one hand, and state weakness or fragility, on the other, has been a central theme in the literature, and Berdal concludes that the general argument in this field can be summarized easily: postwar violence is critically linked to the absence of state institutions that can control and regulate the use of force and provide its citizens with basic security. Accordingly, until state capacity and public authority are reconstituted, violence remains. But, as Berdal points out, of particular interest here are which mechanisms and circumstances may permit state weakness to transform into postwar violence. For instance, when individuals and communities are faced with a situation where the state has lost its coercive capacity and violence escalates, populations try to reduce uncertainty by turning to actors or alternatives that offer the best chance for survival.[14] Richard Hill, Jonathan Temin, and Lisa Pacholek have similarly noted that in most cases individuals and communities in contexts where formal and public security is inefficient or scarce create their own security mechanisms or accept compromised and unaccountable security provided by nonstate actors. Furthermore, individuals and communities forced to take security into their own hands are often also remarkably effective and creative in doing so.[15]

The measures people resort to and the creativity citizens use to protect themselves in states with weak security institutions when levels of violence are high are relevant for my research. How people cope with violence and insecurity is central for this understanding and can be illustrated by the findings of Nordstrom, who has followed the creativity ordinary people showed to survive the war in Mozambique. What she found, even in the epicenters of war and violence, was that people did not resort to an unstructured "dog-eat-dog" survival mentality in the absence of formal governmental and social institutions. Most people were, quite the opposite, actively dedicated to rebuilding their lives and societies. They were also actively engaged in work with others in finding solutions to the war and instituting conflict-resolution measures at the local level.[16] There are no reasons to believe that people in a postconflict setting such as Liberia would not resort to the same levels of creativity found by Nordstrom in the Mozambique war zones to cope with the everyday violence and lack of security in the absence of state-offered protection. This, I would argue, contributes to the explanation for the use of informal security networks. As Baker has suggested, when a state cannot offer a system that protects people from crime and when it cannot guarantee to detect and punish occurring crimes, people are likely to resort to their own policing and courts.[17]

Furthermore, Chabal and Daloz identify two essential forms of violence in Africa: crime and "state" violence. To cope with this violence, survival strategies and countermeasures are required that often demand the protection of organized networks. In such a context, where citizens need to find protection that compensates for a state's failure to provide security but at the same time need to find protection against the very violence performed by the state itself, the management of violence can turn into a resource. It thereby becomes crucially important to examine networks that seek to organize and make the high levels of violence found in Africa productive, Chabal and Daloz suggest.[18] In fact, most of the security and justice in postconflict and fragile states is actually carried out by nonstate security and justice actors, not by the state police and judiciary. Nonetheless, in many fragile states it is impossible to make a sharp distinction between state and nonstate justice and security systems. The delivery of security should rather be described as existing in a continuum between these nodes.[19] Few African citizens see formal and informal security provision as mutually exclusive categories and rarely use either one or the other exclusively. People constantly move from one sphere of security agency to another, formal or informal, to safeguard their protection.[20]

Despite the informal security arena's importance for many African citizens, the dynamics of this context, its links to the formal security institutions, and the mechanisms, rationale, and structures of the actors operating in this sphere appear to be largely unknown to the outside world. To also understand the significance of the informal security context in Liberia, it is vital to understand the dynamics of contemporary postwar violence and the ability (or inability) of formal security institutions to handle this challenge. But the ability, or inability, of the state to safeguard security provision for its citizens cannot be analyzed in a vacuum. As Berdal states, there has been a tendency in the state-building literature to extensively focus on the issue of states' "low capacity." Even though state capacity is critical, the reconstitution of that capacity and the form the state takes have more relevance for the prospect of postwar violence.[21] For example, the Liberian state and its formal security institutions after the war were not essentially in need of regaining the capacity to protect its citizens, since the protection of ordinary Liberians had never been a priority of the Liberian state in the first place. In fact, Liberians have a history of being occupied with protecting themselves against different security threats, including those posed by the state. It is thereby important to not focus only on whether the Liberian state has had, and has, the capacity to protect its citizens; one must also consider whether this ever has been, or is, in the interest of the Liberian state at all.

POSTWAR SECURITY AND INSECURITY IN LIBERIA

As Nordstrom so elegantly put it, "When a war ends, it makes less difference than we might think. No alchemy exists whereby state and society 'naturally' revert to prewar realities with the declaration of peace."[22] In Liberia, since the war came to an end in 2003, major efforts have been undertaken to strengthen and reform the formal security institutions such as the army and the police in Liberia. As the peace agreement was signed, a force of approximately fifteen thousand peacekeepers under chapter 7 of the Charter of the United Nations was deployed to assist the National Transitional Government of Liberia in implementing the agreement, creating one of the largest United Nations peacekeeping missions in the world at that point. The United Nations force was mandated, among other tasks, to advise, train, and assist the Liberian law-enforcement authorities and other criminal-justice institutions and assist the National Transitional Government of Liberia in the implementation of the disarmament, demobilization, and reintegration process of the ex-combatants. The United Nations Mission in Liberia took the leading role in the reform of the Liberian National Police and began the recruitment of cadets for the new police force in mid-2004. By late November 2004 a first batch of the newly trained officers was deployed to the counties.[23] The United States, with a long history of interests in Liberia, focused on the reform of the Armed Forces of Liberia (AFL) through private contractors. But the security-sector reform represented an enormous challenge for Liberia, coming out of fourteen years of war. The process entailed addressing a security sector that has historically been dysfunctional, politicized, and incapable of protecting ordinary Liberian citizens.

According to some observers, the army reform, despite many current challenges, was a provisional success, with its pool of two thousand vetted and trained soldiers.[24] But most observers agree that the police reform has been less than successful, leaving Liberia with an ineffective, badly trained, underresourced, and corrupt police force. The Liberian National Police has both funding and logistical problems and is fundamentally insufficient for the security needs of Liberia. Furthermore, the force was initially unarmed. As this was a political call, based on the past misuse of power, this decision was not necessarily incorrect, but it left the completely unarmed police at risk of being unable to stop armed criminals or even protect themselves. As a result, areas were left that the police were unable or unwilling to patrol. In addition, a police officer earned little more than seventy U.S. dollars per month, leaving officers with few chances to support themselves on this low wage. Corruption thereby became a tool for survival for Liberian National Police officers.[25]

In her analysis of the security-sector reform in Liberia, Sukanya Podder found that the limitations of this process were a result of the gap between international approaches and Liberian local realities of security and justice provision through a mix of formal and informal actors. The attempts to reconstruct a state monopoly on security provision has not sufficiently taken into account that both formal and informal structures and actors operate within this provision. Podder claims that as both formal and informal actors are able to provide legitimate public and private security in areas of low state presence, security-sector initiatives should seize the opportunity to include legitimate informal actors in the institutional rebuilding process that accompanies security-sector reform. Reliance on such actors stems from the trust and efficiency of these frameworks. To exclude legitimate actors simply because of their informal character risks creating low-capacity institutions and conditions for public dissatisfaction that may fuel further conflict. In the efforts to establish a weak state's monopoly over violence, key networks and actors that sustain security provision at the local level are overlooked. In the Liberian case the use of such an approach has failed to acknowledge local perceptions of insecurity, which creates pockets of exclusion and resistance. International efforts to reform the security sector through its focus on formal institutions of security, she argues, remain disengaged with the public perception of who is best placed to offer security.[26]

Accordingly, formal initiatives to strengthen and reform the Liberian postwar security landscape have failed to acknowledge the importance of informal security-providing actors and mechanisms. I do not scrutinize these formal security-sector reform processes further. Challenges and inadequacies in their planning and implementation have been analyzed in detail elsewhere.[27] In the sections to come, however, I give further attention to the informal actors and initiatives of security provision often neglected by formal processes. A broader understanding of the various actors, and perhaps especially the informal ones, can nuance our understanding of postconflict security landscapes.

THE ROLE OF BIG MEN AND WOMEN

In this postwar context of weak formal security institutions, which were not only destroyed by the civil war but also had a prewar history of being inefficient and predatory, the informal security arena is inevitably of great importance for the Liberian people. Furthermore, as Mats Utas has described in his research on informal power and networks of Liberia, a shift from formal to informal power is nonetheless rather difficult to bring about, even though the serious destruction of state structures and bureaucracy caused by the civil wars ought to have made room for rapid social capacity improvements of the state. Accordingly, although the state as a structure was destroyed, the informal powers and the logic that actually ruled Liberia remained very much the same during the years of war. As Utas further shows, the lack of a well-functioning state has made it crucial for Liberians to have good connections with Big Men in a variety of networks. These Big Men are businessmen, military commanders, politicians, civil servants, or outright illegal actors. They use their positions of status for individual extractions of state or natural resources and to recruit followers or dependents. This relationship offers mutual benefits for the Big Men and their followers, as Big Men need followers to attain resources, while part of what is extracted is being channeled from them to their followers.[28] As Clapham points out, clientelism (which this is an example of) must be understood as a rational behavior following from a logic of personal relations, not as a characteristic of particular cultures. It is complex and multifunctional but also competitive in nature, as clients attach themselves to patrons to gain advantages in a contest over scarce resources. Furthermore, even though the clientelist relationship itself is dyadic—that is, between the patron and the client—the dynamic that creates it must be understood in relation to a wider social construct, Clapham argues. Here one must acknowledge the "clientelist system," where the clientelist links are fairly widespread.[29]

Such a perspective on power relations is applicable to contemporary Liberia. In the Liberian case the Big Men Utas refers to operate both within formal and informal contexts, often in both the legal and illegal sphere. As politicians, even at the very highest level, these formal actors can fully be understood only if their roles in informal networks also are taken into account. Utas argues that, because of the centralized nature of power in Liberia, all the current Big Men, no matter what positions they might hold, have connections and are partially loyal to the Biggest Man, or Woman, of Liberia. In other words, the position until recently held by President Ellen Johnson Sirleaf and by Charles Taylor before her. Furthermore, when it comes to President Johnson Sirleaf, she must be seen as a master at maneuvering both the formal and informal context. On the one hand, she has a Harvard degree and a former career within the United Nations system and the World Bank as well as lengthy experience in Liberian politics. On the other hand, she has held important positions in several prewar governments and, more important, been an active player in the Liberian civil wars.[30] In June 2009 the Liberian Truth and Reconciliation Commission found Johnson Sirleaf to have sponsored the rebel group National Patriotic Front of Liberia (NPFL) and Charles Taylor to overthrow the government of Samuel Doe.[31] This background furnished President Johnson Sirleaf with the ability to maneuver the international arena as well as Liberia's formal and informal spheres of power. President Johnson Sirleaf is one of the influential actors within the Liberian elite that have had both incentive and capacity to use the informal security groups, based on lingering wartime structures, for various purposes.

In the same way as Liberian power and politics must be analyzed, bearing both formal and informal structures in mind, so must the aspects of Liberian security and insecurity be explored. Following the logic of how power is exercised in Liberia, influential actors, with the ability of providing security or causing insecurity, are (and must be) based within, or have links to, both the formal and informal arenas. This means that actors within the formal state structures, whether they are politicians or important actors within the formal security institutions such as the army or police in Liberia, must interact, in one way or another, with informal actors. This creates an environment where postwar rebel networks and the actors within these structures inevitably become relevant and are both allowed and called on to linger.

Vigilantism as a Security Provision in Opposition of the State?

The protection of ordinary Liberians has never been a priority of the Liberian state from a historical perspective, and Liberians have been left to protect themselves, in fact, against different security threats, including those posed by the state. As noted by Ebo, for example, Liberia's asymmetrical social relations have created a cleavage between the state and the vast majority of Liberians. The seeds of what grew to become the Liberian security sector were sown by the elite to create a security structure to preserve and protect the interests of the privileged. In other words, the main reason for the Liberian security sector to exist in the first place has been the security of the state, often at the expense of "the state of security"—that is, the extent to which society feels safe, encompassing a broad human security agenda and not merely military, national, regime, or even individual security.[32] To understand the Liberian postconflict landscape, a focus beyond the formal security institutions and practices is therefore required. The practice of vigilantism, an activity that often operates on the border between informal and formal security provision, is thereby identified as an important aspect to analyze in the Liberian context.

Vigilantism can simply be understood as a form of informal security provision that people either actively choose or feel forced to rely on for their basic human security. Nevertheless, in contemporary media and elsewhere, vigilantism tends to be characterized by undisciplined mobs or crowds of young men without any clearly defined social or political identity, acting spontaneously on emotional impulses. As Lars Buur and Steffen Jensen have pointed out, however, viewing vigilantism from such a narrow perspective is not helpful when trying to understand such a complex phenomenon. Although vigilante organizations challenge rule of law and the state's monopoly of violence, this practice cannot be reduced to either expressions of the mob or to mere anti-dotes to formal law. The complexity and the ambivalence lies in the fact that vigilantism addresses issues of security and moral order relevant for people living on the margins of the reach of the formal state apparatus, and thereby also often becomes legitimate at local levels of the state. As such, vigilantism can arguably in many cases be seen as a form of local, everyday policing.[33]

As a result of deep mistrust of the state and formal security providers, vigilantism can emerge and be encouraged. Daniel Nina, for example, has ar-gued that vigilantism arises from the perception that the state is doing nothing to guarantee the safety of a community. The state in this light is thereby seen as limited player with regard to crime prevention. Accordingly, the notion of the state as the sole guarantor of safety and security becomes little more than a myth.[34] Still, as has been pointed out by David Pratten and Atreyee Sen, vig-ilantism must be understood at the same time as something more than a pop-ular response to the vacuum left by state collapse, failure, or instrumentalized disorder, despite the fact that police resourcing and corruption contribute ma-terially to the emergence and continuing legitimacy of vigilantes.[35] Informal security provision should not be understood as something entirely separated from the formal security sphere. These organized attempts to defeat crime or enforce norms and law and order, sometimes with violent measures, are often claimed to be outside of, and in opposition to, an inefficient and even preda-tory state. Yet, Buur and Jensen argue, the links between these informal groups and the state are often more complex. These groups operate at the frontier of the state, blurring the boundaries of what normally falls within and outside the formal sphere. Formal security providers sometimes take part in informal security provision, like police officers in vigilante groups, while state represen-tatives, on the other hand, have used vigilante groups for legally sanctioned violence.[36] In the case of Nigeria, Pratten gives further examples of these blur-ring boundaries between vigilantism and state activities, as he demonstrates how the state itself and individual state governors have provided a significant impetus for vigilante practices. As Pratten shows, in this case state governors sponsored vigilante groups as a substitute for autonomous state-level police forces because the federal police were unable to deal with local conflicts.[37]

ILLICIT, BUT STILL LEGITIMATE

Suzette Heald, in her research on vigilantism in Tanzania, shows how strongly the state and vigilante groups can be connected. In this case villagers in cen-tral Tanzania from the early 1980s and onward began to organize their own from of collective policing, which came to be known as *sungusungu*. Heald shows that these groups, which initially bypassed the official state struc-tures, far from being rejected have instead become an integral part of the administrative structures of rural Tanzania. In northern Tanzania *sungusungu* organizations emerged from the start with strong state support, the administration mandating local communities to codify their own laws and impose their own punishments. This, Heald argues, raises questions about the nature of the postcolonial state in Africa. It is easy to regard the emergence of such unofficial police forces as yet another threat to human rights. But it is important to contextualize these movements in the circumstances from which they arise. These specific informal security groups tend to evoke a positive public response. At the community level *sungusungu* groups have received little but praise, and at this level they are also believed to actually represent the righteousness of the ordinary citizen, as a response to criminals and a guard against corruption in the form of a state officialdom. Even at the state level, the political and administrative wing of the government largely agrees and supports them accordingly.[38] But, as Pratten and Sen question, is it "private" or "public" policing when a government legislates to authorize local defense forces or to sponsor vigilante groups? And when communities grasp opportunities within the law to organize their own protection, without being explicitly authorized to do so, is it then "private policing"?[39] Such questions, I would argue, unavoidably shed light on the complexity of the blurred boundaries and existing links between private and public, state and nonstate, and formal and informal security provision.

Furthermore, as Thomas Kirsch and Tilo Grätz underline in their analysis of vigilantism in Africa, the question of who is entitled to enact justice, to police morality, and to sanction wrongdoings has increasingly been subjected to violent conflict in many African countries.[40] These questions thereby open up opportunities for the analysis of conflicts and contestation between such presumed dichotomies over the authority of security provision and over what parts of these practices are to be considered legitimate or illegitimate. In the words of Ray Abrahams, "The analyst of vigilantes is by definition operating in the shadows rather than the bright light of consensus and legitimate authority, and the boundary between vigilante and criminal, like that between heroes and bandits or patriots and traitors, is both fluid and manipulable."[41] Similarly, Chabal and Daloz suggest that when examining the range of activities informal security-providing networks carry out they should be analyzed from the perspective of "legitimacy" and "accountability" rather than perceptions of "legal" or "illegal." In a context of patron-client relations, the notions of legal and illegal can become irrelevant as accountability takes the form of redistribution. Patrons who manage to provide their clients with the expected resources will largely be considered legitimate, even if illicit. It is only when patrons fail to redistribute resources, Chabal and Daloz argue, that their activities are regarded as criminal.[42] I proceed with the acknowledgement that vigilante groups, or informal security groups in general, may be seen as illegal from one perspective while at the same time be considered as both accountable and legitimate by ordinary citizens and, unofficially, even by the very state.

The links between informal security providers and the formal sphere are, for different reasons, often kept hidden. As Lund points out in the case of Niger, vigilante groups along with various informal actors portrayed the state as their antithesis, as the state was considered distinctly removed from the local arena. These groups had an ambiguous position as they searched for credibility. On the one hand, they emphasized their nonstate status and, on the other, they operated in the formal language of the state. Vigilantes could, for example, sometimes involve themselves in police matters. In this sense these groups, by vying to establish their own public authority, paradoxically become part of the very state they depict as distinct, distant, and exterior.[43] But, as Abrahams reminds us, vigilantism cannot exist alone but operates alongside, and typically on, the structural and cultural frontiers of state power. Vigilantism, furthermore, is typically more critical of the state's actual performance rather than the state itself.[44] In the following section these blurred boundaries between formal states and informal actors, here used for their violent potential but also their ability to protect, is considered further.

THE STATE, INFORMAL SECURITY PROVIDERS, VIGILANTES, AND REBEL GROUPS

To achieve political ends governments on the African continent have used more than community-based vigilante groups. Other informal security-providing networks and even rebel groups have in fact unofficial links to formal states. The Kamajors in Sierra Leone are an important example of this, which Hoffman describes as a web of social relations or patronage networks that became militarized during the war. The ethnically Mende-based Kamajors constituted the largest force of the country's Civil Defence Forces, which served as an umbrella term for disparate Sierra Leonean militias. When the Mende-dominated Sierra Leone People's Party won the election in 1996, the Kamajors became even more influential. Sam Hinga Norman, a key figure in the Kamajor movement was also appointed as the party's deputy minister of defense. As Hoffman argues, the Kamajors thereby became widely perceived, particularly by the Sierra Leone Army, to be the party government's de facto security force. Under the banner of the Civil Defence Forces, the Kamajors, along with other irregular forces, later on during the war helped to reinstate the Sierra Leone People's Party in 1998.[45] But the state-sanctioned use of the Kamajors is not the only example of this practice in Sierra Leone during the war. The usage of the West Side Boys militia during the end of the civil war is another illustrative example, as military commanders and politicians employed them as a tactical instrument in a larger plot to safeguard their own military and political interests. The West Side Boys militia was one of several military actors in the Sierra Leone civil war, which became a useful tool for politicians and which was partly encouraged and managed in a way that benefited sections of the political elite. As President Ahmad Tejan Kabbah and his government in 2000 grew increasingly afraid of the rebel movement Revolutionary United Front, the government of Sierra Leone made the West Side Boys part of an "ad-hoc security force." This force was successfully used against the Revolutionary United Front, eventually forcing them to lay down their weapons.[46]

These Sierra Leonean cases clearly demonstrate how strategically important the unofficial, yet state-sanctioned, use of informal security networks, and even rebel structures, can be. It also illustrates how formal and informal actors interact to gain mutual benefits and to reach political, military, and economic goals in times of both war and peace. But the unofficial state use of informal security providers of different types is clearly a complicated issue. Does such action undermine the state or rather strengthen it? Is it a threat to security or a way to stabilize unsecure and fragile societies? The International Crisis Group, investigating state use of nonstate or vigilante groups, which had taken up arms to protect their communities as a reaction to growing insurgencies, for certain security functions in four African cases, calls such an act a "double-edged sword."[47] They find that such an approach for weak African states at times is viewed as a necessity. But at the same time it is often a dangerous way to act. The more fragile a state is the more dependent it becomes on the vigilante group, but also the less able to police it or prevent abuses of power. Also, the efficiency of a vigilante can be both fruitful and problematic. The more successful the vigilante group is against insurgencies, the harder it is to demobilize when no longer needed. The vigilante groups by their very nature carry an inherent risk, the International Crisis Group finds, while at the same time they can be more efficient than the state in providing local security and enjoy greater legitimacy in the eyes of local communities.[48] Accordingly, state use of a variety of informal security providers on the African continent is a fact and needs to be further analyzed and better understood. Such action can imply a range of consequences as informal security-providing actors represent opportunities when it comes to strengthening security but at the same time can be a threat to stability.

INFORMAL SECURITY PROVISION AND VIGILANTISM IN LIBERIA

How, then, are we to understand informal security provision and vigilantism in Liberia? The analysis by Kirsch and Grätz of African vigilantism has shown us that there is amazing variation in how vigilante groups are structured and organized on the continent. Vigilantes have been influenced by and aligned with institutions as varied as secret societies, community-oriented agencies of policing, the military, traditional assemblies and courts, private security companies, NGOs, sports associations, and hunters' associations. Kirsch and Grätz also note that there is considerable variety in how the different vigilante groups acquire their legitimacy and how they relate to state agencies and other political and legal authorities.[49] The wars in Liberia left the country in ruins, with a state security apparatus far from being capable of safeguarding the basic security of its citizens. Vigilantism, or informal security provision in general, in Liberia could be both an alternative and a response to a state with limited capacity, or even unwillingness, to provide security for its citizens. On the other hand, vigilantism or the mobilization of other types of informal security-providing groups could also be a practice used by the state, the state security institutions, and other actors within the state apparatus to contribute to the overall security of ordinary Liberians. Seen from yet another perspective, vigilantism and informal security provision could even potentially be used by the very same actors and institutions to fulfill personal, political, or economic interests. As Pratten and Sen note, contemporary vigilantism relates both to the fragmentation of the sovereignty of nation-states and to the dependence that states have on the vigilance of their citizens.[50] This mutual dependence, and the links between the state and informal security groups in the Liberian context, is therefore further examined later in this book.

From Rebel Soldiers to Ex-combatants
Finding New Roles and Purpose

No one knows exactly how many they were, the men and women who fought in the many rebel factions in the Liberian civil wars. Some moved from one rebel movement to another, some laid down their weapons when the first war came to a halt in 1996, only to take up arms again as violence resumed in 1999. Some even avoided the whole disarmament, demobilization, rehabilitation, and reintegration process that followed the official end of the war in 2003. Because of the benefits offered, others enlisted as combatants in the process, even though they might not have had that status. According to the official numbers given by the National Commission on Disarmament, Demobilization, Rehabilitation and Reintegration, by November 2004, when the disarmament and demobilization phase ended, 103,019 persons had been disarmed.[51] No matter the exact numbers, the Liberian wars, which according to popular estimations may have taken between 60,000 and 200,000 lives, created a large category of Liberian ex-combatants. To specifically understand the ex-combatants who have remained active in postwar rebel networks, we need to analyze their lives and opportunities (and lack of such) after the peace agreement was signed.

I do not go into detail on the Liberian civil wars here, except for a brief description, and I do not attempt to examine root causes and political developments during the course of wars either; that has been done elsewhere.[52] Instead, my focus here is on *postwar* Liberia and the transition from rebel soldiers to ex-combatants active in postwar rebel networks.

A BRIEF HISTORY OF THE LIBERIAN WARS

On December 24, 1989, the first Liberian civil war began, as Charles Taylor and a group of about 150 rebel soldiers, known as the National Patriotic Front of Liberia, entered the country as they crossed the borders to Nimba County from neighboring Côte d'Ivoire. At this time President Samuel Doe held power. At the age of twenty-eight, Master Sergeant Samuel Doe, of Krahn origin, had come to power on the night of April 12, 1980, as he and a group of noncommissioned officers violently ousted the former regime in Liberia. The coup ended President William Tolbert's rule (1971–1980) and the over hundred-year-old Americo-Liberian political, economic, and military dominance.[53] Doe, described as Liberia's first warlord, became increasingly devoted to consolidating power for himself, and in doing so he had to marginalize other powerful actors.[54] In his first five years in power, Doe executed more than fifty rivals, real and imagined, after secret trials.[55] Furthermore, Doe, in the same manner as the Americo-Liberian elite before him, began immediately after seizing power to systematically promote individuals into key political and military positions from a few selected clans within his own ethnic group.[56]

The NPFL, who had gathered supporters and mobilized fighters within the Gio and Mano communities, in particular because of Doe's violence and suppression against them, soon came to split into two factions. In 1990 Prince Johnson, a former commissioned officer of the Armed Forces of Liberia and commander of the Liberian military police, who joined forces with Charles Taylor, broke away from the NPFL. With Johnson followed several hundreds of Gio and Mano rebels to form the Independent National Patriotic Front of Liberia (INPFL). The two factions, who at times fought each other, both came closer to Monrovia while defeating the Armed Forces of Liberia and reached the Liberian capital in July 1990. In September of the same year, Johnson, seemingly with the help of the newly created West African peacekeeping force, the Economic Community of West African States Monitoring Group, managed to capture President Doe. While being videotaped, the president was tortured and eventually killed. Even though Johnson had been the one who eventually ended Doe's time in power, Taylor had a stronger hold of Liberia. In 1992 Johnson went into exile in Nigeria and the INPFL collapsed. Many of his combatants then joined the NPFL. As the war spread, several new rebel factions also emerged. The United Liberation Movement of Liberia (ULIMO) was one such group, which soon came to split into two separate forces, ULIMO-J and ULIMO-K. Meanwhile other rebel groups were born, such as the Liberian Peace Council, as well as groups with localized regional support, such as the Lofa Defence Force.[57] After seven years of war, Charles Taylor and his political party, the National Patriotic Party—formed out of the NPFL—won the presidential elections in 1997, in competition between the different rebel factions that had emerged, leaving Taylor as the new Liberian president.

In 1999 war broke out again. The security situation had remained uncertain in 1998 and 1999, but it was in late 1999 in Lofa County that a first series of armed attacks occurred. A new rebel group, Liberians United for Reconciliation and Democracy (LURD), emerged and by the spring of 2003 managed to enter Monrovia. The core of LURD's rebel soldiers were Liberians returning from exile in Guinea, but the movement also came to recruit young people in Liberia. LURD also relied heavily on mercenaries from Sierra Leone and Guinea. As fighting continued, the Movement for Democracy in Liberia emerged, eventually operating in the south while LURD was still active in the north. The advancements of these rebel movements, combined with new international pressure on the Taylor government, finally forced Taylor into exile.[58] An interim government was established, and the United Nations deployed its peacekeeping mission to Liberia.

LIBERIA'S LINGERING REBEL STRUCTURES

Even though the first civil war officially came to an end in 1997, much of the everyday wartime reality remained the same for many of the former rebel soldiers in Liberia. War bureaucracy was preserved on an official level, as the NPFL turned into a political party: the National Patriotic Party. The former warlord, Charles Taylor, was elected president, and the security apparatus was maintained by former NPFL commanders. But other ex-combatants also preserved wartime structures in informal networks. Utas did fieldwork among ex-combatants in Monrovia during the first half of 1998. In a deserted factory in central Monrovia, known as "the Palace," a dozen ex-combatants, originating from all over Liberia, had settled after the war. Some had been part of the NPFL or INPFL, and, while some had remained loyal to these groups, others had joined sides with the Liberian Peace Council, the Lofa Defence Force, or the ULIMO factions or even the remnants of the Armed Forces of Liberia later in the war. Utas notes that there were few indications of Palace youth reintegration in larger society. Palace youth, as much of other footloose youth, were part of a subculture at odds with rest of the society. Although they had participated in various NGO-led rehabilitation and reintegration programs at times, and even though they had learned a variety of skills in these programs, very few were able to get stable work. Furthermore, the ex-combatants of the Palace appeared to have no intentions of returning to the communities they originated from. Some had lost their families; others tended to avoid their relatives. Utas found that family networks had been replaced with informal structures of wartime friends and commanders. In this sense the end of war had had little effect on the military structures of the Palace ex-combatants. The military structures were still used for maintaining discipline and to form patron-client networks, populated mainly by former commanders but reaching all the way up to the governmental level. Through these links the ex-combatants of the Palace could be used by Monrovian Big Men for boosting political rallies or carrying out illegal activities.[59]

Many ex-combatants had come from the margins of society, and enlistment with the various rebel factions was a means to escape this position and to gain a place at the center of society. The rebel movements had accordingly been especially successful in recruiting from among the already marginalized and highly dissatisfied urban and semiurban youth. Yet, as noted by Utas, for most ex-combatants remarginalization rather than reintegration awaited them by the end of the war. It is also highly conceivable that when Liberia once again was drawn back into warfare in 1999, many of the ex-combatants living at the Palace, with their military structures still in place, took up arms once more.[60]

What we can see from the example provided by Utas of ex-combatants in Monrovia is that rather than the ex-combatants going home and seeking to restore earlier networks, their wartime experiences, the possibility of drawing on benefits from former commanders and, even more important, from Big Men in the Liberian elite, and the lack of other employment opportunities made them prone to preserve their military structures and keep their close relationships. Since Liberia's postwar reality offered nothing more than remarginalization for many of the youths, remaining somewhat mobilized offered security. This maintained postwar mobilization probably also facilitated the renewed recruitment during the second civil war. The birth of LURD and the Movement for Democracy in Liberia, based on the former command structures of ULIMO, also bore evidence of this.

Evidently, the end of the first civil war did not lead to the dismantling of former rebel structures or chains of command, but neither did the end of the second war nor the signing of the official peace agreement in 2003. In 2005 Hoffman found that the Duala neighborhood at the outskirts of western Monrovia, which had been occupied by LURD during the war, was still a central area for the ex-combatants. At the Johnson Yard, near the main Duala market in the densely packed neighborhood, a former commander of the Civil Defence Forces and later in LURD lived with his family and other former fighters.

Hoffman observed that as in so many other contexts, the ex-combatants from different factions, even this early in the postconflict period, shared the area, as the factionalism that had divided them during the war no longer made any difference. A steady stream of ex-combatants that had served under the former commander came to visit him daily. The former commander had become a Big Man of sorts, and the ex-combatants came to beg small favors, offer patronage payments, or simply to check in. Hoffman had seen the same cycles of visitors during the years of war when the former commander lived in Sierra Leone, Guinea, and later in Liberia, as he had helped rally troops for LURD. During the war he could mobilize fighters for war and assemble combatants for labor on the battlefield. At other times he could gather them for smaller operations like retrieving stolen goods or send them out for work in the region's mines or plantations. The commander thereby effectively controlled the labor of these youths. As Hoffman suggests, areas such as Duala became spaces for organization and deployment of violent labor with ex-combatants, who at any moment, quickly and efficiently, could be called on as laborers in different fields.[61] The former commander's ability to utilize the wartime rebel structures after the war, by mobilizing the former fighters for smaller assignments or work on the rubber plantations or in the diamond mines, and the ex-combatants' need for economic opportunities and societal security, provides an explanation for the lingering postwar rebel structures. In this sense, as was also shown by the example provided by Utas, the peacetime rationale for staying connected and mobilized followed much of the same logic as it had during the war. It shows further how former commanders can remain central nodes, even after the war is over.

Furthermore, Morten Bøås and Anne Hatløy, in their research on militia membership and reintegration in Liberia, based on interviews with Liberian ex-combatants from various rebel factions, found that what caused Liberian youths to fight in the civil wars and join armed factions were mainly security concerns—for themselves and their families and communities. Security, regardless of which armed group they belonged to, was given as the most important reason for joining, based on various ideas regarding protection and opportunity. Bøås and Hatløy point out that even though the motives of the ex-combatants clearly could have changed during the war, their reasons for "getting in" were neither very political nor overwhelmingly based on a desire for personal enrichment or from idleness; it was based on the lack of security.[62] Given that insecurity still prevails in Liberia, preserving wartime networks, either as part of informal security groups or in other constellations, or joining them despite having a past as a rebel soldier seems like a rational strategy for individual, family, or community protection, even though the war is over. Accordingly, ex-combatants and others, at least from the point of view of personal and economic security, might have similar incentives to preserve or to join new informal security networks as during the war.

POSTWAR REBEL NETWORKS AS THE MAIN SECURITY THREAT

Along with the end of war came also the fear of postwar rebel networks. From 2003 onward a series of reports on postwar insecurity emphasized the significant threat to peace and stability that organized networks of ex-combatants were believed to constitute. Many observers linked this to a failed disarmament, demobilization, rehabilitation, and reintegration process.[63] While the government of Liberia itself, by 2008, argued that the reintegration of ex-combatants had gone well, it admitted that some still posed a lingering security threat. According to their estimations, approximately nine thousand ex-fighters remained outside the reintegration and rehabilitation programs, and these were the ones believed to pose local, national, and regional security threats.[64] Postwar rebel networks involved in the exploitation of natural resources was one of the major concerns that observers pointed out. Ex-combatants, organized by former rebel commanders and businessmen, were reported to be exploiting diamond, timber, gold, and rubber resources with virtual impunity, generating significant income. Postwar rebel networks were known to be operating in the Guthrie and Sinoe Rubber Plantations; the diamond mining areas of Lofa, Nimba, and Gbarpolu Counties; and the timber areas of Grand Bassa, River Cess, and Sinoe Counties, among other places, with the purpose of conducting illegal trade. These activities were seen to seriously undermine internal and external security.[65] The fears were that revenue from the ex-combatants' illegal trade in natural resources would be used to fund rebel groups and renew warfare, as was the case in the past, and that postwar rebel networks at the sites of their illegal occupations were behind human rights abuses against other Liberians. The Liberian state could be further weakened by the loss of revenue and thereby be even less capable of dealing with present security risks and challenges. And, finally, postwar rebel networks, regardless of their activities, because of their organized presence and lingering command and control systems, could easily be remobilized as mercenaries in the unstable region. The general, and seldom questioned, view on postwar rebel networks was accordingly that these structures posed such an acute threat to peace and stability that they had to be dissolved immediately.

LIBERIAN EX-COMBATANTS AS INFORMAL SECURITY PROVIDERS

The main focus for this research is to analyze how and why rebel networks, despite years of absence of war, are still relevant in postwar Liberia. The general view on postwar rebel networks has been that these structures remained to illegally exploit natural resources and as a potential source for remobilization for renewed warfare, made possible because of inadequacies in the formal reintegration process. This book does not question such explanations, but I do find such theories incomplete. I therefore search beyond such assumptions of why postwar rebel networks exist. To find answers to my research questions, I examine former rebel soldiers' ability to transform and adapt to the present postwar security political situation while making use of their organization structures and skills in security provision obtained as rebels during the wars.

The security political situation in Liberia, with weak formal security institutions with low capacity and a history of predatory behavior, has created an environment where informal initiatives for security and protection are called on. In such an environment informal security groups or networks have a natural platform. Given that insecurity prevails in Liberia—even though the levels of insecurity and violence clearly cannot be compared to the levels during the wars—some of those men and women who now have the status of ex-combatants might have the same reasons to remain a part of postwar rebel networks and, through them, join vigilante or other informal security groups, as they had during the wars. A contributing reason for them being mobilized could still be out of security concerns, based on ideas of protection for themselves, their families, and their communities, as Bøås and Hatløy write of the incentives of wartime recruits. Seen from this perspective, ex-combatants in postwar vigilante or informal security groups could thereby be perceived as a continuation of wartime mobilization. The postwar rebel structures could be seen in this light as a reflection of the continued insecurity in postwar Liberia.

Yet from another perspective, prewar Liberia also suffered from insecurity, with state structures either incapable or unwilling to provide its citizens with protection. Being organized again in different types of informal security groups could then also be seen as a consequence or continuum of the Liberian prewar situation. As Abrahams noted in his early analysis of vigilantism in Tanzania, although these groups posed problems for the state—with their lack of a formal legal base and illegal activities—one of the most interesting aspects of these groups was the depth of the widely shared desire for peace and order that led to their emergence, which genuinely seems to inform most of their activities.[66] Rebel structures maintained in informal security groups in postwar Liberia paradoxically could be interpreted as both a continuation of war as well as a striving for peace and security.

But I am not interested only in postwar rebel networks that have emerged as vigilante groups and as providers of local informal security for individuals and communities. Networks of former rebels involved in informal security provision owing to political or commercial interests are also a main concern here. Actors within the Liberian elite and the formal state apparatus may have an interest in making use of and gaining influence over these structures. As the ex-combatants have the ability to both provide security and create insecurity, this can make them valuable assets if they stay mobilized. In the following case studies, based on original interview material and findings from my fieldwork in Liberia, I illustrate how postwar rebel networks are organized and operate in the informal security arena and attempt to describe the rationale behind these lingering features of war. By doing so I intend to give further examples of how the adaptive capacity of former rebel soldiers is utilized by various Liberian actors. Based on the arguments here, I attempt to show how and why this remobilization or maintenance of rebel structures could be in line with the interests of former rebels, key influential actors within the Liberian elite, and formal state institutions, as well as ordinary Liberian citizens seeking protection and basic security in their everyday lives. Nonetheless, this analysis also seeks to explore potential risks that this postwar development poses to the general security situation and for renewed fighting and warfare in Liberia and in the wider West African region.

Conclusion

To understand why rebel networks do not simply vanish in the transition from war to peace, despite efforts to demobilize and reintegrate ex-combatants, this book analyzes hidden and explicit motives of ex-combatants (former rebel commanders, specifically), the Liberian political and economic elite, formal security institutions, and ordinary Liberian citizens for wishing these networks to stay organized. Accordingly, the analysis is focused on whether there in fact exists a need among these actors for postwar rebel networks. The theoretical starting point of this research has been the often-neglected informal security context to understand why postwar rebel networks can and do reappear in the shape of informal security networks after the war. Formal security institutions have often failed to provide citizens with basic security in places such as Liberia. Distrust in these institutions has made people turn to alternative solutions to cope with everyday life and safeguard their basic human security. In the Liberian case weak formal security institutions with low capacity and a history of predatory behavior have created an environment where informal initiatives for security and protection are called on. In this environment, ex-combatants have found a way to function as informal security providers by using their wartime networks, connections, and skills in their security and intimidation capabilities.

For *ordinary citizens* the motives behind wanting the continued mobilization of such networks is thereby based on a need to find protection, as postwar rebel networks—among other activities—function as vigilantes in neighborhoods where the police might be incapable or unwilling to operate.

In such cases ex-combatants might be community members' best options for protection. Yet to use ex-combatants as protectors is believed to entail many risks, as the ex-combatants are feared to act more violently than others without a combatant past, and because there is a great risk of impunity if these actors decide to take the law into their own hands.

The motives for *formal security institutions and authorities* to see the continued presence of postwar rebel networks as an advantage might not be so obvious. But as theories on vigilantism explain, formal and informal security institutions often coexist when state capacity is low. In such instances formal authorities can call on informal actors unofficially to act as security providers or to cooperate with formal security providers to strengthen their capacity to protect ordinary citizens. Yet the increasing delegitimization of formal institutions, as well as impunity and mob violence, is believed to be among the risks these actors must take into consideration when using informal security-providing networks.

For the *political and economic elite*, there are often hidden motives for promoting the continued existence of postwar rebel networks. Officially a government, and in this case the Liberian one, would argue that it would do anything in its power to break up wartime networks, as there are great risks of continued violence, or even renewed violence, if these networks are not abandoned and the ex-combatants are not reintegrated. But as the case studies show, there can be both political and financial gains to be made for these actors by unofficially utilizing postwar rebel networks. The forthcoming chapters reveal, for example, how the political and financial elite made financial gains by their unofficial cooperation with the postwar rebel network that had taken over one of the most important rubber plantations in Liberia, while they officially struggled at the same time to evict the ex-combatants from the plantation. Later, when the ex-combatants were finally removed from the command of the plantation, the management continued to use them as informal security providers, both because of their capacity for intimidation (as other workers could be threatened into carrying out their jobs even when the management failed to pay them) and because of their skill and knowledge in security and protection in general. Another example provided in this book reveals how such networks can be used to mobilize votes, show force, or simply supply personal bodyguards for the elite. But beyond these examples, we see in chapter 3 how the political elite in West Africa have also used postwar rebel networks for what is often feared most: renewed warfare.

The *ex-combatants* themselves can have several motives for remaining in or attaching themselves to a rebel network postwar. For example, in a society such as the Liberian one, there are not many employment opportunities, but, through connections, a postwar rebel network can provide temporary informal employment opportunities, often by providing informal security. Relying on other ex-combatants can also be a social security net, as many have spent years with their fellow combatants while their links have been weakened to family or others who could otherwise provide social security. But by preserving their wartime connections and ex-combatant identity, ex-combatants are also at risk of being stigmatized as violent or unpredictable, which in turn might lead to social exclusion or be a disadvantage when it comes to their chances of securing employment opportunities. Accordingly, ex-combatants must carefully weigh the risks and advantages that may come with a preserved ex-combatant identity and a postwar rebel network.

Former *rebel commanders*, if they have managed to preserve good connections to both the elite and ex-combatants, often have a special position in postwar rebel networks. If they manage to attach themselves to the right Big Man, they can secure benefits for ex-combatants in their networks such as employment opportunities and thereby economic support. This can make a former commander strategically important both for the elite actors who use them to mobilize ex-combatants for whatever purpose and for the ex-combatants whom the former commander or leader of the postwar rebel network calls on for such mobilization. Former commanders can thereby have more to gain than lower-ranking ex-combatants, as their direct connections to the elite in turn also can lead to better societal and employment opportunities (even formal ones). But former commanders or others who have leading positions in postwar rebel networks also have more to lose than lower-ranking ex-combatants. If former commanders attach themselves to the wrong Big Man—for example, a losing candidate in a political election—they are at risk of standing without any support after such an event, while they also might be especially targeted by the winning side, as they are more easily identified than other ex-combatants without prominent positions.

Networks are important in most people's lives. In Liberia they are vital. Involuntary independency can be a danger in any society, but in countries where the state and formal institutions are weak, people are forced to rely on other security nets. As Caroline Bledsoe argues in relation to networks of political patronage, people within a political climate of uncertainty and instability seek powerful mediators who can use personal influence to get them jobs and scholarships and protect them from heavy-handed government bureaucrats, for example. Bledsoe uses the notion of "being for" someone else or other people to explain this type of patronage politics. And, in such a context, a patron figure whom one is "for," Bledsoe notes, can be a chief, landlord, teacher, parent, senior wife, or older sibling. Whether such a person is kin is, however, less important than his or her capacity to perform mediative and protective functions.[67] Under such preconditions networks are shaped and sustained. People need patrons and the networks that come with them for their everyday security, whether it be for livelihood, protection against violence, or for other social reasons. Most people have several Big Men and are simultaneously attached to several networks. For my informants, postwar rebel networks have become one of their most important safety nets. They rely on kin and other important relations as well, but these networks can from time to time provide them with employment opportunities that otherwise would be closed to them, which is one of the key factors behind ex-combatants' decisions to attach themselves to such structures. But because many actors—not only the ex-combatants themselves but actors from the elite to ordinary citizens—find postwar rebel networks useful, they have remained important to Liberian society, for good and bad.

Furthermore, these networks' informal character is key for their continued survival. For the ex-combatants this means that they can use them when they need them or be more or less active within them with each opportunity. A big political event such as an election, for example, can expand such networks, as this can bring new opportunities for ex-combatants. At other times other networks might be more important for individual ex-combatants. For the elite the informal character of such networks is crucial for their use of these structures. Elite actors can continue to use these networks unofficially under such circumstances when it serves their purposes, without having to declare this publicly. The elite can use them unofficially from time to time without formally having to bear the responsibility for the risks of doing so. Postwar rebel networks can, in other words, be perfect political tools because of their official invisibility, as they have been formally demobilized but unofficially maintained. In such circumstances postwar rebel networks can remain relevant long after war has been declared over.

CHAPTER 2

Regional Wars and Recycled Rebels

THE REMOBILIZATION OF POSTWAR REBEL NETWORKS
IN TIMES OF WAR AND CRISIS IN WEST AFRICA

This is a book on the forces and mechanisms allowing, and calling for, postwar rebel networks to linger long after war has come to an end. In the following chapters I illustrate the continued importance these networks have, for both the ex-combatants themselves and the Liberian economic and political elite, several years after the peace agreement was signed. Accordingly, the emphasis is on *postwar* Liberia and the period after 2003, when war had been declared officially over. Yet this chapter commences elsewhere: it takes us back to the emergence of the Liberian civil war in 1989 and continues through the turbulent and violent years that followed in the whole region until the end of war in 2003. This chapter begins with the stories of three young Liberian men, whose backgrounds, as sons of high-ranking army officers under President Samuel Doe's rule, came to shape their lives and war trajectories. Having belonged to the ethnic Krahn minority, favored by Doe, Michael's, Simon's, and Jacob's lives dramatically changed when war began in 1989 and their Krahn identity and fathers' military positions were turned against them. Difficult circumstances, coincidence, and active choices drew the three young men into active combat. They became soldiers, rebels, commanders, regional warriors, and eventually ex-combatants. One of them also spent years in prison. They became part, but also mobilizers, of strong networks based on wartime rebel structures that came to affect their lives long after the wars in Liberia were over.

From the early 1990s not only was war raging in Liberia but large parts of West Africa were in different stages of crisis. Civil war had broken out in Sierra Leone in 1991, as the Revolutionary United Front (RUF) rebels, backed by Charles Taylor, eventually came to challenge President Joseph Saidu Momoh's and later Ahmad Tejan Kabbah's rule. Guinea and President Lansana Conté had to face the consequences of the neighboring wars, as hundreds of thousands of refugees fled the violence across the Guinean borders throughout much of the 1990s. President Conté and the political and military elite were also actively involved in these wars. As a result of their taking sides against Taylor, incursions on Guinean soil were one of the results that became a reality for Conté and the Guinean population. By following the young Liberian men in this chapter, through this time of war and crisis, we move across West African borders and discover how the mobility of the rebels, in addition to the antagonisms or loyalties between the ruling political actors in the region, entangled the conflicts to such a degree that it was impossible to tell where one stopped and the other one began or whether the different conflicts in fact were just one great West African war with different battlefields.

The logic behind postwar rebel networks and how individual ex-combatants like Michael, Simon, and Jacob, on the one hand, and the Liberian political and financial elite, on the other, made strategic use of these structures following the end of the war is at the very center of analysis in this book.[1] We follow these networks as illegal plantation occupiers, informal security providers, neighborhood vigilantes, and security forces mobilized for the Liberian presidential elections. Each case gives us further insights into why these structures simply did not vanish with the end of the war, how they function, and why they have become so relevant in the postwar context. But the postwar rebel networks were in these cases not used in their capacity as combatants or with any obvious attempt at renewed warfare. The use of the very same networks in this chapter differs. The young Liberian men and their network of former rebels became valuable to regional elites *specifically* because of their combatant past and their readiness to be used in warfare, as soon as the first Liberian civil war had come to an end, in a still turbulent time of violence and crisis in West Africa. The ongoing war in neighboring Sierra Leone, the crisis in Guinea, and the instability in the whole Mano River region continued to impact the young men's lives, despite the recently acquired peace in Liberia following Charles Taylor's coming to power as the new Liberian president in 1997.[2] In fact, Taylor's success, and later election victory, forced ex-combatants who had been opposed to him into exile. But the forced exile did not shatter the networks of rebels. Outside Liberia, at least for these men, their links to one another were instead strengthened.

In this chapter, with its point of departure in Michael's, Simon's, and Jacob's stories, we discover how postwar rebel networks in regions of instability can be used for what is often feared the most in relation to ex-combatants: renewed warfare in neighboring conflicts. Through the trajectories of Michael and Simon in particular (Jacob's story as a combatant took quite a different turn) and other young Liberian rebel soldiers, we see how actors within the regional elites efficiently tapped into the networks of Liberian rebels in exile, using former commanders as entry points and mobilizers. These networks were drawn into the regional dimension of the ongoing West African wars and crises, where combatants were moved over international borders, recruited and mobilized by the political elite in the region in their struggle for power and influence.

Nevertheless, the approach to use individual narratives to understand a bigger picture of remobilization has its limitations. Michael's, Simon's, and Jacob's stories do not reveal all aspects of the extremely complex phenomenon of the recycling of postwar rebel networks, nor all motivations for individual remobilization of combatants during this turbulent time of war and crisis in West Africa. These three individual stories alone are not the basis for a complete and fully overarching illustration of the use, motivations, and movements of such networks. Yet individual stories and these leading narratives give us much-needed, and seldom acknowledged, grassroots perspectives that undoubtedly contribute to a more comprehensive understanding of the phenomenon. The narratives provide for a point of entry to these and similar experiences of individual rebel recycling and the use of larger networks postwar. By using individual stories, we identify important pieces of a bigger puzzle on how individual ex-combatants can relate to postwar rebel networks and how these networks in turn are used by important actors on a strategic level. Their stories are thereby valuable contributions for the illustration of how postwar rebel networks, even after the first Liberian civil war, proved to be of significant importance to the regional elites—if they stayed mobilized, well connected, and willing to once again use their skills in warfare, that is. We also discover how essential these networks can be for the individual combatant, both in times of war and afterward and how devastating it can be for a former rebel soldier to be excluded from such a network, as the story of Jacob bears witness to.

Becoming a Rebel

Growing up in Liberia in the 1970s, Michael, Simon, and Jacob were only young boys when the military coup that brought the twenty-eight-year-old master sergeant Samuel Doe to power in 1980 came to change their lives dramatically. Doe had been one of the seventeen soldiers who murdered President William Tolbert on April 12 that year. He was also the one who became accepted as nominal head of state and cochair of the new junta, known as the People's Redemption Council, who declared that power now was in their hands. Even though coups occurred frequently in West Africa at this time, the events in Liberia in 1980 were quite different from what people had been accustomed to because of the bloody and highly public manner in which the former government representatives were killed. Thirteen leading members of the former government were passed before a tribunal and convicted of corruption a few days after the coup, then executed in a public display on the beach in Monrovia. The new administration, however, purported that they had liberated Liberia and were acting on behalf of indigenous Liberians repressed by the Americo-Liberian elite. The junta was thereby initially very popular, and people celebrated in carnival mood on the streets of Monrovia.[3] But Doe, himself an ethnic Krahn, soon revealed that it was not the indigenous Liberians, but himself and his own group in particular, that he intended to favor. As noted by Amos Sawyer, for example, Doe's military dictatorship was responsible for extensive assaults on vital institutions of Liberian society, reaching all the way down to the level of villages, where chiefs and elders were replaced. Doe's brutal regime was challenged by students, religious leaders, and even fellow military officers, but many opponents were murdered, imprisoned, or forced to flee the country.[4] For Michael, Simon, and Jacob, as sons of generals and a major in Doe's army and being of Krahn origin, the new change of regime meant that they became part of the small privileged minority promoted during Doe's years in power.

The Armed Forces of Liberia (AFL)'s senior leadership, like other institutions, had been dominated by Americo-Liberians, and resentment was strong among the indigenous lower ranks, who lacked the opportunities enjoyed by the officers corps. Yet Doe's seizure of power did not bring about the change the lower-ranking soldiers might have hoped for. On the contrary, Doe set out to use the old discriminatory system to his own advantage. It was soon evident that Doe had no intention of getting rid of ethnic divisions. Instead, he manipulated them in a new manner, filling the most important military positions with his ethnic Krahn, while at the same time purging the army of ethnic Gios and Manos. As expressed by Adekeye Adebajo, Doe effectively turned the AFL into an "instrument of Krahn oppression." This label came to follow the AFL throughout the civil wars. The Executive Mansion Guards, the Special Anti-Terrorist Unit, and all four infantry battalions were headed by Krahns soon after the coup.[5] And it was especially the Gios and Manos who were victimized under the rule of Doe and at the hands of the army.

One incident that stands out, and from which Taylor and his rebel forces could easily rally popular support owing to the hatred of the Doe regime and the AFL it had created, was the massacre of an estimated three thousand Gio and Mano citizens in Nimba County by Doe's Krahn-dominated army in 1985. The former AFL commander and Doe's fellow coup maker, Gen. Thomas Quiwonkpa, a Gio from Nimba County who Doe had forced into exile because of his growing popularity, had returned to Monrovia in November 1985 with his men, crossing the Sierra Leonean border to overthrow Doe from power. But the coup failed, and Doe unleashed the AFL massacre of Gios and Manos in Nimba County in revenge, both within the AFL's own ranks and among the civilian population. The Krahn-dominated soldiers burned villages and killed indiscriminately. And even though Nimba County was the epicenter of the purge, the killings of Gios and Manos were also reported in Monrovia and Grand Gedeh County.[6] But Doe lived to regret his brutality, as Gios and Manos thereby mobilized against him when Charles Taylor and the National Patriotic Front of Liberia (NPFL) rebels gave them the opportunity in 1989. For Michael and Simon, who had grown up with the privilege of being Krahns and as the sons of army generals, and Jacob a son of an AFL major, the NPFL rebellion and the subsequent fall of Doe in 1990 put their lives in great danger. Krahns were now among those targeted by the rebels, and the hatred of the AFL had grown strong.

Michael and Jacob were first cousins, sons of two brothers. They grew up far from each other, Jacob in a quarter near the army barracks where the AFL men were living with their families in Monrovia and Michael in Sinoe County. Nevertheless, during his whole childhood, Jacob was sent to Sinoe during the holidays, which made Michael and Jacob good friends from an early age. Simon was Jacob's best friend growing up in Monrovia, while Michael and Simon also knew each other well, both through Jacob and their fathers. But the war was to bring the three young men even closer. Michael's and Jacob's fathers were killed in battle with Taylor's forces early on in the war, while Simon's father fled the country. With their families shattered and war on them, the three young men had to find protection. For Michael, Simon, and Jacob, this meant taking up arms. As violence escalated in 1992 and as several rebel factions emerged, Michael, who had now reached the age of seventeen, voluntarily joined the AFL. At this point the Liberian army recruited heavily among young Krahn men to get a stronger force against the rebels, as most men of the other ethnic groups had already left the army. From 1990 the AFL was able to mobilize support by promising to protect Mandingos and Krahns. Mandingos, like the Krahns, were regarded as Doe collaborators and targeted in revenge for the systematic violence and previous massacre on Gios and Manos in Liberia. But, as noted by Stephen Ellis, by 1993 at the latest, the army, as other armed factions, had ceased to credibly represent the interests of any ethnic group or any ideology. As Ellis argues, all factions were at this time best identified by reference to their leaders' personality and public profile and the identity of their external alliances.[7]

During these developments Michael decided to follow a new leader. In 1993 a small group of fighters broke away from the army to form the predominately Krahn rebel group Liberian Peace Council (LPC), led by George Boley. Michael, now an eighteen-year-old rebel soldier, was part of the group, which fought mainly Taylor's forces in southeastern Liberia. Boley, a Krahn politician, had served as a minister under both Tolbert and Doe and had been able to gather about 2,500 combatants for his LPC. While Michael continued to fight for Boley and the LPC, Simon, only a few years older, had chosen a similar path. Just like Michael, following in their fathers' footsteps, Simon had joined the AFL after the war had started, as the unleashed violence was now turned against the Krahns. But as Michael followed George Boley at the emergence of the LPC, Simon came instead to fight the NPFL from within the other main rebel group at that time, the United Liberation Movement of Liberia (ULIMO). The ULIMO had been founded in 1991 in Sierra Leone by leading Krahn and Mandingo politicians. In early 1994 ULIMO had split into two factions along ethnic lines. The roughly 3,800-man-strong Krahn-dominated ULIMO-J was headed by Roosevelt Johnson, while the Mandingo-dominated ULIMO-K, with about 6,800 fighters, was led by Alhaji Kromah.[8]

Jacob's destiny during the war was entangled with both Michael's and Simon's. In 1991, when he was only seventeen, Jacob, like Simon, joined ULIMO. An army officer called Charles Dent had left the AFL for ULIMO, and this man became Jacob's entry point to the rebel movement.[9] Dent was commanding a unit of illiterate rebels. For this reason Dent approached Jacob, whom he knew through his father. Jacob had been just about to graduate from high school when war broke out and the life he knew drastically changed. With his family shattered and violence all around him, Dent instead became his chance to find protection. Jacob was recruited to become what he himself calls commander Dent's "first sergeant," and in this position he kept records for Dent and therefore followed him everywhere, taking notes and documenting all that Dent needed for his ULIMO unit. In this way Jacob climbed the hierarchies of the rebel system fast, and he soon became a commander himself.

In 1993 Jacob was reunited with Michael again. A peace conference had been held in July the same year, and a cease-fire had been agreed on. But Taylor was slow to disarm, and renewed violence was soon a fact. During this turmoil the LPC was born. According to Jacob, it first consisted of fifty-two men, with George Boley as their leader. Both Jacob and Michael had, despite their young age, been successful during the war. They had managed to climb the hierarchy and were chosen as two of the main commanders close to Boyle. And their close relation to the rebel leader continued during the time Boley himself gained a new formal status, which happened only a few years later. On August 19, 1995, the Abuja Agreement was signed, in yet another attempt at achieving peace in Liberia. The peace treaty set up a Council of the State of Liberia, to consist of five members and a chair, a position Charles Taylor insisted on gaining. Two of the other invited members came from the warring factions: Alhaji Kromah from the ULIMO-K and Michael's and Jacob's leader, George Boley of the LPC.[10] Boley thereby held a formal state position once more and new authority that was to bring new benefits for men like Michael and Jacob who had remained loyal to him during the war. Boley saw to it that Jacob got a position as a police captain in 1995. Jacob had gone from being a young rebel soldier to now being part of the formal security system. Things were looking good for him, and he was enjoying his new influence. But the situation was to change rapidly.

The invitation of warring faction leaders into the new government did not bring about the long-awaited peace in Liberia this time around either. Fighting continued between Taylor's NPFL forces and Boley's LPC in the southeast, between the two wings of ULIMO in the west, and between the NPFL and ULIMO-K in Bong County.[11] Finally, in 1996, after thirteen broken peace deals and seven years of raging civil war, the Abuja II talks were initiated, and a political climate emerged in which elections could be held. The security situation was far from perfect in Liberia, but there was a presence of Nigerian peacekeepers and relative stability within the coalition government. Charles Taylor, however, dominated the Liberian political environment. This was clearly reflected in the election results, as the former rebel leader and his National Patriotic Party won a landslide victory in 1997. It has been debated whether Taylor won because of the Liberian public's fear of postelection violence and a return to conflict were he to face an electoral defeat or simply because this was a result of Liberians finding Taylor and the National Patriotic Party to be the only likely candidates to control a deteriorating security situation.[12] For Michael, Simon, Jacob, and others who had been opposing Taylor during war, the election result was nothing short of a disaster.

The Camp Johnson Road Combatants

War had separated Simon from Michael and Jacob for years, but Taylor's success brought the three childhood friends together again. In September 1998 fighting broke out at Camp Johnson Road in Monrovia. The antagonists were mainly ULIMO-J and LPC combatants on the one side and Taylor's forces on the other. Krahn fighters from different warring factions had gradually been building up an increasingly strong presence around the ULIMO-J leader, Roosevelt Johnson, in the Camp Johnson Road area after Taylor's election victory in 1997.[13] According to Michael, the Krahn fighters had gathered around Roosevelt Johnson not on the basis of former rebel affiliation but simply for protection from targeted violence and intimidation by Taylor's forces. Taylor was using his new presidential powers and reconstituted national army to move against Roosevelt Johnson, and it was said that anyone associated with him and his base in the ethnic Krahn region of the southeast was being picked up and "disappearing" from Monrovia.[14] As Taylor's powers grew, the Krahn fighters felt more and more unprotected, which both strengthened former alliances among them and created new ones as they assembled at Camp Johnson Road. The new government nevertheless claimed that Johnson was building up a new force to launch a coup. Whether this was true or not, on

September 18 Charles Taylor ordered the paramilitary Special Operation Division to attack the camp. After intense fighting, leaving over fifty dead, Roosevelt Johnson and a group of combatants took refuge at the U.S. Embassy. From there they were evacuated to Sierra Leone and Nigeria.[15] Hundreds of Krahn soldiers, along with civil servants and civilians, over the coming months, left the country after being hunted by Taylor's forces.[16] Michael and Simon, who had been caught up in the heavy battles, were among those who managed to escape Taylor's forces and reach the embassy. Along with a group of about twenty other Liberian fighters, they were flown to Freetown, the capital of Sierra Leone, by the U.S. Embassy.

The Camp Johnson Road incident had a quite different ending for Jacob, who had never managed to escape Taylor's forces and was shot in the spinal cord. Still, Jacob was lucky. His men quickly took him to a hospital. Jacob was told that he would never walk again. But several weeks later Jacob nevertheless managed to stand up and walk out of the hospital. He was, however, in the worst imaginable condition, and he was frightened. He knew that Taylor's men were after him, and he knew that he had to go into hiding. But in his fragile condition Jacob could not travel far. Together with seven other men from his former rebel unit, he took refuge at his aunt's house in the outskirts of Monrovia. But Jacob and the other men were soon found and arrested. They were taken to Monrovia Central Police Station, where they were imprisoned immediately. They spent six months there without a trial, Jacob says—nineteen men connected to the Camp Johnson incident, most of them Krahn. He, like many others, was later convicted and sentenced for treason.

Jacob came to spend years in his prison cell, at times so ill that he feared for his life. But against the odds, Jacob survived this ordeal as well. Meanwhile, Taylor still held power in Liberia, but across neighboring borders a rebellion against him was rising. The Liberians United for Reconciliation and Democracy (LURD)—a movement with external support and resources but consisting of many of the very combatants forced into exile after the Camp Johnson Road incident—was born. From 1999 and onward the rebels came to pose an increasing threat to Taylor's newly won power, and he needed to use every means at his disposal to fight them. In this way Jacob and the combatants taken as prisoners at Camp Johnson Road became of interest to the Liberian president. Michael, Simon, and many of the combatants whom Jacob knew and had fought with for years were part of the new rebellion. Many of them, just like Michael and Simon, had strong links to the imprisoned Camp Johnson Road combatants, a fact Taylor calculated that he could possibly use. In March 2002 Charles Taylor suddenly announced that he was to release twenty-one prisoners convicted of treason who had been held at the Monrovia Central Prison since the Camp Johnson Road battle on September 18, 1999.[17] Taylor was under pressure as LURD was pushing deeper into Liberia.

Taylor's decision to now release the Camp Johnson combatants could therefore have been seen as a gesture aiming at creating an environment for peace talks. Yet Taylor could have had multiple, if not ulterior, motives.

Jacob was notified about the developments in prison, and he was told that he was to be released at once. But when Taylor's men came for him, he was not released but escorted to Taylor himself. Jacob was taken to a compound in Monrovia, where Charles Taylor received him in the garden, surrounded by his main commanders. These were men Jacob knew and saw as his main antagonists. Taylor approached him, Jacob said, and told him the following, "I am the commander in chief, and your brothers are not here now. You will fight for me instead. I order you to take this money." With that Taylor gave Jacob USD 7,000 and keys to a car that had been parked outside the compound. In that moment Jacob knew that he was trapped. There was no way he could say no to Taylor. He had been imprisoned for years, he was far away from the men he knew and trusted, and he felt alone and vulnerable. If he refused Taylor's offer, he knew he would be killed then and there. But if he joined him, he would lose the people most important to him, people he had grown up with, like Michael and Simon and others whom he not only had fought with but had shared his life with for years. And Jacob knew what the money was all about. People would see him, a man freed by Taylor, with money and a new car, and there would be no doubt that his loyalty had been bought. Jacob realized that no matter what he did he would lose. In this way Jacob came to fight for yet another leader. Under Taylor, Jacob came to command a unit of about 150 men based at the presidential mansion, protecting Taylor until the president was forced into exile in 2003 at the end of the war, following LURD's advances and international pressure.

Things were never the same for Jacob after he joined Taylor. As the war ended, Jacob was once again on the losing side. While Michael and Simon came to win great benefits from being part of a strong postwar rebel network, Jacob was never fully trusted by his former fellow combatants again. Michael and Simon still regarded him as their brother and helped him when they could. Yet Jacob was never trusted with any inside information, and he was never invited to take part in any of the network's activities. Jacob had lost access to what proved to be vital for many ex-combatants following the end of the Liberian civil wars, his postwar rebel network.

Fighting in Sierra Leone

After the Camp Johnson Road incident in 1998, it soon became clear that Michael's and Simon's lives as combatants did not end along with the termination of the first Liberian civil war, following Charles Taylor's election victory, or by their forced exile. In Sierra Leone the Liberian fighters were drawn into the regional dimension of the ongoing West African wars. Like other combatants, they were moved across international borders, recruited, and mobilized by different actors within the political elite in the region who were battling one another for power. What happened to the two young men next shows how the networks of rebel soldiers created in Liberia during the first civil war immediately proved to be very useful for powerful actors within the region. As the situation was far from stable in West Africa, and violent struggle for power continued in neighboring countries, postwar rebel networks that stayed mobilized and organized and continued to be willing to use their skills in warfare became highly valuable.

For the first three months, the group of Liberian fighters that had been flown to Sierra Leone after the Camp Johnson incident were brought to the West African peacekeepers of the Economic Community of West African States Monitoring Group's base at Lungi airport outside Freetown. But the Sierra Leonean political elite soon proved to have plans for the Liberian ex-combatants. From Lungi Michael and Simon and the other Liberians were relocated to a place called Brookfields Hotel. The situation in Sierra Leone was highly unstable at this time. The country had been at war since 1991, as a guerrilla force calling itself the Revolutionary United Front (RUF) had launched a rebellion intent on overthrowing President Joseph Saidu Momoh of the All People's Congress. But Momoh was deposed by his own army officers in a coup in 1992—and Capt. Valentine Strasser became the new head of state, establishing the National Provisional Ruling Council. Even though the RUF's proclaimed reasons for fighting were gone, the war continued to rage between the rebel movement and the new regime. The council started a heavy recruitment campaign among marginalized and excluded youths and quickly expanded the army and succeeded in pushing the RUF back. By 1994, however, the RUF had regained its strength, and fighting continued. Nevertheless, neither the rebels nor the government was strong enough to achieve a total military victory, which opened the way for peace negotiations. In February 1996 the first democratic elections were held, and Ahmad Tejan Kabbah of the Sierra Leone People's Party took power. Despite the official end of war, neither side seemed much devoted to the peace, and no serious attempts to demobilize or disarm fighters were undertaken. In 1997 yet another military coup was carried out by the army, and a new regime—the Armed Forces Revolutionary Council under the leadership of Johnny Paul Koroma—was installed. The council invited the RUF to join the military junta, and, for more than eight months, the Armed Forces Revolutionary Council and the RUF held power. But with the help of the West African peacekeeping force, the Economic Community of West African States Monitoring Group, the Kabbah regime was reinstalled by March 1998.[18]

But the RUF rebels were not yet broken, and the Kabbah government was now looking for ways to use the exiled Liberian combatants to their advantage in the ongoing war. Representatives of the Sierra Leonean government approached the group of Liberians that Michael and Simon were part of, offering them a chance to take sides in the civil war against the RUF. The rebellions in Liberia and Sierra Leone had been intimately interlinked from the start, and one important aspect tying the wars together was the relationship between Charles Taylor and the RUF leader, Foday Sankoh. Before the emergence of the wars, both Taylor and Sankoh, like other key actors in the conflicts to come, had been hosted by the Libyan president, Moammar Gaddafi, as they prepared their troops for battle. Later, during the Sierra Leonean rebellion, Taylor's and Sankoh's regional cooperation continued, and Taylor came to constitute a considerable source of support for Sankoh fighting the Kabbah government and was said to have committed his fiercest troops to the RUF.[19] Naturally, the Sierra Leonean president and the exiled Liberian combatants now approached by Kabbah's representatives had a common enemy.

Ex-combatant Recruitment at Brookfields Hotel

Before the war the Brookfields Hotel, the place the exiled Liberian fighters were taken to, had been a meeting point for both local elites and international tourists, but beginning in 1997 the hotel was first used as barracks for RUF rebels. When the rebels were driven out of Freetown in March 1998 and the Sierra Leone People's Party government and President Ahmad Tejan Kabbah were put back in power, the Civil Defence Forces, who had been allied with the Sierra Leonean government, took Brookfields Hotel as its own barracks. Several hundred combatants permanently or temporarily lived at the hotel with their dependents. Danny Hoffman, conducting field research at the barracks among the combatants at Brookfields Hotel before they were finally evicted in 2002, has described the hotel as a location that concentrated the labor force of a violent economy and oriented it toward deployment throughout Freetown and Sierra Leone and even the whole region if necessary. The combatants at the hotel became a force that the Sierra Leone People's Party government could use as insurgents against a renewed rebellion into the city or a coup by the state's armed forces. The forces meant to protect the Sierra Leonean leadership were hosted there, and the hotel served as a base for the Special Forces, the most professionalized contingent of the militia. From Brookfields Hotel combatants were sent out to the front lines in Sierra Leone, but it also became the major transit point for redeploying combatants into warfare in the wider region.[20] Michael and Simon, along with the group of Liberian combatants flown out of Monrovia, were based at Brookfields Hotel in early 1999 when the Sierra Leone People's Party government mobilized them for what came to be one of the most violent periods of the Sierra Leonean war, starting with the January 6 rebel invasion of Freetown. The group of Liberian rebels thereby came to fight on the Kabbah government side during the attacks.[21]

Nevertheless, the newly established alliance between the Sierra Leoneans and the exiled Liberian combatants soon crumbled. According to Michael, the Liberian fighters later in 1999 fell into a dispute with the Sierra Leonean authorities over the payment for their contribution during the January 6 invasion. The Kabbah government refused to pay them in weapons and ammunition, as had been agreed on. Kabbah and Taylor were enemies, but Kabbah was clearly anxious about Taylor's power and influence. Possibly, Kabbah feared provoking Taylor by arming the exiled Liberians, knowing that this eventually could lead to a large-scale armed response on Sierra Leonean territory. The dispute between Kabbah and the Liberian combatants was not resolved; instead, several of the Liberians were imprisoned in Freetown. Some of them nonetheless managed to escape the authorities. While Michael took refuge in Ghana in 1999, Simon somehow made his way to Guinea. Yet the two young men's trajectories as combatants were once again to be shaped by the regional aspects of the West African conflicts and by the regional elites' mobilizing postwar rebel networks, as well as by new recruits for the ongoing power struggles.

Liberian Mercenaries, Regional Mobilization, and LURD

In Guinea President Lansana Conté was facing a rebellion believed to be supported by Charles Taylor.[22] Since the wars started in the neighboring countries, hundreds of thousands of Liberians and Sierra Leoneans had taken refuge in Guinea, which had been entangled in the neighboring conflicts from the start but had still enjoyed relative stability. But in the late 1990s the security situation quickly deteriorated, as a series of cross-border raids were carried out from Sierra Leone. The attackers came across the borders, killed civilians, burned and looted villages, and then retreated back to Sierra Leone. A furious President Conté immediately blamed Charles Taylor for being behind the attacks carried out by RUF rebels. But the attackers were not only foreigners. Guinean rebels calling themselves the Rassamblement des Forces Democratiques de Guinée claimed that the attacks were the work of the Guinean opposition.[23] Accordingly, Conté found himself facing Sierra Leonean, Liberian, and domestic rebels on his territory from the late 1990s onward.

The turbulence in Guinea and the hostile relationship between the two West African presidents Lansana Conté and Charles Taylor came to give Simon and other Liberian combatants in exile in Guinea new opportunities to make use of their skills as combatants. Together they joined the Guinean army, hired as mercenaries by the Guinean president seeking to strengthen his army against the rebels. At this point the situation in Guinea was extremely tense. In September 2000 a coalition of Taylor-sponsored Guinean rebels, the Rassamblement des Forces Democratiques de Guinée, and RUF fighters had been carrying out attacks in the country near the border with Sierra Leone and Liberia. The Rassamblement rebels now claimed they were intent on reaching the capital, Conakry.[24] Liberian mercenaries consequently became a valuable asset for Conté, as tensions between Guinea and Liberia rose and the security situation in Guinea deteriorated. For Simon and the exiled Liberian fighters, the situation in Guinea meant a way to make a living, using their experiences as rebels. They thereby continued their paths as mercenaries for a few months, aiding President Conté and the Guinean army. But they were soon needed for yet another war. Taylor's regime was threatened as exiled Liberians, predominantly former ULIMO-K rebels, formed the rebel movement LURD. Moreover, LURD leadership was closely linked to the Guinean government. Sekou Conneh, a former Liberian politician and businessman, had emerged as the rebel movement's chair. Yet, with all certainty, a more important player for the establishment of the rebel movement was Conneh's wife, Aisha, the spiritual adviser of President Conté. Aisha Conneh was not only one of the most important mobilizers of the new rebel group; she was also a key force behind President Conté's decision to back the rebellion.

In Guinea Simon soon became part of the initial core force of LURD, and he was once again mobilized as a rebel commander. Meanwhile, it soon became evident that the destiny of Michael—who instead had taken refuge in Ghana—was also to be determined by the emerging rebel group. The new movement needed to mobilize combatants, and the leadership strategically sought to make use of postwar rebel networks. Michael, who had proved himself as a commander during his years of combat with the LPC and as a mercenary in Sierra Leone, was contacted by one of the movement's coordinators, a Liberian living in the United States at the time. Michael was tasked with recruiting former Liberian fighters, and for this assignment he could use the network of combatants he had established during the first Liberian war and during his time in Sierra Leone. In a highly organized manner, the commanders that had been chosen as recruiters for the emerging rebel movement were sent out to different regions of West Africa. Michael was responsible mainly for recruiting in Côte d'Ivoire. He was given USD 1,500 for the assignment through his contacts in the United States. His travels were paid for, and money was sent to him via Western Union for paying his recruits. The recruits Michael had gathered were thereafter sent to Guinea. In Guinea Aisha Conneh was at the center of the coordination of the new movement.

Aisha Conneh, a former market woman in her midthirties, had grown up in Kakata, a small town in Margibi County in Liberia. But when war came she, like so many other Liberians, was forced to flee, and in 1990 she came to Guinea. The stories of how this young woman came to gain the trust of the Guinean president differ, but there is no doubt that she did do so and that, with the help of her powerful connections, she came to play a vital role in the making of LURD. Michael, who came to work under the woman who was sometimes called the "Iron Lady," was curious about how Conneh had gained her power and influence. His years at war had made him accustomed to always doing his own background research on the people he worked with. Aisha Conneh was known at the time as a spiritual adviser or soothsayer of the president. But the circumstances of how she had gained this prestigious position were less known. According to what Michael found out, Aisha Conneh's first husband had either been aware of or had even taken part in the planning of a coup against President Conté. But Conneh's husband had fallen ill, and on his deathbed he had revealed the plans to her. With her husband dead, Aisha decided to turn to the president with the information. But Aisha was clever, Michael argues, so instead of telling the president the whole story, she presented the plan of the coup as a vision that had come to her in a dream. With the information provided by Aisha Conneh, the Guinean authorities were able to thwart the coup, and from that moment Conneh could take her place as the new soothsayer of the president.

"That woman could have been president herself," Michael laughed when he told me the story, "if she had had formal education too." "She is very intelligent," he says, "and she was far more valuable to LURD than her husband ever was."[25] After her husband's death Aisha Conneh married his brother—Sekou Conneh—who subsequently became the chair of LURD, which secured the emerging rebel movement's connections all the way to the highest level of the Guinean political elite. But even though Sekou Conneh was the chair of LURD, it was Aisha Conneh who the new recruits often passed through after having been contacted by Michael or the other recruiters in the region. From time to time Michael and these other recruiters were also called to meetings she organized in Conakry. Aisha Conneh's good connections with President Conté helped channel the Guinean support to LURD.

As William Reno rightly has pointed out, LURD's leaders sought external patronage on an opportunistic basis and, in this way, involved neighboring states in their cause. But foreign politicians had become more adept at using Liberian rebel groups such as LURD to serve their own purposes.[26] Accordingly, Conté had good reasons to support the newly established rebel movement and, of course, had his own agenda for doing so. The hostile relationship between Conté and Taylor was well known, and Guinea's assistance to the new rebel movement was an open secret. LURD's activities in Conakry were reported to be based at Aisha Conneh's house, heavily protected by presidential guards under Guinean government supervision. It was also in the garden of Aisha Conneh's house that Michael and the other recruiters met with her. Through Aisha Conneh Guinean authorities helped facilitate the recruitment of LURD forces. There were no doubts that the president's spiritual adviser was to have great influence on the Liberian war to come. LURD needed manpower and loyal combatants, preferably with fighting experience, and with Aisha Conneh's elite network such a mobilization was easier to facilitate. One episode that illustrates Aisha Conneh's influence occurred during the mobilization phase of LURD. According to Michael, Aisha Conneh convinced President Conté to contact Sierra Leonean president Kabbah, persuading him to release the Liberian fighters who had been imprisoned after the January 6 rebel invasion—the group Michael and Simon had both been part of. But Sierra Leonean support for the emerging rebel group was not as straightforward as that provided by the Conté government. Possibly fearing attacks from Taylor, Kabbah supported the new rebellion in a more discreet manner than the Guinean president.[27] Nonetheless, after the unofficial Guinean request to release them, the Liberian fighters were flown to Conakry, where they were united with Simon and the other combatants mobilized for LURD.[28]

In exchange for their role as mercenaries in the Guinean army, Michael argues the exiled Liberians decided not to ask for money. Instead they wanted "humanitarian assistance," as he called it, from the Guinean political leadership to return to Liberia to fulfill LURD's only political aspiration: to oust Charles Taylor from power. "Instead of financial payment, we chose the weapons," Michael explains. They were thereby allowed to keep the weapons they had been given as mercenaries, to start their war against Charles Taylor. Yet there were additional terms for the Guinean military supplies the Liberian dissidents had been given. According to Nicholai Hart Lidow, President Conté insisted that LURD assisted Guinea against cross-border attacks on Guinean soil. Thereby, LURD had no choice but to also, in essence, function as a paramilitary for the Guinean government.[29]

In the beginning the new rebel movement was composed of only two hundred to three hundred men, Michael states, but they "recruited and trained" along the way, as they pushed farther into the country, and he believes that they could have been as many as ten thousand to fifteen thousand troops at their height. While Michael never took active part in the fighting this time around, Simon, now as a LURD general, once again entered Liberia in 1999, crossing the border from Guinea and entering Lofa County. According to estimations, LURD controlled about 30 percent of Liberia by December 2002, from Voinjama and Zorzor in Lofa County and the Guinea border area, south to Saint Paul's Bridge, southwest to the town of Bopolu, and east along the Sierra Leonean border to the outskirts of Foya. By early 2003 LURD forces had expanded their military presence considerably and were now also in control of Tubmanburg, Klay Junction, Foya, Robertsport, and key strategic areas in the immediate vicinity of Monrovia. James Brabazon, in his analysis of LURD, found that, contrary to media reports on the rebel movement at the time, LURD was not composed of isolated groups of loosely affiliated rebels but was instead a coherent and integrated mobile irregular army. According to Brabazon, LURD's military structure operated along protocols established by the AFL and involved a coherent system of ranks and titles that appeared to be respected. Combatants were promoted and awarded ranks based on length of service and ability in the field in addition to previous military experience or affiliation. Former AFL or ULIMO fighters who entered LURD also kept their former ranks.[30] LURD was according to such analysis, contrary to a common prejudice regarding African rebel groups, a well-organized and well-coordinated movement.

LURD's military strategic capabilities were also illustrated by the way in which the movement's coordinators outside Liberia recruited former Liberian rebel commanders, like Michael, and gave them responsibility over specific geographic areas, where these commanders' networks of former rebel soldiers were used to remobilize combatants all over West Africa for the emerging rebellion. Another illustration is found in the movement's ability to use and channel the Guinean political elite's interests in a rebellion against Taylor in their warfare. Yet, on the other hand, as has been pointed out by Ilmari Käihkö in his in-depth examination of LURD, the movement was still characterized by loose cohesion. It was unified more by a shared identity than by a strict chain of command and suffered from continuous internal power struggles and lack of formalization. Despite this, contrary to what has been suggested, it was not a strategic, predatory group of criminals.[31]

During the summer of 2003, fighting had reached the capital, which was one of the factors forcing Taylor into exile in August as peacekeepers arrived. The result was the signing of the Comprehensive Peace Agreement in Accra, putting an end to the civil wars in Liberia. But the end of the war or the subsequent disarmament, demobilization, rehabilitation, and reintegration process did not manage to shatter the wartime networks that Michael, Simon, and Jacob had been part of this time around either. Instead, these networks became the means by which many ex-combatants secured a living postwar and a powerful instrument for the Liberian elite to enrich themselves and secure power. One example of this dynamic was evident as former rebels took over one of the country's largest rubber plantations at the end of the war.

Networks of Ex-combatants as Threats to Peace

One of the most fundamental aspects driving disarmament, demobilization, and reintegration efforts in postconflict environments is the fear that groups of ex-combatants will be mobilized for renewed warfare. This aspect has been identified within conflict-resolution research and has been clearly visible in actual peace-building interventions. Since the end of the Cold War, international efforts to end prolonged conflicts in parts of Africa, Central America, and Southeast Asia have all included initiatives and programs to disarm and demobilize combatants after years, and often decades, of war and military service.[32] As Anders Themnér notes, former fighters can pose the gravest threat to postconflict societies if they participate in organized violence as members of illegal armed groups. This type of violence not only inflicts the greatest loss in lives and property but also has the potential of undermining the legitimacy of the newly established peace. And in the worst case ex-combatant violence can have a detrimental effect on regional security.[33] Similarly, Mats Berdal has argued that in the short to medium term, arms and combatants recently emerged from war are potential sources of both domestic and regional instability.[34]

But networks of ex-combatants can also be a source a continued instability in a wider region long after war has been declared to be over. Networks of ex-combatants, for several reasons, tend to linger many years after peace agreements have been signed, despite the disarmament, demobilization, and reintegration process. Yet these networks are mostly used not in their capacity as combatants or with any obvious attempt to start new warfare but for other security-related assignments. This chapter differs from the subsequent cases in this sense. In this chapter postwar rebel networks have been used *specifically* in their capacity as combatants, as mobile warring networks with the ability to be used in a wider context of regional conflict. Themnér, in his research on why some communities of ex-combatants reengage in organized violence while others do not, argues that there is an increased risk for renewed organized violence if the ex-combatant community is remarginalized after the arrival of peace from a lack of political influence, personal security, or economic assistance. He also notes, however, that such reengagement in organized violence often requires the involvement of domestic and regional elites, as well as lower-level actors such as local politicians, communal leaders, or former midlevel commanders who can serve as a link between the elite and the ex-combatants.[35]

This assumption is well in line with the reasoning in this chapter. One of the main and overall arguments of this book is that postwar rebel networks tend to linger long after peace agreements have been signed and despite disarmament, demobilization, and reintegration initiatives. But contrary to what is often assumed, and usually taken as a given, the maintenance of postwar rebel structures is not *necessarily* a bad thing or a threat to lasting peace. Of course, it can be, but such a negative development where networks of ex-combatants are used for renewed warfare never occurs without the involvement of elite actors and substantial financial resources. If this happens, lingering networks can have a great and devastating impact on the development of conflict within a large regional context.

A Regional War with Regional Warriors

Hoffman notes that accounts of the wars in Liberia and Sierra Leone, as well as the periods of violence in Guinea, often explore the influence of one conflict on another but that they are more rarely treated as *the same* war. Hoffman questions this. In his analysis of warfare in the Mano River region, he focuses on the seminal role that border crossing and movement played in this context, referring to movements of personnel, war materiel, financing, plunder, refugees, tactics, ideas, and so on.[36] And as Reno has pointed out in his analysis of the wider interstate political contexts of this (or *these*) war(s), regional politics of personal alliance shaped what became more than just a fight for the next Liberian presidency. Whether warfare in the Mano River region should be seen as one or several intimately connected conflicts does not concern me here. But in line with Hoffman's reasoning, this chapter is focused on how movements across the regional borders, with specific focus on combatants, affected the course of events and conflict development during this turbulent time. At the same time I take into account Reno's emphasis on the importance of regional personal-alliance politics, both at the highest political level as well as on grassroots level in the actual actions of the rebels. By following individual Liberian combatants like Michael, Simon, and Jacob and their networks of rebel soldiers, I have shown how networks of combatants can easily be used in a wider context than their original theater of conflict. I have illustrated how actors within the absolute top of the regional elite at this time, like Taylor, Conté, and Kabbah, did their best to use these mobile networks of combatants for their own personal gains as well as against one another. I explore these dynamics, however, with a point of departure in, and the main emphasis on, the experiences of combatants on the ground. My informants' stories nevertheless shed light on how even individual combatants could become important to these powerful actors, precisely because they were part of larger rebel network that in turn had the ability to change the course of conflict in the whole Mano River region. As Reno has pointed out, Taylor was a far more sophisticated strategist than most reports were willing to acknowledge. He was not only extremely bright; he was also a careful collector of data on people and events that he found important for his situation.[37]

Jacob's personal encounter with Charles Taylor in 2002 not only supports Reno's statement about Taylor but could actually be seen as an example of how a powerful actor, even at the presidential level, felt the need for, or saw advantages of, using individual combatants to cause disturbance in or manipulate networks opposing him. This is a good example of how such actors within the Mano River regional elite acknowledged these networks as valuable tools to be used in their own interest as well as significant threats if turned against them. This also shows what tends to be forgotten: the elite is actually quite close to the combatants on the ground in a conflict like the Liberian one simply because they need to be well connected to the actual fighters to control and influence the outcome of war. These combatants, organized in often well-structured networks, were strong forces to be reckoned with, and the elite actors were fully aware of their potential.

Conclusion

When it comes to the frequency and actual occurrence of regional use and remobilization of postwar rebel networks, Morten Bøås and Kevin Dunn recognize, in their edited volume on "African guerrillas," the recycling of warriors from one place to another as an important aspect of civil war in Africa. But they note that the concern that these recycled combatants can be used as seasoned mercenaries and further destabilize the region is somewhat exaggerated. While it is correct, they argue, that some fighters from Liberia have fought in Sierra Leone, Guinea, and Côte d'Ivoire, these professional warriors constitute only a small minority of the total population of combatants in these countries, as the overall majority of the fighters fought only in their own country.[38] That argument is not contested here. As already stated, and as the following case studies show, the most important aspects of why postwar rebel networks like those Michael, Simon, and Jacob are all part of seldom have something to do with their will to take part in renewed warfare specifically. Nevertheless, rebel networks, like the ones followed in this chapter, *can* clearly be used across regional borders as these mobile warring networks, with elite-level support, can be easily mobilized if the right channels are used. As Michael once told me, "You know Mariam, some people used to call us the Mano River Unit! Because we were fighting all over the place." Michael's story shows what rarely is accounted for: how such mobilization and recruitment can actually be carried out in practice. He highlights the importance of individual commanders and how they can be used as entry points for efficiently and rapidly mobilizing rebel networks. No matter whether the recycling of rebel networks occurs less frequently than is often assumed, it *does* happen, and we therefore need to learn more about such mechanisms and how individual combatants on the ground are tied to the most powerful mobilizing actors within the elite. Furthermore, by following an actor such as Michael in particular, the commonly held prejudice regarding African rebel movements as badly organized and undisciplined is challenged by the way the mobilizing LURD made use of his skills and extensive rebel network. LURD, at least initially, had an efficient and well-structured way of mobilizing and organizing its troops, to a great extent consisting of Liberian postwar rebel networks with high-level Guinean support.

CHAPTER 3

From Rebels to Security Providers

POSTWAR REBEL NETWORKS AT THE GUTHRIE
RUBBER PLANTATION / SIME DARBY

The events at the Guthrie Rubber Plantation, or Sime Darby, as the Liberian plantation came to be known after January 2010, are used in this chapter to illustrate some of the mechanisms allowing rebel networks to linger long after the wars came to an end in Liberia and the neighboring region. These events attempt in particular to show how political and commercial interests, but also security concerns and disappointment in the disarmament, demobilization, rehabilitation, and reintegration (DDRR) process, have contributed to the maintenance of wartime structures at this location. The developments at the plantation, from the time of war until the present, show how postwar rebel networks have actually continued to be of strategic importance for the ruling political elite in Liberia, despite the end of wars in West Africa and throughout a time when the Liberian authorities were officially part of international efforts aiming at demobilizing and reintegrating such structures. But the situation at the plantation also shows how former key rebel commanders themselves have been able to strategically preserve and use their influence gained during the wars, not only during the initial period just after the peace agreement had been signed but also several years following the official break with war. Accordingly, the power dynamics at the plantation display an unofficial lingering mutual dependence between the political elite, commercial investors, and the networks of ex-combatants, having clear implications on the postwar security context in Liberia, with the rebels being involved first as illegal occupiers, then as an unofficial informal security force, and finally as recognized formal security providers.

In this chapter we also further scrutinize the meaning of security provision. We explore whether former rebels who have been the ultimate instruments of causing insecurity and perpetrating violence during years of war can instead become providers of security in the postwar phase, or whether these networks simply are used because of their violent potential, as a source of intimidation toward those who could question or disobey or otherwise pose a threat to the political and economic elite making use of these networks. Furthermore, this specific case also illuminates how formal and informal security provisions are intimately interlinked in a postconflict country such as Liberia, while at the same time displaying the ex-combatants' striving to move from the informal sphere to the formal by gaining official status and recognition for their work as security providers.

Three individuals in particular are the focus of this chapter, three former rebel generals, controlling networks of ex-combatants who had been present at the plantation for years. At times these former rebel generals have been in full control of all aspects of the management of the plantation; at other times they have been deeply involved in the elite's management. Two of these former generals we already know from previous chapter—Michael and Simon, the young combatants who navigated both the first and the second Liberian war and the West African crisis during the 1990s and early 2000 as soldiers, rebels, mercenaries, and regional warriors. These two experienced combatants, alongside another former rebel general, Alpha, presented in this chapter, all came to play important roles in the preservation of postwar rebel networks at the plantation. I illustrate these three former generals' internal interactions, the coordination of their former fighters at the plantation, and their interactions with the political and economic elite in Liberia, to explain the function and the logic behind these lingering postwar rebel networks.

Guthrie Rubber Plantation and the Civil Wars

In 1981 the Malaysian Guthrie Rubber Company was hired to operate a three hundred thousand-acre government-owned plantation area, located in the Bomi and Grand Cape Mount Counties of Liberia. Rubber is one of the main exports of Liberia, with the first plantation established as early as 1906, and with one of the world's largest rubber plantations, owned by Firestone Plantation Company, located in the country. The civil wars came to affect the situation at the country's rubber plantations, with several actors trying to get a share of the lucrative industry. Charles Taylor, as the new president of Liberia, installed an interim management in December 2000 to control Guthrie. The new management mainly comprised the same management as before, but now the plantation was under the direct leadership of Taylor. But renewed warfare challenged Taylor's control over Guthrie. During 2002 and 2003 Liberians United for Reconciliation and Democracy (LURD) rebels carried out several attacks in and around the plantation area, and by July 2003 the rebel takeover was a fact.[1] As the war came to an end, ex-combatants established full control and management over the Guthrie plantation, initially under the leadership of one ex-LURD general in particular: Simon.

In June 2006, three years after the signing of the Liberian peace agreement and LURD's takeover of Guthrie, an estimated five thousand ex-combatants were still in full control of the rubber plantation area. The command structures were still intact, as the ex-combatants maintained allegiance to their former commanders. Rank determined control over rubber tapping. No one could operate at Guthrie without the permission of Simon, and taxes had to be paid to the self-established NGO, the National Veteran Rehabilitation Project, which was run by a five-member committee of ex-combatants and was also controlled by the two ex-LURD generals. Control over Guthrie implied control over great economic interests. The rehabilitation project was said to generate up to USD 18,000 a month, in addition to significant sums made by individual ex-combatant tappers. The ex-combatants themselves claimed that rubber tapping was their only means of survival while awaiting the RR component of the DDRR process to take effect.[2] In February 2006 President Ellen Johnson Sirleaf and the special representative of the secretary general of the United Nations Mission in Liberia (UNMIL), Alan Doss, established the Rubber Plantation Task Force (RPTF) to assess the situation of Liberia's rubber plantations and to make recommendations for future action. The RPTF concluded that the illegal occupation of rubber plantations had to be stopped. The government was recommended to evaluate options for implementing reintegration and rehabilitation packages for registered ex-combatants at Guthrie to establish a government-run interim management at the plantation.[3] President Johnson Sirleaf formally requested the RPTF to concentrate its efforts on reestablishing state authority and rule of law on the plantations occupied by ex-combatants or other illegal managements. Negotiations between the RPTF and the ex-combatant leadership followed. After promises of reintegration benefits for the ex-combatants, the government with UNMIL military and police support claimed to have repossessed Guthrie under an interim management team (IMT) on August 15, 2006. Following negotiations between the Liberian government and the Malaysian palm oil–producing company Sime Darby, an agreement was finally signed in April 2009.[4] The takeover was delayed, but Sime Darby finally took over the management of the Guthrie Rubber Plantation on January 1, 2010.

According to a United Nations report from October 2009, individual negotiations launched by the RPTF with ex-combatants helped to break down the ex-combatants' chains of command to repossess the Guthrie plantation in 2006.[5] Nevertheless, chains of command and rebel networks were far from broken. Even though control officially once again lay in the hands of the Liberian government and the current IMT, the former LURD generals were still influential, with their network of ex-combatants remaining active at the plantation long after this date.

LURD Generals and the Rubber Plantation

When war came to an end in Liberia, ex-combatants had to face a new type of challenge. Having survived war, they now needed to survive peace. Former rebels like Michael and Simon, for example, who had been drawn into the wars as young combatants, had first taken up arms with the need to find protection.[6] Later, with few alternatives open to them, this had also become a way to secure a living. Michael and Simon, and whole networks of ex-combatants, could use their skills in warfare in different conflict contexts all over the West African region affected by war and crisis as long as political elite actors were willing to use them in their proxy wars and struggles for power. But, with the end of the wars, ex-combatants had to find new strategies to fight for survival in a war-torn Liberia. For Michael and Simon, whose war trajectories had often been entangled during the many years they had been combatants, postwar life came to offer quite different opportunities for them, and their lives would eventually look very different. Yet the situation at Guthrie after Taylor had fallen from power was to bring them together.

Michael and Simon had both been active in LURD during the second Liberian civil war. Yet, while Simon had been a general fighting on the ground, Michael instead had a more strategic responsibility, mobilizing combatants for the rebellion from different parts of West Africa. With this responsibility Michael also had a more direct link to the rebel movement's leadership. This link, between the movement's highest level and combatants on the ground, opened up new opportunities when the peace negotiations eventually came about in 2003. Michael came to be part of the group of combatants representing LURD who traveled to Accra for the signing of the peace agreement. He had been assigned as a "liaison officer" between the military and political factions of LURD. His task, as Michael sees it, was to protect the interests of LURD combatants and to see to it that the fighters were not left out of the process for subsequent reintegration benefits. The first disarmament, demobilization, and reintegration process in Liberia, following the first war, had completely left out the reintegration components for the combatants, and no real rehabilitation or reintegration had come out of the Abuja accord. Therefore, the ex-combatants, at least from the military wing, were determined to work for the rehabilitation and reintegration aspects to actually be emphasized after the 2003 peace accord. But, such a scenario, Michael argues, never materialized. This was the reason the postwar rebel network of an estimated five thousand ex-combatants, initially under Simon's command, who had managed to take control over the plantation in July 2003, stated that they had no interest in cooperating with the official Liberian DDRR process if they were not given sufficient reintegration benefits. "We decided to just use the government resources directly instead," Michael explains, to compensate for the benefits that they saw they were entitled to—and so began the ex-combatants' illegal management of the Guthrie Rubber Plantation, where they officially remained in control for the following three years.

The LURD Generals' Rule of Guthrie

Michael had initially no role in the ex-combatants' plantation occupation. He had left the battlefield, taken part in peace negotiations, and was looking for new postwar opportunities. Simon, on the other hand, as a LURD general, had led the rebel attacks against the Taylor government in and around Guthrie in 2002 and 2003, resulting in the rebel takeover of the plantation in July 2003. Yet both men's fates, as during the days of war, were once again to be shaped by the political elite. With Charles Taylor in exile, new actors with a taste for power had stepped forward. The 2003 peace agreement called for the establishment of a National Transitional Government of Liberia (NTGL), a government that was to be led by Gyude Bryant. A Liberian businessman, Bryant had not been directly involved in the civil wars and was chosen for the powerful position because of his perceived neutrality. The NTGL was composed of a mix of representatives from the warring factions: LURD, the Movement for Democracy in Liberia, and Taylor's National Patriotic Front of Liberia (NPFL). This was a coalition with one apparent focus: to enrich themselves during the two years they stayed in power. Their misdeeds were also later investigated by audits in the European Commission and the Economic Community of West African States, revealing that corruption was rampant and the justice system in shambles. This led to arrests and a series of trials that nevertheless ended in acquittals on all charges relating to economic sabotage.[7]

During the NTGL's time in power, undoubtedly in line with their quest to enrich themselves, the ex-combatants' takeover of Guthrie soon became an important issue for the transitional government, as the rubber industry at the plantation had the potential of generating significant economic resources for those in control of it. Bryant called for a meeting with the rebel leadership at Guthrie, but before he did so he contacted Michael. Bryant was well aware that Michael knew Simon and the other leaders occupying the plantation and probably figured that he could use Michael to his advantage in the negotiations. But what Bryant may not have calculated on was that Michael also saw this as a strategic opportunity. In their meeting Michael realized what he had always known, that Simon was a skilled leader of men in battle but that he had no clue how to handle the political elite. Michael took his chance and decided to join the occupiers. He was welcomed by Simon and the rebel leadership, who probably understood the benefits of having a leader among them who had been able to establish links to the absolute elite of the Liberian political system. But Bryant "was a wise man," Michael states, when discussing his relation with Bryant after the meeting. As Bryant understood the importance of Guthrie and its resources, Michael recalls, he called on Michael and Simon to further discuss the situation at the plantation and to come to a solution. In Michael's own words, "we made him understand the situation" as they demanded reintegration programs for their former fighters at Guthrie, which Bryant agreed to.

Some five hundred ex-combatants from Guthrie were thereby sent to Bong County to participate in agricultural training programs. The leadership, Michael and Simon, were employed by the DDRR commission as facilitators of the reintegration of their former fighters in Bong. They were to make sure that the ex-combatants went through the process. But in this way the two former commanders in practice also became the gatekeepers to the benefits the ex-combatants at the plantation could get, further strengthening their positions. At the same time Michael and Simon with their network of ex-combatants kept their positions at Guthrie, undoubtedly generating significant resources both for the rebels and the NTGL, as the whole question of control over the rubber plantation came to be postponed because of the upcoming 2005 Liberian national elections.

As the elections came and Ellen Johnson Sirleaf became president in 2005, and while the international community celebrated the democratic developments in Liberia, "everything stayed the same at Guthrie," Michael says. "Individuals changed, but the same institutions remained in control of Guthrie." After Johnson Sirleaf had been elected president, she—like Gyude Bryant before her—called for meetings with Michael and Simon. "Ellen was wise and decided to use the same formula as the NTGL had used," Michael states. But President Johnson Sirleaf and the UNMIL special representative of the secretary general, Alan Doss, established the Rubber Plantation Task Force and called on the reestablishment of state authority and rule of law on the plantations occupied by ex-combatants or other illegal management. Negotiations between the RPTF and the ex-combatant leadership followed, and, after promises of reintegration benefits for the ex-combatants, Michael and Simon and their postwar rebel network officially handed over control of Guthrie to the government of Liberia, under an interim management team (IMT), in August 2006. In practice the ex-combatants and the rebel leadership remained active and very influential at the plantation.

The role that Michael and Simon and their postwar rebel network played at Guthrie Rubber Plantation should not be underestimated. For three years, from 2003 until 2006, Guthrie and the nearby villages were completely under their command. Such influence, during this relatively long period, would have been impossible if the commanders did not have the ability to satisfy, or to a certain extent coerce, the dependents below and the elites above. First, relying on the former rebel structures and chains of command, the former rebel commanders could maintain control and loyalty by keeping lower-ranking former commanders in key positions under their direct control. Furthermore, the postwar rebel networks' organizational structure went beyond LURD's former chains of command. Within their ex-combatant network at Guthrie, former rebels, as well as followers from NPFL and the Movement for Democracy in Liberia, were organized and fully integrated into the command structures. In this way the commanders could avoid internal divisions and the combatants' previous factional associations never became a real issue at the plantation. Second, the rubber industry and Guthrie generated significant amounts of money. Global Witness estimated that the commanders' ex-combatants organization made up to USD 18,000 a month in addition to the money the individual ex-combatant tappers earned.[8] A large number of authorities, including top local and central officials of the transitional government, were known to receive bribes from the ex-combatants to ignore the situation at Guthrie.[9] And, as was revealed by Michael, the cooperation with the NTGL reached all the way to its chair, Gyude Bryant.

Since the former commanders had the ability to keep the plantation running while at the same time generating a significant income for many influential actors, the rebel leadership gained the crucial unofficial political support needed to remain in power. In the words of Simon himself, "I was the government, the management, everything. You see, I created a system that everybody was benefiting from. In that way I could keep the control, and everybody was satisfied." Despite Simon's choice of words, he and Michael exerted shared leadership. When I first started to research and map the ex-combatant networks and the informal security structures at Guthrie in 2009, I failed to see Michael's full role. Simon and a third commander, Alpha, were the visible ones. Michael was, nevertheless, the one that the three commanders themselves regarded as the highest in their hierarchy. Simon was notorious and feared. He was known to be dangerous and very violent, which explains his visibility. He was the one who most active on an operational level at the plantation during the time of the rebel occupation but also in the period that followed, as he was incorporated into the informal security structures after the official governmental takeover in 2006.

The dynamics between Michael and Simon are interesting to analyze to understand how they were able to maintain control of Guthrie between 2003 and 2006 and currently remain influential at the plantation. Michael and Simon's relationship is undeniably close. They grew up together, fought together, and then managed to take full control over Guthrie together. Furthermore, even after the official reestablishment of government control of the plantation, they stayed influential, as the structures of security providers, based on networks of ex-combatants, that they had established more or less remained. While Simon was the one who became the most visible of the two commanders with regard to the informal security provision of ex-combatant networks that lingered after 2006, Michael was, and is, the one with the closest political connections. He is also the one who, during the plantation occupation years, successfully negotiated with contemporary political and economic elites in Liberia. As the two former commanders have shared their leadership, they have been able to divide the tasks between them in mutually beneficial ways. While Michael has connected them to the political and financial elites in Liberia, Simon has had the operational responsibility and skills to organize the ex-combatants. The loyalty between Michael and Simon and the combination of their different skills have made them a successful duo when it comes to making use of their postwar rebel networks and their connections to the ruling elite.

Guthrie and the Influence of Former Rebel Commanders

When I first conducted research at Guthrie in October 2009, men and women guarded the entrances to the rubber plantation day and night and kept record of all persons and vehicles entering the plantation. They were called the "monitors" at the time, because that was what they were supposed to do: monitor, observe, and report suspected illegal tapping without taking any action themselves. Those who entered Guthrie unauthorized or who were caught stealing rubber or tapping illegally were to be immediately handed over to the police. As I was told by several United Nations officials, the IMT, and the police during my stay at Guthrie, the monitors were not to be considered a security force. In reality, the situation was much more complex.

During my stay at Guthrie in 2009, the workers and inhabitants at the plantation were once again under the management of a new IMT. The IMT was led by Boakai Sirleaf (at that point deputy minister of agriculture and a relative to President Johnson Sirleaf), while awaiting the expected, but delayed, handover to Malaysian investors. Since the government's takeover from the rebels in 2006, new IMTs had come and gone. They were often characterized by mismanagement and regularly failed to pay the workers, causing tension and occasional violent demonstrations. Yet, when it came to informal security provision, some structures appeared to have lingered. The current monitors had worked for the new IMT only for a couple of days in early October. This was not a new constellation. The IMTs all needed to protect their interests at Guthrie, and apparently the small unarmed and underresourced police force, the monitoring United Nations police force, and the present United Nations peacekeepers were not regarded as fulfilling this task satisfactorily. Already during Taylor's time in power, he had brought in ex-combatants to attend to security at Guthrie, and the IMTs had chosen to take the same action following the government's takeover. A significant part of the monitors had always been ex-combatants, operating within former rebel structures.

In 2009 Guthrie Rubber Plantation was divided into three estates: Grand Cape Mount Estate, Lofa Estate, and Bomi Estate, which is subdivided into two sections, Bomi 1 and Bomi 2. Each estate was then further divided into divisions and camps, where the inhabitants lived and worked. The monitors numbered nearly 160 altogether, including three women. They lived and worked in all sections of the plantation and were organized somewhat like a military unit. Each division had one commander (in total four commanders), which in turn had responsibility for the lower-ranking monitors. The estate commanders were all accountable to three main commanders, the first commander, and his two deputies.[10] Another man also appeared to still be influential: the ex-LURD general we know as Simon, who, together with Michael, had officially handed over the control of Guthrie three years earlier, in 2006.

The monitors were not all ex-combatants; indeed, many were not. Yet ex-combatants were present in every monitoring group at Guthrie. The constellation was not a new one. Many had been working as monitors for years. Some had been working since the government takeover in 2006 and for several different IMTs. Others had been there since the war or even before it. The current IMT had simply kept most of the monitors. Following UNMIL's advice, the IMT was said to have excluded the most notorious ex-combatants. But this was evidently not entirely true, as the presence and influence of two men in particular, the former commanders Simon and Alpha, proved otherwise.

ALPHA, THE FORMER NPFL GENERAL

Alpha first came to Guthrie in 1998.[11] The civil war was over, and Charles Taylor had become the new Liberian president. To protect and monitor every aspect of Liberia's financial resources, President Taylor also assumed direct control over Guthrie and the interim management. To secure the area against illegal tappers and rubber thieves, then as now, a security force was installed. The security providers were called the Plantation Protection Department, or simply the PPD. Alpha, a former NPFL general, was directly installed by Taylor as head of the PPD, with the title of chief of security. Alpha remained in this position until the Taylor regime left power in 2003.

At the age of twenty, in 1990, Alpha had joined Taylor and the NPFL rebels. After three years with Taylor's forces, Alpha had advanced within the ranks of the NPFL and became a general. But, despite his new status, Alpha was still outranked by his twin brother, a well-known NPFL general who had eventually been executed after orders by Taylor in 1994.[12] The twin brothers gained a reputation early on in the war. A former PPD member, who worked at Guthrie under the command of Alpha for a year, described the twin brothers as "really notorious and well known. Those who have lived beyond the NPFL lines during the war know them. Alpha's twin brother was one of the NPFL generals and a close friend to Charles Taylor, and therefore Taylor chose Alpha as head of the PPD. But I think it was mostly because he was so notorious. You know, that was needed to keep the security at Guthrie. When you saw him you wouldn't believe what he was capable of doing. Alpha could be very violent."[13] Even though Taylor had been the one who had appointed Alpha directly for the position at Guthrie, Alpha found it hard to trust the leadership of NPFL after his brother had been executed by their own forces. He heard rumors that Taylor had learned that Alpha was only awaiting to avenge his brother's death, and therefore Taylor was after his life. Nevertheless, Alpha stayed at the plantation until July 2003, when he decided to go into exile in Ghana, as LURD forces, under the leadership of Simon, took over the rubber plantation. But, as the Liberian government regained control over Guthrie in 2006, Alpha saw new opportunities to return to the plantation. According to UNMIL officials I spoke to in 2009, Alpha was one ex-combatant they surely did not want to see at the plantation, since they said he was known to cause trouble and harass workers and inhabitants at the plantation. In October 2009 Alpha was nevertheless the deputy commander of the monitors. He himself claims that he had returned to Guthrie only after having been called on by the former interim management to provide security, in the same way he had done before. As I spoke to workers at the plantation in 2009, some told me that Alpha was power greedy and corrupt, others that they respected him as their leader. Alpha's influence and authority were never questioned.

SIMON, RETURNING TO GUTHRIE

In early October 2009 I heard a rumor among the plantation workers: Simon was back at Guthrie. He had been seen in several camps, and the atmosphere became immediately tense when the matter of the former rebel general was brought up. That Simon was present at Guthrie once again was clear, but not many knew why he was there, and this caused worry and distress among the workers. Yet the monitors were better informed than the regular tappers. One of the young monitors told me that Simon had come to their headquarters a few days earlier and said that he was now responsible for security at Guthrie and that the monitors once again were under his command. The monitor, however, had not confirmed this information with his commanders. When I discussed the return of Simon with one of the plantation workers' supervisors, he not only confirmed the rumor but also claimed that the very person who had brought Simon back was in fact the head of the new IMT, the deputy minister of agriculture at the time, Boakai Sirleaf. The supervisor was not surprised at all by Sirleaf's actions. Simon possessed the ability to make tappers and monitors obey, either out of fear or respect. With Simon on his side, Sirleaf could control Guthrie. According to the supervisor, Simon had already started to resume his commanding position as he supervised the plantation at night time, driving around the camps in one of the estate manager's car, and he knew of at least one recent incident where Simon had threatened a plantation worker suspected of illegal tapping.

Sirleaf's relationship with Simon was, at least at Guthrie, not a well-kept secret since the monitors as well as the Liberian National Police commanders and the stationed UNMIL soldiers confirmed seeing them together. According to one of the stationed UNMIL soldiers at Guthrie, Sirleaf had said that Simon had been brought back to offer him advice on which ex-combatants were trustworthy and that Simon thereby should be included in the new security structures for Guthrie. This, he said, had caused deep tensions among the workers at the plantation who feared the return of the ex-combatant leadership. When I had the opportunity to ask him about this matter, Sirleaf himself denied that Simon had, or was to have, anything to do with the security provision at Guthrie. He claimed that the only reason he had brought Simon back to the rubber plantation was so that the workers could see a good example of an ex-combatant who was now a fully reintegrated man.[14]

The first time I met with Simon was in mid-October 2009 in Monrovia. We had talked on the phone a few times and had arranged a place to meet. Simon, however, did not turn up alone. He came accompanied by those he called his "boys," a couple of ex-combatants he always kept around him for his security, in the same way he had always organized his personal protection during the wars and when he controlled Guthrie. The ex-combatants in his network were not all former LURD fighters. His ability to unite the ex-combatants irrespective of their previous allegiances during his years at Guthrie was still prevalent, as some of his closest men came from other warring factions. Since a couple of weeks back, Simon and his men had once again been active at Guthrie. He had returned because he was requested to do so. In September, when the new IMT claimed responsibility of Guthrie, Boakai Sirleaf had called Simon, telling him that the Liberian government needed him to secure peace at the plantation. Otherwise, they risked new protests among the plantation workers, he was told. Since then Simon had traveled back and forth to Guthrie, showing his support for the new IMT by "encouraging" tappers and monitors to remain loyal to the new management. According to Simon himself, his new position in no way implied that he was inferior to the monitor commanders; instead, they once again were under his command.

Simon reported directly to Boakai Sirleaf. But he was not the only one Simon reported to. As we talked, Simon's phone rang and, according to him, Fombah Sirleaf—the stepson of President Ellen Johnson Sirleaf and the director of the National Security Agency—was the one who had called to request a meeting, wanting the latest report on the situation at Guthrie.

As I met with Michael and Simon in 2011, we discussed the developments after the government had taken over their leadership at Guthrie in 2006 and the events leading up to Simon's unofficial return to the plantation in 2009. Michael described what happened after the government took over as a "leadership vacuum." The IMTs were unable to control the ex-combatants and the tappers at the plantation, and several violent protests were staged against the new leadership. Boakai Sirleaf, as head of the new IMT at Guthrie in 2009, therefore felt the need to do something. He turned to both Michael and Simon to ask them to return. He wanted them to talk to the ex-combatants and the other workers at the plantation and encourage them to work (as the situation was, the IMT had often failed to pay the tappers their monthly salary, resulting in violent protests and strikes). As Michael, who once again had used his skills to maneuver the postwar political climate and found new opportunities, was too busy to attend to the situation at Guthrie, the two former commanders decided that Simon would be the one who would return to Guthrie, keeping Michael fully informed about the situation.

Knowing the history of the rebel leadership at Guthrie, the new management must have assessed the risk of bringing the commanders back within the informal security structures at the plantation. According to Michael, this was also why the National Security Agency and Fombah Sirleaf got involved. They knew that Simon had the ability to take control over Guthrie, and they feared yet another rebel occupation. But in this way the government could use Simon's reputation of being violent to make tappers work, despite their difficulties in providing the workers with regular salaries, while at the same time supervising him by keeping him close to the National Security Agency to minimize the risks of the rebel leadership regaining control over the rubber plantation. Despite these measures, the cooperation with the former rebel generals was far from uncomplicated for the plantation management. Not only did Simon's return to Guthrie cause distress and fear among the plantation workers, but the two commanders also soon fell into disagreements with the management. As Michael explained about the situation at Guthrie, "We wanted to run our own kind of operation." The two commanders considered that since they had been responsible for security at Guthrie for years, they were not interested in taking orders from the new management about how security was to be run. The disagreement, however, never turned into an attempt at another rebel occupation. Instead, the dispute between the former rebels and the new management resulted in Simon leaving his unofficial position within the security force in December 2009.

New Management at Sime Darby, Same Lingering Rebel Networks

In January 2010 the Malaysian palm-oil producer Sime Darby had taken over the management of the former rubber plantation, and in September 2011 I traveled back to the plantation. In one of the nearby villages at the outskirts of the plantation, I was to meet with Alpha, the former NPFL general who had been one of the commanders responsible for the plantation's informal security provision.[15] As I came to learn, some things had changed when it came to the structures for security provision at the plantation with the new management. But much had also stayed the same. The monitors, who now operated under the name Sime Darby Security (SDS) had become the formal security providers for the new management. The members proudly presented their ID cards, showing me their new formal status. The group had expanded and was composed at this point by a little more than two hundred security providers, approximately 10 percent of whom were women. The SDS had kept most of their former organization structures, and the wartime rebel links were still visible, as about 75 percent of the security providers were ex-combatants from all factions active in the Liberian civil wars. Five main commanders were responsible for the different plantation estates, each having subcommanders for the smaller divisions of the plantation. Alpha had risen to the highest security commander and had personally chosen the men and women who worked below him. He had known many of them during the war, as they had fought below him during his time as an NPFL general. Former fighters often came looking for him, knowing he now had the potential to provide them with paid employment by recommending them to the management.

Since the security group gained its official status and the Sime Darby management took over, Alpha and the security providers, as well as the other workers, had been paid without delay every month. This reflected a new kind of stability that had never been seen at the plantation during the Guthrie days. This development had, of course, brought with it several positive aspects, and one was that it thereby reduced the incentives of the ex-combatants to be used as threats of violence against other plantation workers. Alpha had thereby also strengthened his own position in the community around the plantation. Tappers and other planation workers did not need to fear the ex-combatants in the same way any longer, and the men under his command could be assured that work within the security force also would provide them with an income. Alpha was proud to show me around in his new house under construction, and he told me about his plans to start a new business on the side. He was thinking of starting a small nightclub, using a part of his house. His house and such plans would have been completely impossible only a few years earlier. But in his new position Alpha was empowered. In this way Alpha retained his network of ex-combatants, which the new management, like their predecessors before them, made good use of. But, despite the improved situation for the security providers, among the workers at the plantation the security force had always been prioritized when it came to the payment of salaries. As one of the security providers explained, the former management, despite failing to pay the tappers, always saw to it that at least the security group received some payment. In this way the government could secure their incomes generated from the plantation, as the security group could be used to make tappers work even when their salaries were delayed. According to this security provider, the group did not use violent measures against the workers, since many of the tappers and the other workers came from their own families and communities. But, as he explains, the security force was still able to "encourage" the tappers to work simply because many of them were ex-combatants. As he said, "the people had fear for us," but it is always like this: "If you're in security, you become the public enemy in Liberia. That is how people see it." He then stated that Liberians have good reasons for this perception, considering the history of the country and how the people have always been abused by the security institutions.[16]

When it came to the actual protection of Sime Darby, not much had changed since the first time I visited the plantation. The sds carried out security in the same way they always had done. They guarded the entrances to the plantation and patrolled the area day and night, reporting all events to their immediate commanders. They were still unarmed, but the new management had provided them with cutlasses. For personal security, the group members stated. The area they patrolled was vast and, with only little more than two hundred security guards, there were often not more than two or three individuals in each patrolling group, and sometimes they were forced to work alone. Several incidents of violent attacks had occurred, as rubber thieves and illegal tappers often operated in larger groups, outnumbering the small patrolling teams. The Liberian National Police had only a few unarmed officers in the area, and the unmil force at the plantation before the new management took over had left, leaving the sds as one of the few security actors operating in the plantation area and the surrounding villages. The management had promised security training courses and uniforms for the members, but at this point the only thing that reflected the group's official status was the id cards. Instead, it was very prominent that the group, for better and for worse and for lack of other means, still used their wartime skills and chains of command to organize and operate at the plantation.

Ex-combatants in the Postwar Political Economy

As the case demonstrates, there are clearly not only political reasons for the elite's use of postwar rebel networks at the plantation. The potential of substantial economic gains was one important part of this development. As Berdal and Dominik Zaum have argued, war, and civil war in particular, transforms the relationship between state and market, creating its own political economy. Because of war, new structures of political power and authority can arise; new actors controlling resources can emerge; and new forms of interaction between political and economic life can come about. Civil war implies the emergence of different, or alternative, kinds of order. And as Berdal and Zaum conclude, war economies persist into peacetime and are likely to shape the character of the postwar political economy.[17] I would argue that such a development has clearly occurred in Liberia, and that the case of Guthrie / Sime Darby is an illustrative example of this. Several actors have been used to, or even dependent on, the wartime logic on which the economy of this plantation has been built, making it rather difficult, or even undesirable, to change the way things are despite the established peace.

Furthermore, in the specific Liberian case, William Reno—in his analysis of the warfare in Liberia and what he calls "warlord politics"—finds that the Liberian war did follow a clear logic. Strongmen used commerce to consolidate their political power within a coalition of interest among themselves, businessmen, and local fighters. Taylor, he notes, controlled commerce in gold and diamond mining, timber, and, as we have seen in this case study, rubber. Such warlord politics, Reno argues, is not a result of the collapse of state authority and capacity. Instead, this situation emerged as the result of a social coalition of enterprising strongmen, small-scale foreign commercial operators, and a segment of the country's youth. The history of governance in Liberia and the elite's social arrangements, along with external conditions, have given strongmen the political and financial autonomy to seek their own fortunes at the expense of a central authority.[18] Even though the wars were over, many aspects of this old logic referred to by Reno remained the same in postwar Liberia, despite the absence of warlords in presidential positions. Thus, the Liberian government under the leadership of President Ellen Johnson Sirleaf, just like the governments led by Bryant and Taylor preceding it, rather than demobilizing all ex-combatants—which is the entire point with the DDRR process—had strong reasons for *re*mobilizing influential ex-combatants. This appears to have been done out of both political and financial considerations as well as from a security point of view. The plantation has always had the potential of generating a significant income for the Liberian state. Yet during the time the plantation was under the government's management, they were unable to provide employment and basic social services for their workers. Therefore, protests and strikes were a constant threat to the government's authority. In this context the influence of notorious ex-combatants was used to make people work. Considering Liberia's violent past and history of attaining power by war or coups, the efficiency of this strategy should not be underestimated. But ex-combatants are per definition potential destabilizers; as they once were the instruments of warfare, they could just as well become so again. By unofficially using the violent potential of the ex-combatants, President Johnson Sirleaf and the ruling political elite could, on the one hand, secure their political and economic interests to remain in power, but, on the other hand, they were at risk of maintaining structures that could be used for renewed warfare.

Postwar Transformation of Rebels into Security Providers

When the rebels took over the plantation in 2003, it was clearly nothing but an illegal occupation. Still, the official transitional government cooperated with the rebel management and benefited from the illicit economy generated at Guthrie. Later, when the Liberian government under the leadership of President Johnson Sirleaf regained control of the plantation, many aspects of informal structures, like the remaining postwar rebel structures, stayed the same and actually ensured that Guthrie kept generating financial resources despite the inadequate management. The plantation in this sense, after the government takeover, still operated in the borderlands between the formal and informal, and the legal and illicit. Carolyn Nordstrom, in her research on "shadow networks"—that is, extrastate exchange systems in and in relation to war—and on how economic transactions take place on nonlegal platforms as well as the shadowy illegalities and legalities that sustain war, finds that there is a profound irony in such shadow realities. Nordstrom notes that the realm of the unregulated is a realm of both possibilities, where great fortunes can be made, as well as a realm of danger, where great cruelty is possible. The arena of the shadows, she argues, is a place where power regimes are contested and where new forms of capital, access, and authority arise. Not merely illicit systems bent on rapid and potentially immense gain, shadow networks also offer a means of development for people with few alternative means of survival, making them a serious source of power in the contemporary world.[19]

When it comes to the unofficial use of postwar rebel networks at Guthrie / Sime Darby, I believe that one must also keep in mind this notion pointed out by Nordstrom. There is no doubt that the ex-combatants in this case study were used in a manner that involved clear risks and had severe unethical implications. They caused fear and were potential sources of violence in and around the plantation area. But they did so mainly when the elite called for it. This was evident as the situation was much calmer after the Sime Darby management took over. The incentives of violent and threatening behavior against the plantation workers were clearly reduced by this change of management, since the elite no longer had any need to use ex-combatants as intimidators against their own workers, as they were now able to pay salaries and provide better working conditions. The overall question I pose is whether a rebel can become a security provider or, in other words, if a perpetrator can become a protector, and the answer is, of course, yes. But it all comes down to the elite actors' intentions when using postwar rebel networks, no matter whether the use is informal or formal, official or hidden. These networks do have a violent potential, but they also have a potential for providing good security and for being well organized and disciplined. They are not simply good or bad in themselves.

The transformation of the security providers at the plantation from times of war, rebel occupation, and postwar interim managements until the Sime Darby management took over also reflects this interaction and the dynamics between formal and informal security provision. The trajectory of Alpha is interesting in this regard, as he has been active at the plantation since the time of Charles Taylor, with only a few years' interruption. Alpha, along with many men under him, have gone from being rebel soldiers to becoming informal security providers and have now finally reached a state where they can call themselves the official security force of the plantation. Their transformation, while operating at the borders between the official and unofficial, shows how the ex-combatants have strived to find employment opportunities in an insecure postwar environment through the use of their wartime networks and skills. In this sense they have also succeeded, as they have finally found a position within the formal security system, because the economic and political elite, in times of war as well as afterward, and regardless of who has been in power, has taken advantage of these postwar rebel networks, despite the risks and perils of keeping them mobilized. The work as security providers, both informally and formally, at the plantation after the government had regained control in fact also gave ex-combatants, who often struggle to make a living in postwar situations, something to do and a way to support themselves. Giving ex-combatants a chance to survive from activities other than warfare does work as a conflict-management effort, even in settings where their links to one another are preserved.

Furthermore, to understand in depth how postwar rebel networks operate and how the elite make use of such structures in practice, one needs to follow and focus on individuals within these networks. The three commanders, the former rebel generals Michael, Simon, and Alpha, represent important nodes, linking formal and informal regimes of power by connecting the political elite to their networks of former rebel soldiers, networks, as we have seen, with the ability to both create security and cause instability. The Liberian political elite's interaction with these former generals, as illustrated by the case of Guthrie /

Sime Darby, gives evidence of the elite's strategy to win the loyalty of the ex-combatants through former key rebel commanders who still have influence over their wartime networks and, as in this example, use them mainly for financial gains. The individual ex-combatants can link themselves to the formal regimes of power within postwar rebel networks and through their former, or newfound, rebel commanders in the hope of finding employment opportunities or economic gains in a way that would never have been possible otherwise.

Michael in particular is a good example of an actor who has been able to benefit from this mutual dependence between the political and economic elite and the ex-combatants. By keeping his network of ex-combatants close to him, even after he and Simon had handed over control of the plantation, he remained important for the political elite. He became a gatekeeper to these lingering war structures, who politicians and others in power need to go through if they wish to use these actors. Michael also managed to use the contacts he gained during his time managing the plantation to secure employment within the official security structures of Liberia, through a position with the Intelligence Department of the Liberian National Police. Michael has continued to climb the hierarchies of the formal state security system, using his good connections to the elite and his postwar rebel network. In addition, Michael has done what few ex-combatants have had the ability to do: he has invested some of his resources in university studies to obtain a degree in criminal justice. While using his skills and contacts, Michael has continued to pursue a postwar security career and has attained a senior position within one of Liberia's formal security institutions. At the same time, in addition to running an ex-combatant organization, Michael and Simon continued to visit the plantation, the new Sime Darby management, and the headquarters of the ex-combatants within the plantation security group led by Alpha several times a week. Michael was thereby safeguarding his interests and influence through his position within both the formal and informal power structures of Liberia.

Conclusion

The developments at Guthrie / Sime Darby Plantation, from the time of Charles Taylor's regime at the end of the first civil war and throughout the years of renewed warfare and the postconflict and preelection period, reveal some of the reasons why postwar rebel networks remain relevant in Liberia today, regardless of the fact that many years have passed since the signing of the peace agreement. What we have seen in this case is that, paradoxically, the networks of former rebel structures that President Ellen Johnson Sirleaf officially set out to disrupt were the very same that she and the Liberian government were using unofficially to maintain control and stay in power. The case of the ex-combatants at the plantation gives us insights into why the continued presence of wartime structures, in the shape of postwar rebel networks, can become so important from a political and economic perspective, both for the individual ex-combatants—for lack of other livelihood opportunities—and the elite looking to secure power and ensure financial gains. Through the analysis of this mutual interdependence, between the political and economic elite on the one hand and the ex-combatants on the other, the links between formal and informal regimes of power shaping the contemporary security situation in Liberia also become visible. By looking at the case of Guthrie / Sime Darby from the perspective of the political elite, it appears that it simply was never the true intention to completely demobilize all former rebel structures. Postwar rebel networks were much too valuable mobilized for such an undertaking. In the words of Magnus Jörgel and Mats Utas, politicians are Big Men with powers only as great as their networks. Party politics thereby can be seen as a form of patronage, whereby politicians obtain "wealth in people" in exchange for assuming responsibility for their followers.[20] The logical action to take from such a perspective could hence arguably be to preserve, rather than destroy, such networks created out of warfare.

Throughout this book I have attempted to show that the maintenance of postwar rebel networks and the actual use of such structures are quite complex issues. Postwar rebel networks can, and are, used for both good and bad and can be both providers of security or violent perpetrators. In this chapter the elites' initial use of remaining wartime structures of ex-combatants appears to have been well connected to these actors' violent potential. In this case postwar rebel networks were undoubtedly used because they can have a very intimidating effect. Ex-combatants were used to make workers do their share even when the management itself had failed to fulfill its end of the deal of paying salaries on time or providing good working conditions. Nevertheless, postwar rebel networks are at the same time also used because ex-combatants connected to such structures can be good workers: disciplined and already well organized. Although the plantation occupation was an illegal venture, networks of ex-combatants also had the ability to turn their military organization into a structure managing all aspects of this Liberian rubber plantation. The later use of postwar rebel networks at the plantation, as Sime Darby had taken over the management and working conditions in general had become more stabilized, appears to be more connected to the fact that the former rebels could actually become well-organized security providers if used for this specific purpose.

CHAPTER 4

Nothing Left for the Losers in Winner-Takes-All Elections

REPURPOSED REBELS, POLITICAL MANEUVERING, AND THE 2011 LIBERIAN ELECTIONS

It was September, just before the elections. It had proved rather difficult to get hold of any of my informants, but to get hold of Michael had been nearly impossible.[1] We spoke on the phone and arranged to meet, but it often ended with Michael texting to apologize that he couldn't make it; something had come up again: "election-business," he said. Michael was busier than any of my informants in Liberia, but, then again, Michael's situation was very different from all the other ex-combatants I know. He has done what the others only dream of; he has managed to secure employment in the formal sector, a senior position within one of the country's security institutions. If "reintegration is the process by which ex-combatants acquire civilian status and gain sustainable employment and income," Michael has certainly been socially and economically integrated into civil society.[2] But Michael's success lies not in his abandonment of his wartime rebel networks but rather the opposite.

In October 2011 Liberia faced one of the country's toughest postwar challenges—the second general and presidential elections following the civil war. These were the first postwar elections organized by the Liberians themselves. The previous elections had been run by the United Nations peacekeeping mission; now the Liberian state took over. The elections were widely seen as a test of the state of the country's security-political situation and as an opportunity to consolidate Liberia's fragile peace. Yet there was also a fear of renewed instability or even violence. The elections would be telling, not only in terms of the final electoral results. More important, the preelection political mobilization and the manner in which the elections were conducted would, it was thought, be a powerful indicator of Liberia's security system and how far the country had come since the peace agreement. In most postconflict countries much is at stake, and tensions are high during elections.[3] The 2011 Liberian elections were no exception. In this chapter I use the elections as a point of departure for analyzing the contemporary role of Liberian ex-combatants and how such a political event can highlight the relevance of talking about postwar rebel networks, eight years after the war came to an end. I explore why a lingering temptation to mobilize such networks as potential perpetrators of electoral violence still existed during the time leading up to and during the elections and what consequences that had for the contemporary security situation in Liberia.

For this chapter I have followed ex-combatants in support of the presidential candidates who, ultimately, were the most important candidates to the 2011 Liberian elections: the incumbent president Ellen Johnson Sirleaf from the Unity Party and Winston Tubman, presidential candidate from the Congress of Democratic Change (CDC), before, during, and after the elections.[4] The Liberian presidential elections serve to illustrate both how the political elite used postwar rebel networks for different purposes, including informal security provision and voter mobilization, and how the ex-combatants themselves made use of this political event and their wartime links to one another. My analysis takes the experiences of two men in particular as a point of departure, two Liberian men closely connected to ex-combatant networks. The first one, Michael, we know from the two previous chapters as the former rebel commander who, through his involvement in the illegal occupation of the Guthrie Rubber Plantation, managed to secure important political connections leading all the way up to the incumbent president, Johnson Sirleaf. The other main protagonist, Alex, a former vigilante leader who, despite not having been a rebel soldier himself, managed to establish a network mainly of ex-combatants that was later mobilized by Winston Tubman during his electoral campaign. These two men's stories are very different, mainly because Johnson Sirleaf won and Tubman lost the elections. For these men and especially for the ex-combatants around them, who had few opportunities to make a living in a postwar society, the elections were crucial. These political events are the moments when the otherwise distant political elite have to listen to the Liberian people. During elections Liberians, and perhaps ex-combatants in particular, see opportunities otherwise closed to them. But the difference between winning and losing in Liberia can be immense, something that can be demonstrated by following networks on both sides of the dividing line. For my informants political involvement was very advantageous, for one side— for the other, disastrous. The 2011 Liberian elections came to provide yet more evidence of the long-term effects of the war and of remaining rebel structures still used for political purposes, despite all initiatives for demobilization and reintegration. It revealed how important it is for many ex-combatants to become what they regard as "politically active," but, more so, it highlighted the importance of supporting the "right" political candidate—that is, the next president of Liberia.

Postconflict Elections and the Final Break with War

Elections in postconflict countries are often seen as important markers of a state's transition from war to peace. Elections are therefore prioritized within international efforts aiming at rebuilding states and promoting democracy after violent conflicts. Especially in high-profile international interventions, elections also have an important symbolic value, signaling in both the domestic and the international arenas that a legitimate government authority has been put in place. This is seen as representing an essential step in the process of state reconstruction and thus a central part of postconflict state building.[5] Successful elections—that is, elections that are peacefully conducted and considered "free and fair"—become milestones symbolizing a break with a violent wartime history. Yet when electoral violence still occurs, it naturally makes us question the sustainability of the newly acquired peace and the state of the democratization process in general. Electoral violence and its causes, perpetrators, and consequences have been given increased attention for these reasons in recent years.[6]

Such research is of great value, not least because it can tell us something about the level of stability that a country has reached after a conflict. But would that then lead to the conclusion that the absence of electoral violence is a sign of a state's final break with war? In this chapter I suggest otherwise. Mary Moran, in her research on violence and democracy in Liberia, notes the Western tendency to view these two concepts as opposite ends of an evolutionary scale, whereby the successor to widespread violence is imagined to be democracy. Through the lens of the particular case of Liberia, Moran questions whether democracy and violence really are separate, or even separable, states or whether there is violence in democracy and democracy in violence. Moran asks if a people really can be said to "choose" democracy over war and vice versa. As answers to these questions, she argues that in Liberian political discourse violence and democracy are not conceptually opposed, but aspects of the same understanding of legitimacy. Liberian history can be understood as an ongoing interplay between themes of democracy and violence enacted at both local and national levels.[7] In this chapter I approach the 2011 Liberian elections from a similar perspective. I suggest that the elections, despite the relatively low levels of violence that occurred, cannot be seen as a final break with war. Instead, the elections in this case rather make Liberia's wartime past more evident. War and peace are entangled, not opposite ends, and the elections illustrate this continuity. For instance, as pointed out by David Harris and Tereza Lewis in their analysis of the Liberian elections, many of the political actors with popularity built on war records returned in 2011, illustrating how the time passed since the war, compared to the 2005 elections, did not appear to have altered the political environment.[8]

Liberia's Recent History of Electoral Violence

The use of wartime structures and ex-combatants to win elections is not a new phenomenon in Liberia. As Terrence Lyons, among others, observed during the 1997 elections after the first civil war, the former National Patriotic Front of Liberia rebel leader Charles Taylor converted his military organization into an efficient mass-mobilizing political party, where patronage replaced guns and rallies roadblocks, to win the political competition.[9] Taylor's political party provided a civilian platform from where he could compete for votes during the elections, but in reality the organization remained fundamentally militarized.[10] Taylor furthermore convinced United Nations monitors to accept the result of the elections, in which his party had intimidated voters, and was elected president.[11]

As noted by Benjamin Reilly, the easiest way to attract voters in postconflict societies is often to appeal to the very same insecurities that generated the original conflict in the first place. In such cases instead of attempting to win support with policy appeals, postconflict parties have a strong incentive to downplay policy choices and instead mobilize voters along identity lines.[12] In the Liberian case this seems to be true, as wartime insecurities as well as aspects of identity appear to have played an important role in all postconflict elections. But a remarkable aspect of the 2005 elections that later followed was the virtually complete disappearance of rebel groups in the political process, as neither the Liberians United for Reconciliation and Democracy nor the Movement for Democracy in Liberia transformed into political parties. Sekou Conneh, the former chair of Liberians United, did reappear in the elections as a presidential candidate of his own political party, but the attempt was rather ineffectual, as his estranged wife and former coleader Aisha Conneh decided to support Johnson Sirleaf and the Unity Party instead.[13]

According to Harris, many rebel generals and leaders of insurgent forces seemed to have been satisfied with unseating Taylor and pursuing lucrative deals within the National Transitional Government of Liberia and in business.[14] Still, the war and former rebel soldiers continued to have a significant impact on the elections also after the peace agreement had been signed in 2003. As demonstrated by Amos Sawyer, the ending of the war and the removal of the oligarchy and warlords did not make Liberia a political tabula rasa. During the 2005 elections the candidates who could claim to have provided security for local people during the wars were favored by the voters.[15] Candidates associated with armed groups with credible records among their people were elected. In Nimba County both elected senators had a past as combatants. Prince Johnson, the former leader of the Independent National Patriotic Front of Liberia, who constantly reminded voters of his protection during the conflict and his ability to defend them again should there be another war, won the senior senate seat by a landslide. The National Patriotic Front commander Adolphus Dolo, who won the second senator seat, campaigned on his record of defending Nimba County against the Liberians United for Reconciliation and Democracy forces in 2001.[16] Additionally, Sawyer notes, a similar pattern, although to a lesser extent, could also be seen in other parts of the country during the elections.[17]

The political maneuvering of postwar rebel networks during postconflict election processes, whether or not this leads to the use, or threat of use, of violence, is an illustrative example of war and peace entanglements that have been observed in the Liberian elections in the past. And the elections of 2011 was no exception. The analysis here, however, does not emphasize electoral violence as such, but rather the category of actors often associated with this type of violence, namely the ex-combatants. Yet the mobilization of former rebels and other actors associated with a past war during elections, contrary to what is often assumed, is not *necessarily* done with the purpose of committing violence, nor does such mobilization necessarily lead to large-scale outbreaks of violence. The case of the 2011 Liberian elections illustrates that while such actors can be used for violent purposes, as they have been in many postconflict elections in Africa and elsewhere over the years, their violent potential is far from the only reason the political elite was interested in them.

Winston Tubman and the Vigilante Leader

It was so hot that April day. The rainy season had yet to begin, and there had been no rains the night before which would have cooled the morning hours slightly. I was in Sinkor, Monrovia, on one of the streets off Tubman Boulevard. I had not been walking for more than half an hour to get to our meeting point, but I was still covered in sweat and dust. Two young men selling telephone scratch cards at the street corner noticed me and offered me some shade underneath their parasol by their small fair booth. I was grateful to find cover from the hot Liberian sun and took a seat on the floor beside the friendly young men. I was probably early, or Alex was late—either way I could see him approaching from afar after I had chatting with the men for some time. Alex sticks out in a crowd. He is taller and bigger than most Liberian men, and he dresses according to basketball fashion. He walked slowly, though, not in the same determined way he usually did, and for a moment I thought he looked more tired than I had ever seen him before. But I forgot about that when he saw me, cheered up, and came to greet me. This meeting would turn out to be very different from when we last saw each other. That time, only a few months before, the Liberian national elections were approaching, hopes were high, and Alex had big dreams for the future. Winston Tubman's run for the presidency had opened up new opportunities for him and a network of men around him, men who could be used as security providers, men with a background in rebel movements or vigilante groups.

The very first time I met Alex, in 2009, he had emerged as a leader of a vigilante group in Sinkor, Monrovia, a few years earlier. The group saw themselves as local defenders of their community in an area were the Liberian National Police did not dare to enter at night. At dusk the young men of the group gathered. After Alex's instructions they were divided into smaller groups and took turns to patrol the neighborhood until the early morning hours. Anyone not belonging to the community found wandering their streets was stopped and questioned. Suspected criminals, or anyone caught committing a crime, were to be brought directly to Alex and thereafter be handed over to the police for further investigation. This did not always happen, however. From time to time the vigilantes took it on themselves not only to be the neighborhood's watchmen but to determine the captured individual's guilt or innocence after an on-the-spot interrogation, as well as the punishment.[18]

Alex himself had not been a rebel soldier. Among the approximately fifty men who made up the vigilante group, that made him an exception. The men came from different backgrounds, ethnic groups, parts of Liberia, and rebel factions. What they now shared was not only their community and their status as ex-combatants but also poverty and unemployment. The members of the community could not afford to pay the vigilantes, but most contributed a little money or food to keep the group going. In this way being a vigilante was for some of these young men a way to secure a daily meal, but it was also a way to make use of skills learned during the war somehow. According to vigilante members and other members of the community, Alex had been chosen because he was well respected, well known, and trusted. He in turn made good use of the ex-combatants' skills as informal neighborhood security providers. Years in wars and rebel movements had taught them how to organize themselves and secure an area and where to take positions to protect their neighborhood and ambush suspected criminals. They knew how to fight, but, more important, as Alex and others in the community often pointed out, they were fearless and feared for their violent nature. The knowledge that the vigilante group was primarily composed of ex-combatants had a deterrent effect on outsiders.

But the advantages of having former rebels as vigilantes also came with its perils. The ex-combatants were more likely to take the law into their own hands when it came to punishment. The rule that the suspected criminal was to be brought to Alex first and then to the police was, as discussed, broken from time to time. The ex-combatants' past experiences from war and their fearless attitude toward violence made them unpredictable and difficult to control. Catching a person in the act of committing a crime, the ex-combatants were more likely than others to resort to violence immediately. The community's attitudes toward the vigilante group were thereby ambivalent. As a community member who was not part of the vigilante group told me, the vigilante group enjoyed strong support in the community because the alternative was nonexistent: the Liberian National Police were neither present nor trusted. The ex-combatants' skills in security and fearless attitude made them valuable vigilantes in the eyes of the community, even though the ex-combatants were often treated with suspicion because of their past in the war and their presumed violent nature.[19] Nevertheless, the community would rather have them organized in the vigilante group than not. Their skills proved to be useful, while they, at least to a certain extent, could be controlled, as they worked for the community instead of constituting a threat against it.

CDC Mobilizing

When I met Alex again in September 2011, life had taken a new turn for him and the vigilante group. Alex and the men around him had, as they saw it themselves, "gone into politics."[20] Or, as one could also see it, Liberian politicians had reached out to ex-combatants. Alex had been approached by Winston Tubman—the man who, in May 2011, had been chosen as the presidential candidate for the CDC party. After being nominated, Tubman set out to cater for his personal protection and establish his own informal security group. Tubman wanted men around him who could work as his personal bodyguards, men who could protect him when campaigning but possibly also show force, power, and status. To find men suitable for the job, Tubman turned to Alex. This was not the first time Tubman had run for president and not the first time he had turned to Alex either. Like Johnson Sirleaf, Tubman, the nephew of Liberia's longest-serving president, William Tubman, was part of and brought up within the old Americo-Liberian elite. He had degrees from London School of Economics, Cambridge, and Harvard University and had owned his own law firm. During Doe's years in power, Tubman served as Liberia's minister of justice. After the fall of Doe, Tubman had continued his career as a diplomat within the United Nations and had just left a position as the United Nations special representative of the secretary general for Somalia in time for the 2005 elections to compete for the presidency.[21] Tubman came to run for Doe's old party, the National Democratic Party of Liberia.[22]

Tubman had come to know the vigilante leader and had called on him to establish an informal security force of ex-combatants to surround him during his campaign in the 2005 elections. Tubman had lost the race against Ellen Johnson Sirleaf back then, and Alex and his men had returned to their normal life and business. But for the 2011 elections, Tubman needed the vigilante leader and his network once again. The security force established around Tubman and the CDC party in many ways came to resemble a military unit. Alex and four other men, the others being former rebel generals, were chosen as the main commanders. Some of these men had also worked for Tubman once before in 2005, while others were new recruits. Each commander had a specific task and main responsibility for areas such as Tubman's overall day and nighttime security, campaigning and motorcade security, private house and party headquarters security, and so on. Under each commander Alex assigned ex-combatants from his vigilante group to work as security providers. The closest group to Tubman was composed of approximately twenty-five men. But the overall mobilized informal security network around CDC was much larger than this. George Weah, the well-known footballer and former CDC presidential candidate from 2005, who during the 2011 elections ran for the vice presidency under Tubman, also had his own personal informal security force, resembling in structure the one organized for Tubman.

Above all this, there was an additional informal security group working for the CDC party, which some informants called the "Battle Cry." The Battle Cry was a much larger group, composed of approximately a thousand men and a few women, most of them ex-combatants. The Battle Cry was not operating autonomously but instead was under the command of Tubman's security group. The group had their members both in Monrovia and out in the counties and worked as a reinforcement of Tubman's security group during his campaigning. The group was, for example, to check and secure an area before Tubman and his closest security men arrived in towns and villages to campaign. The members of Battle Cry never received any regular payment from the CDC party but were often given food and drinks and, sometimes, small amounts of money. The members of Alex's security group closest to Tubman could count on somewhat more regular payments from the CDC party, but for them, as for the members of the wider security structures of the party, it was the hopes and promise of an eventual electoral victory for Winston Tubman that mattered. When I talked about this with Alex and the other commanders of the security group, they all were very enthusiastic. If Tubman were to win in the elections, they all felt sure that the victory would imply permanent security jobs. At least the commanders were to be incorporated into the official security system, either as bodyguards or in other positions within the formal security institutions, since Tubman as president would surely be able to provide for this. Where they would end up if Tubman was to lose, they did not even want to think about. But they were sure this would mean that their struggle with unemployment and poverty would certainly continue. A victory for the incumbent president Ellen Johnson Sirleaf, they argued, would not give them any benefits at all.

Ellen Johnson Sirleaf and the Former LURD General

As the 2011 elections came closer it became more and more evident that the network of ex-combatants at the Guthrie / Sime Darby plantation who had remained there since the end of the war had a role to play in the political developments in Liberia. Through the three former generals who had kept active at the plantation following the government takeover, the ex-combatants within the plantation's security force were connected to influential political actors. By following the trajectory of Michael as one of the three main commanders at the plantation, we can see the mutual dependence between key political actors on the one hand and key former rebel commanders with the ability to influence postwar rebel networks on the other. Through Michael the ex-combatants at the plantation could be used for political purposes and through him the ex-combatants themselves could take advantage of this political event.

During the time he was in control of Guthrie, Michael had already successfully managed to secure and leverage political connections. Authorities and politicians, even at the highest level of the National Transitional Government of Liberia, cooperated after the war with the rebel leadership occupying the plantation. In doing so they managed to take advantage of the financial resources generated by the rubber industry. Also after the 2005 national elections, Johnson Sirleaf's government negotiated with the rebel commanders to regain control over Guthrie, and Michael was the main negotiator on the occupiers' side. He became the gatekeeper between the political and economic elite and the ex-combatants at the plantation. The elite needed the ex-combatants and the ex-combatants needed the elite. Michael could thereby operate as the link between these actors, making cooperation possible and a mutual dependence fruitful for both sides. Even after he and the other ex-combatants had officially handed over control of Guthrie in 2006, Michael remained an important actor for both the politicians and the ex-combatants. He successfully negotiated reintegration benefits for his former combatants with the Johnson Sirleaf government but also stayed in close contact with the ex-combatants who remained at the plantation as informal security providers. Moreover, Michael also managed to use the contacts he gained during his time managing the plantation, after the rebels had handed over control, for his own benefit to secure employment within Liberia's official security structures. Furthermore, Michael had done what few ex-combatants have had the ability to do: he had invested some of his resources in university studies to obtain a degree in criminal justice.[23] While using his skills and contacts, Michael has continued to make a career within the official security structures, as he later attained a senior position within another one of Liberia's formal security institutions.

Unity Party Mobilizing

For the 2011 elections Michael once again became important for both the political elite and the ex-combatants in his network.[24] In March 2011, during
the voter registration process, he launched an ex-combatant organization
based around the plantation area. When Michael first had the idea, he presented it to a senior local politician in Johnson Sirleaf's government in Bomi
County, where the rubber plantation is located, who decided to sponsor the
project. Michael said that he came up with the idea because he wanted an
organized network for ex-combatants' rights. He wanted to keep them away
from trouble, drugs, and criminal activities, and he wanted to work for their
employment opportunities by using his links to the political elite. But whatever motives Michael had for starting the organization, it was evident that for
the politicians facing an upcoming election, supporting Michael's organization was a very strategic way of gaining votes. Michael soon had more than
a thousand ex-combatants enlisted in his organization and the network and
was approached by politicians at the highest level.

Michael and the leadership of the organization, composed of himself and
two other former rebel generals, even had a few meetings with the president
herself. The outcome of these meetings was that Michael and the former commanders promised to promote Ellen Johnson Sirleaf and the Unity Party in
the elections and during the preelection phase in exchange for financial support and promises of scholarships for higher education for some of the ex-
combatants should the Johnson Sirleaf government stay in power. As Michael
explains, he first encouraged the ex-combatants to register for the elections;
then, as he says, "I told them why, when, and how to vote." Michael's influence
on the ex-combatants also as voters was accordingly significant.

The Losers

When I met Alex again in Monrovia in April 2012, his outlook had changed
dramatically from the time I last saw him, only a few months earlier, just before the 2011 Liberian elections. Before the elections Alex and the network of
ex-combatants around him had been confident about the future. As Tubman's
VIP security group, they were not only able to secure an income but also felt
proud to have a job and to use their skills in security for something they saw
as a positive cause. Having known Alex and some of the other men in his
group for a few years, I found that the difference in their attitudes in the preelection period was remarkable. They believed that there was a role for them
as formal security providers in the future and that Winston Tubman and the

CDC party would open doors for them. But this required an election victory for their candidate, something that did not happen.

The results of the first round of the presidential elections, held on October 11, 2011, were released on October 25, giving incumbent president, Ellen Johnson Sirleaf, the lead with 43.9 percent of the votes, followed by Winston Tubman with 32.7 percent. The former rebel leader Prince Johnson, now a presidential candidate for the National Union for Democratic Progress Party, took the first round's third place with 11.6 percent of the votes.[25] As none of the candidates managed to secure an absolute majority, Johnson Sirleaf and Tubman faced a runoff that was to be held on November 8, 2011. But Winston Tubman and the CDC claimed that the election had been rigged in Johnson Sirleaf's favor. Tubman and the CDC pulled out of the second round and urged their supporters to boycott the runoffs. For Alex and my other informants supporting Tubman and the CDC, this decision had immeasurable consequences. They felt cheated out of the election victory and were convinced that the elections had been fraudulent, regardless of the approval of international observers. Their frustration grew rapidly, and Liberians and election observers now started to fear renewed violence, despite the relatively calm preelection period. On November 7, the day before the second round of the presidential elections, the protests eventually turned deadly, on a day that my informants refer to as "Bloody Monday." Thousands of CDC supporters had gathered outside the party headquarters to urge voters to boycott the runoff. Violence broke out as police backed by United Nations forces blocked a road to prevent the CDC activists from marching into the city. Tear gas was used but also live bullets, and at least one young man among the CDC activists died after being shot in the head.[26] These events in many ways marked the beginning of the end of the hopes and dreams about a better future that Alex and the men around him had held during the preelection phase. President Johnson Sirleaf's victory was declared a few days later.

Alex was broken when I met him after the elections. Tubman had left the country, leaving Alex and his men without work. But not only was Alex without a job; he seemed to be unable to get a new one because of his former commitment. Alex's strength, which Tubman clearly had taken advantage of, that he had been a well known and respected man in his community with the ability to mobilize whole networks of ex-combatants, was now turned into a weakness. The opposition knew him very well, and no one wanted to employ him. With the victory of Johnson Sirleaf, security positions within the formal security institutions were now completely out of reach, Alex and all my pro–CDC informants argued. But these positions were not beyond reach for ex-combatants on the winning side, those who had supported the president before and during the election process. Now Johnson Sirleaf had to pay them back with whatever means she had, leaving nothing for the losing side. As Alex explained, "CDC can do nothing for the ones they mobilized. They are left with nothing. And now things are even worse than before, as the winning side don't want to have anything to do with them." Not only had Alex looked for jobs at the formal security institutions; he had visited almost all the private security companies, but no one was willing to offer a position to a man who so clearly was connected to the losing side. For Alex and the ex-combatants working for him, this was a "winner-takes-all" situation, and they had been supporting the "wrong" candidate.

Furthermore, Alex was not only miserable from his inability to find a job; he was also scared. In December, only a few weeks after the Johnson Sirleaf victory, Alex's house was attacked. Masked men broke into the house in the middle of the night. They took everything of value and smashed the rest, leaving Alex' small home completely devastated. Alex and others in the neighborhood strongly believed that this was an act perpetrated against Alex as retaliation because he was a CDC man and had not been loyal to the ruling elite of Liberia. The police, he says, had not investigated the incident and could even have been involved. He had no evidence of this being so, but this was what he and others believed. From this night on Alex did not dare to spend another night in his old house. He feared another attack; he feared revenge and retaliation; he even feared for his life. For six months he had been moving around all over Monrovia, spending the nights at different friends' houses. He never wanted to stay in the same place for long, and he was careful not to let too many people know his whereabouts. Alex, in all those years I had known him, had been proud to be a well-known man in his neighborhood. Now he saw this as his biggest disadvantage. He and many ex-combatants around him had put everything at stake when they took sides in the elections. This political event had been their most promising option, a risk they considered worth taking. But they had lost it all.

The Winners

For Michael the elections meant something entirely different. As I could see when we met again in April after the elections, Michael and his network of ex-combatants had clearly benefited from Johnson Sirleaf's victory. The victory meant that Michael could feel more secure in his position at the security institution, a position he most likely would have lost given a new political leadership. For his ex-combatants Michael had used his personal contacts with senior politicians to get funding for more than twenty scholarships for university studies. He had been the one appointing the candidates for the scholarships, choosing among those ex-combatants in his network who already had a high school diploma and whom he saw as promising. He had managed to recommend several others for different informal security positions through his contacts at various institutions and private organizations. This was the government's way to pay him back for the support he had mobilized during the electoral campaign. The official election results from the first round of voting in Bomi County, where Michael's ex-combatant organization was based and where he had the main part of his network, gave Ellen Johnson Sirleaf 65.3 percent of the votes, as compared to Winston Tubman's 28.7 percent. For the second round, as Tubman had boycotted the elections, Johnson Sirleaf won a clear victory of 92.4 percent.[27] Michael often laughed and told me that *he* had won Bomi for Ellen. He said this jokingly, but it was not hard to tell that he saw some truth behind his statement. It is of course impossible to say precisely how much influence Michael and his network of ex-combatants actually had on the Liberian elections, but what is evident, judging from how much the politicians invested in their contacts with him and his former fighters, is that the impact was significant.

Michael has remained important for a large network of ex-combatants, despite the war being over for many years. They come to him for favors and small handouts, but, most important, if they are lucky, they have the possibility of finding employment through him. For the Liberian elite Michael is just as valuable. His network of ex-combatants is large and loyal, and through him politicians and others can access these postwar rebel structures, whether for personal gain, votes, unofficial security providers, or for other social, financial, or political purposes.

Postwar Rebel Networks Used for Their Violent Potential during Elections

During the Sierra Leonean general elections in 2007, Maya Mynster Christensen and Mats Utas followed what turned out to be a remobilization of ex-combatants into "security squads" for the political parties. The exact motives for mobilizing ex-combatants were never officially specified, but the former fighters themselves argued that, alongside a lack of trust in the formal security institutions, political leaders chose to employ them because they were afraid of the consequences of *not* mobilizing them. The politicians feared another uprising and were therefore forced to work with them. Other statements indicated that the task forces, in addition to providing security for the politicians, were also used to intimidate and at times to "create a general state of panic," with opposing political parties' task forces being used against one another. Furthermore, Christensen and Utas's informants also regarded the elections as an opportunity to benefit in ways the end of the war never offered them.

But the most important motivating factor for the ex-combatants was their expectations for the future. Their participation in the security squads, they believed, could bring future benefits such as jobs and education.[28]

Many of these incentives were also relevant for my informants in the 2011 Liberian elections. But during the elections Liberia witnessed far fewer violent encounters than Sierra Leone. I do not speculate on why the outcome of the use of postwar rebel networks was more violent in Sierra Leone here. Yet the issue of time passed since the war might be a factor worth mentioning in brief. As was later to be discovered in the Sierra Leonean 2012 elections, the levels of violence decreased compared to those of 2007 and were a matter of only small-scale and localized incidents, which did not suggest a high level of central planning, as noted by Felix Conteh and David Harris. As the same authors have pointed out, it may be that violence in the Sierra Leonean case was no longer an efficient vote-collecting strategy for the main parties.[29] More important for this study is that the Liberian case questions the assumption that the use of postwar rebel networks is done simply with the motive of mobilizing electoral violence—a conclusion one might otherwise be tempted to draw analyzing the Sierra Leonean case from 2007 in isolation.

In the Liberian case the use of networks of ex-combatants does not seem to have been intended to create an overall state of panic in any sense, even though the politicians surrounded by ex-combatants while campaigning could have had an intimidating effect on the public. For Winston Tubman for example, campaigning in the company of the network of the ex-combatants Alex could secure for him could also have been a way to show force, power, and status, thereby attracting votes. Danny Hoffman found examples of a similar logic during the 2005 Liberian elections, when a businessman from Grand Cape Mount County decided to run for the House of Representatives. The businessman found a former rebel commander an indispensable ally, as he had the capacity to mobilize "supporters" in Monrovia. From his connections higher up in the Liberian hierarchy, the commander, who kept a network of ex-combatants close to him, learned that the businessman needed young men who could rally for him on appointed days, taking to the streets wearing his party colors and face on T-shirts. The businessman needed, as Hoffman argues, a display of force and support. With ex-combatants dancing, shouting, and marching in his name, he manifested power. With his army of "violent labour" he could make it clear for the Liberian people that he had the strength to govern.[30] Tubman's mobilization of the ex-combatants in 2011 could be seen from a similar perspective, as a way to publicly show force and power, partly through displaying the ability to control ex-combatants. But, maybe even more important, in the case of the 2011 elections, given that the networks of ex-combatants and their dependents were still well connected, operational, large, and loyal, having access to them could be an effective way to mobilize votes in exchange for promised benefits. This shows how the violent potential of postwar rebel networks is only one, and not necessarily the most important, aspect of why the political elite finds these actors valuable during political events such as elections even long after the war ended.

At the same time the strategic use of postwar rebel networks by the political elite should not make us overlook the equally strategic use of the political elite by postwar rebel networks. As noted by Liisa Laakso, researching electoral violence in Africa, groups mobilized as potential perpetrators of violence should not be disregarded as a passive reserve manipulated by political leaders. Instead, violent campaigning for the winning party can be a strategy for marginalized groups to gain political power after elections.[31] This argument fits well with the case of the Liberian ex-combatants during the 2011 elections, despite the Liberian postwar rebel networks' not being used for the specific purpose of violent campaigning as such. The fact that the political elite wanted to make use of and manipulate postwar rebel networks for their own benefits does not take away the ex-combatants' own agency and ability to make strategic choices in their support of political candidates. Yet at the same time not all the ex-combatants within the postwar rebel networks had the same freedom of action when it came to taking sides in the political game. An actor like Michael, who ultimately had become a gatekeeper between the two sides, obviously had more room to maneuver than most low-ranking ex-combatants. Still, these postwar rebel networks were far from passive tools in the hands of the political elite in this regard. The elections were an opportunity, albeit a risky one, to take advantage of their wartime pasts as rebel soldiers, both for ex-combatants who had secured more influential positions in postwar Liberia and among the majority who had not.

Postwar Rebel Networks as a Resource for Stability and Livelihood

Lyons, researching political mobilization during postconflict elections in militarized societies, emphasizes selective incentives—such as patronage—as one of the major ways for political parties to mobilize support. Selective incentives may take the form of material benefits, such as salary or employment, or nonmaterial benefits such as prestige or a feeling of efficacy. Individuals might be willing to join a political party, social movement, or insurgency because the selective incentives are available only to those who participate. To maintain the benefits of selective incentives, a difference between the treatment of one's in-groups and out-groups is required. Patronage distributed only to supporters of political parties is an example of this.[32] In the case of the 2011 Liberian elections, it is clear that politicians used this strategy to mobilize support among the ex-combatants and that both the material and nonmaterial benefits of the selective incentives were significant for the mobilized ex-combatants. For my informants the elections were, above all else, an opportunity to find employment. As pointed out by Kathleen Jennings, among others, in Liberia the language and expectations of what the reintegration process was to bring about was clearly incompatible with the implementation and the resources assigned for this task. The reintegration concept in itself is vague and could refer to either a more ambitious or minimalistic reintegration agenda. In the Liberian case this led to heightened expectations, followed by frustration and dissatisfaction among the ex-combatants. Many were unable to find paid employment after completing the disarmament, demobilization, rehabilitation, and reintegration training course and then accused the DDRR process of failing to improve their situations and leaving them with unfulfilled promises. By as early as December 2003, disappointment in the process had led to riots causing the death of nine people and a temporary suspension of the DDRR.[33]

One of the fundamental issues was that the ex-combatants were under the impression that completion of the DDRR would automatically lead to employment. But this was in fact impossible for the weak Liberian state and economy. Ex-combatants, like most Liberians, had to find their own way to rebuild their lives and secure their livelihood. For some of the ex-combatants, who had spent years in the war among their fellow combatants, leaving their closest network, their wartime rebel structures, was not a realistic alternative. Jairo Munive has analyzed the concept of unemployment in Liberia in relation to youth and ex-combatants. With an estimated 85 percent unemployment rate, this is of course an enormous challenge. But, as Munive concludes, since most of the economy is informal in Liberia, the term "unemployed" is of questionable utility. The international community has viewed ex-combatants and young people in general from a bureaucratic perspective, casting those without formal employment as unproductive, making it imperative to transform "unruly" ex-combatants into productive citizens. But in reality, contrary to these representations, young people are actively engaged in economic activities for survival, constituting the backbone of the Liberian postwar economy. As formal employment is not an option for Munive's informants, informality becomes the sole means of survival.[34]

For the Liberian ex-combatants I have followed, before, during, and after the elections, the use of their wartime rebel structures has become a way to access the informal employment market in postwar Liberia. Their particular labor was in high demand during this time. Ex-combatants draw on their skills in security learned during the war, they are potentially violent, and they can be rather influential and efficient in mobilizing support for their candidate, as their networks are often large and loyal to former commanders. For many ex-combatants it thereby becomes strategically important to *preserve* rather than abandon wartime rebel structures to find employment. The 2011 elections undeniably illustrates that the reintegration of the ex-combatants and the dissolution of postwar rebel structures would be counterproductive to the interests of the Liberian political elite, contrary to the message of official policy. In this way a mutual dependence between the ex-combatants and the elite still existed even eight years after the war had been declared over. And during events such as national elections, this mutual dependence becomes even more visible. Nonetheless, the stakes are incredibly high for the ex-combatants when they take sides in political events such as elections. While this can be an opportunity to sometimes gain formal employment, it may also end disastrously, as survival in Liberia in many ways is connected to having the right connections to the political elite.

The disbandment of rebel structures is commonly considered vital because of the general view that ex-combatants in lingering rebel structures constitute an imminent security risk with the potential to drive a postconflict country back into warfare. The perceptions of ex-combatants in general, and of postwar rebel networks specifically, are not only a consequence of violent acts committed by them during the war. In fact, such perceptions are also products of the stereotypical, superficial, and often misleading way the war and its combatants have been described and represented in the media and elsewhere. As Jaremey McMullin points out, ex-combatants are predominantly portrayed as inherently and naturally threatening to postconflict peace, and as such they are monitored and discussed merely on the basis of how their disappointment could lead to renewed warfare. All ex-combatant activity is thereby monitored in terms of the risk it poses to war recurrence.[35]

Following this critical reading of preconceptions against ex-combatants, we cannot assume unconditionally that the use of postwar rebel networks in the 2011 Liberian elections necessarily contributed to a risk of renewed war. Such an assumption would rely on the notion that organized networks of ex-combatants would automatically lead to violence. In fact, the involvement of postwar rebel networks during the election process could possibly have had conflict-*mitigating* effects, as the elections gave many ex-combatants some form of employment opportunity, albeit informally. Furthermore, there were no signs of any remobilization to new rebel factions during the elections. Clearly, as pointed out by Kieran Mitton, success in politically reintegrating ex-combatants should not be judged solely by the absence of renewed violence or the conduct of free and fair elections. The extent to which ex-combatants hold faith in the political system and peace to deliver solutions to problems of social and economic disparity is more relevant.[36] Applying this understanding to the 2011 Liberian elections, we must conclude that the relatively peaceful completion of the elections is not enough to say that a successful demobilization of ex-combatant networks has been brought about, nor that these first postwar elections organized by the Liberians themselves signaled a final break with the county's wartime past. Former fighters were instead politically useful in their capacity as *ex*-combatants, highlighting how war and peace continues to be intimately linked in Liberia. Morten Bøås and Mats Utas come to a similar conclusion. With a point of departure in the historical background of the country's conflict, they conclude that Johnson Sirleaf's electoral victory should be interpreted neither as an indication that the country has entered a new stage of peace and reconciliation, nor as evidence of the strengthening of the country's democratization. Instead, the authors suggest, the electoral results could even be seen as cementing old cleavages leading to the civil war in the first place.[37] The "winner-takes-all" effects of the Liberian 2011 elections for my ex-combatant informants support this analysis.

Conclusion

The Liberian 2011 elections never brought the envisioned final break with past wars. The lingering presence of postwar rebel networks and their continued usefulness to the political elite are clear indicators of this continuity. Rebel networks can remain relevant long after war has come to an end, despite years of demobilization and reintegration efforts. In times of elections they can become important pawns in the political game. The elections proved to be an opportunity for Liberian ex-combatants that led to postelection advantages, though only on the winning side. In this sense a genuine democracy was far from strengthened.

Yet these continuities with Liberia's wartime past in itself might not be the real problem at hand, which leads us to a second overarching conclusion of this chapter: that the presence and use of postwar rebel networks in times of elections may not necessarily, or automatically, result in violence. The past wars are part of Liberia's social and political reality, and the country must continue to deal with, and sometimes incorporate, both actors and structures responsible for past atrocities, as they do not simply vanish at the end of war. From the perspective of ex-combatants themselves, their mobilization for the 2011 elections was primarily part of an entrepreneurial strategy to secure employment rather than a desire to take part in potential electoral violence or renewed warfare. The Liberian case shows that the involvement of organized ex-combatants in political events such as elections, or for other tasks and contexts, is not a straight pathway to violence, as is often assumed. This is a central finding, as the general perception of postwar rebel networks is that their mere continued existence may automatically lead to renewed violence—either in connection to important political events such as elections or, in the worst case, a return to war. This chapter has shown that the use of postwar rebel network can have positive outcomes for the ex-combatants themselves but also for postwar stability, as these actors are given opportunities otherwise closed to them.

We might therefore be forced to view postwar rebel networks in a rather different light than traditionally has been the case. Their continued presence, in times of postwar elections and postwar societies in general, is a far more complex issue than often assumed. During elections and in postwar contexts in general, postwar rebel networks can be used for violence or merely as intimidation by their violent potential. Nevertheless, they may also be used for entirely nonviolent purposes. The spectrum of postwar activities these networks can engage in is broad and needs to be analyzed from such a perspective to be fully understood. If we assume that all actors with a history of active engagement in war, including postwar rebel networks, are predetermined to resort to violent methods, we fail to appreciate how such constellations could be used in positive ways. We also fail to understand the circumstances that may lead to these networks being used for violent ends, as we should not forget that they are accustomed to and capable of violence and warfare. Used in the wrong way by the political elite or other financially powerful and influential actors, they are potentially dangerous to future stability and peace in Liberia. There is no doubt that the Liberian political elite was playing a dangerous game with their strategic use of postwar rebel structures during the 2011 elections. And as can be seen from the experiences of ex-combatants on the losing side of the elections, so too were they.

CHAPTER 5

Once a Rebel, Always a Rebel?

EX-COMBATANTS AND POSTWAR IDENTITIES

In this book we have followed former rebels who have survived peace by clinging to their ex-combatant identity, wartime links, and postwar rebel networks. Through their identity, links, and networks, they have been able to secure their livelihood, temporary jobs, and some form of a social safety net. But these former rebels have also been identified as people to fear, as a menace to society or as violent labor. They have often been associated with crime and insecurity and, in reports and research, have more often than not been perceived as the real threats to lasting peace. There are, in other words, normative perceptions of who the ex-combatants are and what ought to be expected of them. This chapter explores what it means in practice to be an ex-combatant in contemporary Liberia, given such perceptions. More precisely, I consider the consequences of being identified, and of identifying oneself, with a category still so emotionally charged as the ex-combatant one and of living with this identity today, years after peace has been declared.

When it comes to the meaning of such an identity, it is herein assumed that any individual possesses several different identities or social roles. These identities or roles can be used by the individuals themselves or by others to express their belonging to or dissociation from a certain group or social category. According to this conceptualization of identity, being an ex-combatant can be *one* of an individual's many identities. It can be a more or less important part of that person's self-image and a more or less vital aspect of how others view that person. When I discuss an ex-combatant identity, it is something more than a group's shared past as actual combatants. I take as a point of departure that these individuals themselves, as well as others, ascribe certain *characteristics* to this group, characteristics that in theory can be both positive and negative in nature. In other words, what it means to be an ex-combatant and to live with this identity depends to a great extent not only on the past experiences shared by this group of having been combatants but also, and maybe more important, on people's notions and understandings of characteristics *believed* to be shared by this group.

Research within the disarmament, demobilization, and reintegration literature, from academic articles to more policy-oriented reports, tell us that after wars are over ex-combatants are vulnerable and often stigmatized and that they tend to be feared and hated but also that they are among the few in war-affected countries who actually get assistance and support following conflict. This, however, can lead in turn to jealousy and feelings of injustice among civilians, causing ex-combatants to be even more disliked.[1] Findings have shown that some do best by hiding their ex-combatant status to better blend in with civil society. But for others, having access to postwar rebel networks can be the key to getting by in their everyday struggle to make a living in a context where there are few other opportunities.

I do not attempt to analyze the situation for all of those many Liberians who could be identified as an ex-combatant in a general manner. In this book we have followed individuals within this group who, for different reasons, have kept their links to wartime structures, individuals who have chosen not to hide their ex-combatant status, their militarized backgrounds, and their skills within security provision. Instead, they have chosen to make use of these experiences in a variety of ways. I explore what the identity as an ex-combatant means for these individuals specifically. To what extent does their combatant past shape their lives today? What do they themselves associate with the notion of being an ex-combatant? And how does the way that others—such as fellow community members and other Liberians, the elite, international communities, and media—view and perceive them affect their lives and who they are today? What doors and opportunities can such an identity close or open?

The transition from war to peace has not been an easy journey for many ex-combatants. As Abby Hardgrove has found, many Liberian ex-combatants lost their sense of direction at the end of the war. The transition out of armed groups caused confusion, as such processes lacked the clarity and purpose that transition *into* armed groups had. The combatants had quickly learned what their role was, what was expected, and to whom they must answer going into war. But as they came out of armed groups, they experienced much the opposite. Hardgrove found that among the ex-combatants there was almost a sense of being dumped out of armed groups and into an ambiguous postwar social terrain.[2] The question of how to relate to one's ex-combatant identity in such a transition further adds to the complexity of coming out of war and armed groups. And there are neither easy answers to such questions nor one common trajectory that these ex-combatants are bound to take. Yet to come closer to an understanding of the postwar reality that this specific group of ex-combatants are faced with, and ultimately how they themselves impact society at large, we once again follow former combatants for whom postwar rebel networks in different ways have been central to their postwar struggles. This chapter provides some insights into three ex-combatants' postwar lives in particular: Abraham, Malcolm, and Jacob. These ex-combatant narratives hopefully add a deeper understanding of the postwar reality ex-combatants may face. Malcolm and Jacob have a background as commanders, while Abraham does not. Although this is not a main focus for this chapter, it may provide valuable insights on whether a background as a commander brings specific postwar advantages or whether such a background only makes the ex-combatant identity a heavier burden to carry.

Furthermore, in this chapter we follow these ex-combatants under rather different circumstances than in the previous chapters. Here I seek answers to what it means to be an ex-combatant and part of a postwar rebel network when there are no wars to be fought and no important political events to be mobilized for, when community members cannot pay them to work as vigilantes, or when there are no big security assignments to be carried out for elite actors. Does the identity as an ex-combatant then partly fade? Or does this identity for some reason become even more relevant under such circumstances? Do these situations shatter, or even strengthen, postwar rebel networks? And if they do continue to exist, can such networks simply be dormant, or do they remain active but in new ways or shapes? These are complex issues, and peacetime offers for these ex-combatants of course vary depending on a series of different factors, making it difficult to seek general answers. But by focusing on a few individuals, with the experience of facing peace as ex-combatants and as part of postwar rebel networks, we can come closer to an understanding of what former rebels are and do several years after the end of war and thereby what relevance such networks have in contemporary Liberia, both for individuals and the society at large.

The former rebel soldiers I have followed in this book have one important thing in common: all of them are men. This is an important factor that needs to be taken into serious consideration when analyzing postwar Liberia for the simple reason that many of the rebel soldiers fighting in the wars were women. Yet within the postwar rebel networks I have followed during the years, women have remained largely absent or invisible. We therefore simply need to ask ourselves, where are the women? In this chapter I explore the possibility that the postwar identity as an ex-combatant might be more problematic for a former female rebel soldier than for a male one and that women for this reason have chosen to stay away from postwar rebel networks to a larger extent than their fellow male combatants. In other words, I consider that women in general, contrary to many men with a combatant background, have more to lose than to gain by being identified as an ex-combatant or to actively use this identity, or networks attached to it, themselves. In line with such reasoning, I therefore also seek answers as to why militarized masculinities in this case appear to be less problematic than the equivalent femininities.

Images of War and Rebels

There is a true danger to the acceptance of stereotypes. As Nigerian writer Chimamanda Ngozi Adichie so elegantly puts it, "The single story creates stereotypes, and the problem with stereotypes is not that they are untrue, but that they are incomplete. They make one story become the only story."[3] Yet the tendency to view rebel soldiers, especially those in African wars, in rather one-dimensional ways is unmissable. Following the end of the first Liberian war in 1996, Philippa Atkinson sets out to analyze what she claims to be false images of chaos and pathos that had been projected by media coverage of war in West Africa. What she finds in the Western media, the few times the Liberian conflict was mentioned, is how Liberia, alongside Rwanda and Somalia, was used as an example of the nightmare scenario the West both fears and expects much of Africa to descend to. The focus within articles and reports on the crisis itself emphasized the anarchy and brutality of the war and the atrocities perpetrated against civilians and foreign nationals, often by child soldiers. The reports were often accompanied by photographs of rebels dressed up in unusual battle gear or of skulls and bones decorating rebel camps. Atkinson sees a will in the media coverage to depict a "weird" war, fought with unique ferocity, by mad princes, warlords, and manipulated and drug-crazed children.[4] In Atkinson's examination of the media reports, she finds a significant focus on the atrocities committed, yet a poor analysis of which side was responsible and to what end. There were almost no discussions of the different tactics by the various actors and rebel groups or of the violence perpetrated and the economic realities of the war economy.

As Atkinson notes, the portrayal of the Liberian war as brutal and chaotic fits in well with the more general picture of Africa as depicted by the media. There is a tendency in media reporting to create an image of anarchy when Africa and African conflicts are being discussed—a tendency with potentially serious consequences. This image, without much real analysis, is conveyed to members of the international community, which in turn influences that community's political action. As Atkinson points out, this influence and importance that the media have in informing experts and decision makers in the international community cannot be underestimated. As she so rightly emphasizes, those who make funding, business, diplomatic, and military decisions cannot avoid being influenced by what have become stereotypical views of African countries at war. There is, therefore, a real danger in the insinuations of such descriptions—that crises in Africa are beyond the experience and understanding of the modern Western world.[5]

Liberian combatants have been objects of the same stereotypical portrayals through which the Liberian war has been understood (or not understood). It is probably not controversial to assume that when people in Western societies think of Liberian rebel soldiers—or more likely African rebels in general, as Liberian rebels presumably would be too specific—they tend to have a picture that corresponds to that of the stereotypical view of African wars, in short, that these individuals as well are beyond understanding. As further discussed by Stephen Ellis, when the world's press became aware of the crisis in Liberia in the mid-1990s, it was through the coverage of an international journalist who traveled with the advancing rebel forces associated mainly with rebel leader Prince Johnson and his Independent Patriotic National Front of Liberia. The focus of this reporting was the bizarre nature of the rebels and their accoutrements: wigs worn by male fighters along with grotesque decorations such as human bones. The journalists were fascinated by what they understood as an incomprehensible slaughter carried out by rebels looking like freaks in a primeval savagery. They wanted to describe the "real nature" of Africa, Ellis explains, that had so often been romanticized. Instead, they offered a picture of Liberia as the scene of the wackiest and most ruthless of uncivil wars, where rebels were high on drugs, fighting naked, in Halloween masks, or in bizarre makeup, believing that African magic could save them from bullets.[6] The journalists did this without seeking explanations for why this might be or wanting to find the reasons behind the rebel soldiers' behavior or even causes of war. Instead, what was seen was mere sensational journalism.

Along the same lines as Atkinson's argument, Ellis underlines that even though such descriptions can be dismissed easily after a more thorough look at the situation, one should not underestimate what implications and influence this type of journalism can have. This is the case no matter how superficial the coverage might be, as not only the world's reading or viewing public might be affected, but policy makers and politicians risk taking action in reaction to information provided through such sensational journalism.[7] The 1994 analysis of the wars in West Africa from U.S. journalist Robert Kaplan strongly contributed to the public notion, which also impacted policy makers, of West African rebels and young men in the region in general as mere violent, lost, and criminal gangs without a political agenda. But the critique against Kaplan's simplistic and stereotypical way of viewing wars and war-affected inhabitants in Africa has been substantial. An important response came from Paul Richards against this so-called New Barbarism thesis, in his analysis with a main focus on the Sierra Leonean war. As Richards argues, whereas it cannot be denied that the war in Sierra Leone is one of terror, involving horrific brutality against civilians, this fact still cannot in any way be taken as a proof of a reversion to some kind of essential African savagery as suggested by Kaplan. The whole point of terror, as Richards underlines, is to unsettle its victims. Accounts of terrorized victims of violence do not constitute evidence of the irrationality of violence. Instead, this shows the opposite: that the tactics have been carefully calculated. Richards strongly criticizes the idea that violence was perpetrated by criminal gangs without a political agenda. In fact, he argues, the war had a clear political context, with belligerents who had perfectly rational political aims, however difficult it may be to justify violence perpetrated to pursue these aims. As in any other war, opportunist individuals and groups commit atrocities and looting, yet these opportunistic acts are insufficient in explaining the conflict, which instead dragged on because of social and political factors. Richards concludes that there is no inherent trend toward anarchy in today's West Africa.[8] Although much research following Richards' early response to theories such as Kaplan's has been devoted to the many and often complex reasons for becoming a rebel and taking part in the wars in West Africa, and many nuanced analyses have been carried out to reach a better understanding of the brutal violence committed during these wars, the notion of the Liberian rebel (or African rebel in general) as a mere greed-driven, barbaric young man will not easily vanish from people's minds.[9]

The Problematic Ex-combatant Identity

The image of a rebel, and consequently that of an ex-combatant, is not only a consequence of the often very violent acts committed by combatants during the war but maybe even more a product of the stereotypical, superficial, and often misleading way the war and its combatants have been described and represented in the media and elsewhere. Ex-combatants in Liberia all know this. Being violent and unpredictable is often associated with an ex-combatant identity, and ex-combatants who cannot, or have chosen not to, hide their past or in different ways take part in postwar rebel networks must always relate and adapt to such stereotypes. These perceptions are held by actors ranging from researchers and policy makers to NGOs, international community representatives and other actors taking part in planning and conducting programs aiming at reintegrating ex-combatants or writing reports, analyses, and risk assessments of this group's violent potential and likelihood of being used in renewed warfare. Jaremey McMullin has pointed out in his assessment of the discourse and practice of disarmament, demobilization, and reintegration in Liberia that a threat narrative, which portrays ex-combatants as inherently and naturally threatening to postconflict peace, dominates the debate on ex-combatants. Ex-combatants tend to be monitored and discussed in terms of how their disappointment could lead to renewed warfare, independent of other variables that could lead to war and independent of how this dissatisfaction of the ex-combatants might be linked to these other variables. This produces a threat narrative in which the rationale for reintegration is not integration or reconciliation of postwar communities but rather the management and mitigation of ex-combatant threats. All ex-combatant activity is thereby monitored in terms of the risk it poses to war recurrence. As McMullin argues, the view of ex-combatants as such threats are anchored in the assumptions that ex-combatants are antisocial, irrational, barbarically violent, apolitical, greedy, and nihilistic and lack education, ideology, and political beliefs. After the end of war, ex-combatants are said to gravitate naturally toward criminal lives.[10]

The views held by fellow Liberian citizens also matter and impact the reality ex-combatants face. An example from neighboring Sierra Leone, drawn by Catherine Bolten, illustrates this often tense and complex relationship between ex-combatants and communities at large. Bolten, conducting fieldwork in Makeni, notes that receiving communities found a way of accepting ex-combatants living among them, while at the same time refusing to incorporate them into the social order. NGO sensitization training, aiming at getting civilians to accept ex-combatants as "normal" men, was rendered a success since civilians and ex-combatants could live side by side without ex-combatants being harassed because of their background. Yet, as Bolten finds, a quiet marginalization of ex-combatants still existed. Ex-combatants were tolerated, but not seen as "just ordinary men." By refusing the ex-combatants this status, community members were protecting themselves and the youth of the society against the threat to social order that ex-combatants were seen to constitute. The ex-combatants were, according to Bolten's findings, seen as the vanguard of youth who disdain manual labor and elder control. And by quietly marginalizing the ex-combatants both socially and economically, the community had found a strategy of not accepting the same behavior among its civilian youth and thus protecting themselves against the threat to their social world that the ex-combatants were understood as posing.[11] In this way people's views and opinions of former combatants, even when they are only expressed quietly, away from large-scale public confrontation, shape the public notion of an ex-combatant identity, which is often intimately associated with negative characteristics.

Yet, although the ex-combatant identity is indeed problematic, or even dangerous, to hold on to, many ex-combatants still choose to do so. Godfrey Maringira found that ex-combatants in postapartheid South Africa have kept a "militarised mind," both at individual and collective levels, despite the transition to democracy in 1994. The danger in this lies in the ex-combatant's perception of the gun as an alternative avenue for making a living in a highly unequal and violent society and as a way to redress the inequalities that have remained in many townships. But ex-combatants also see the gun as a way to meet their families' and communities' expectations of them as providers and defenders. These ex-combatants cling to their military skills and ability to perform violence, which they view as a means to maintain social status, make a living, and protect their families and communities, who often expect them to use violence and military skills, in response to their perceived marginalization by the state. At the same time the ex-combatants also use the social networks emerging from their military identities to mobilize around community issues. For example, ex-combatants used their military skills to recruit youth involved in crime into development projects. Accordingly, identities forged during resistance and combat were reproduced in postconflict society at times because the ex-combatants viewed their military identities as the only way to establish themselves or gain recognition as "defenders" of the community or just as respectable community members. As Maringira argues, military identities are often viewed as sources of future violence, but they are also sources of recognition and status. To view such identities as purely violent, he claims, hides the fact that these identities are also productive in the community. How are we to expect ex-combatants to leave behind their military identity as they continue to be marginalized by the state and remain in violent neighborhoods and when their military identities also can allow the ex-combatants certain privileges in their communities? Military identity provides a social framework in which the social network remains intact. In this way ex-combatants can mobilize one another to collectively meet the challenges they face as a group.[12] Accordingly, although the ex-combatant identity can be highly problematic, especially in the light of the negative perceptions attached to it, there can be good reasons for the ex-combatants' wanting to preserve it. As in the Liberian examples in this book, the ex-combatant identity can also be a valuable tool in a postconflict society.

Turning the Ex-combatant Stigma into a Positive Brand

Having a past as a rebel and a reputation of being capable of committing violence is something that can be turned into an advantage. The ex-combatant identity, even though to a limited extent and only in specific contexts, has been turned into, if not a positive label, then at least a profitable one. For those who are part of a postwar rebel network, such a reputation can be the very factor that secures employment. Ex-combatants in such networks can use this part of the perceived characteristic of the ex-combatant identity in an advantageous way. It is, then, possible to turn a social stigma into a positive brand. Jesper Bjarnesen has done fieldwork on "Diaspo youth"—children of parents from Burkina Faso, who grew up in Côte d'Ivoire but who were forced to flee to their parents' country of origin during the civil war. He shows how this group, which faced social stigmatization as newcomers in Burkina Faso, partly because of their perceived association with the civil war, were able to turn this identity into a positive social marker. "Diaspo" as these newcomers were called, was indeed a label initially ascribed to them by others as a negative stereotype but one that these young men and women now embrace as a positive label. Through what Bjarnesen refers to as a "process of social branding" the Diaspo youth have been able to exploit their Ivorian upbringing to distinguish themselves from the competition. Many have succeeded in creating livelihood opportunities as traders, performers, radio hosts, and other publicly profiled professions. And they have in fact been more successful than local youths. By not hiding their past or trying to blend in, the Diaspo youth embraced their Ivorian backgrounds by publicly displaying what is believed to be a specific Ivorian way of talking, dressing, and even acting in public spaces. This performance provoked resentment in urban Burkina Faso but also inspired admiration. And, more important, in an environment of scarce employment opportunities, the Diaspo identity has also opened doors.[13]

Former fighters of Liberia who have been objects of social stigmatization because of the negative perceptions of the ex-combatant identity have also been successful in turning their stigma into something positive, at least when it comes to finding employment. Networks of ex-combatants are, despite the many negative assumptions, also believed to be hardworking, well organized, and disciplined. Considering how hard it is for any Liberian to find employment and secure livelihood, the ex-combatants have had considerable advantages when it comes to paid employment within the security arena—an arena we also need to remember is intimately connected to the real center of power in Liberia. Here the ex-combatants are sometimes considered to be the most reliable when it comes to getting the job done. The ex-combatant identity in this specific context has thereby been turned into a positive label in the sense that this group is considered to have acquired the qualities, experiences, and networks but also the mind-set for certain types of assignments. The negative perceptions of former rebels still have significant consequences for how they lead their lives in postwar Liberia. What it means to live with an ex-combatant identity in contemporary Liberia has of course as many answers as there are former rebels in the country. Yet all those who have chosen or have been forced to reveal their rebel past are bound to face the, often very negative, perceptions of what it means to be an ex-combatant. In the subsequent sections we follow a few individuals for whom the ex-combatant identity, for better and worse, shapes their everyday life.

Ex-combatant Identity from a Gendered Perspective

It is difficult to know exactly how many they were, and numbers differ. But we do know that women constituted a significant part of combatants in the Liberian civil wars.[14] According to some estimates, young female fighters composed about 30 to 40 percent of all the fighting forces in the country.[15] Yet within the postwar rebel networks—the vigilante and informal security groups I have followed over the years—women have been largely absent. Given the high number of women active as combatants during the war, this is remarkable. The question is thus: Why do the numbers of women in postwar rebel networks not at all correspond to the numbers of female fighters in the Liberian wars?

It is unquestionably so that the ex-combatant identity has functioned through postwar rebel networks as a way, and for many the only way, to secure jobs in postwar Liberia, if only temporarily. Yet being identifiable as an ex-combatant can be a very difficult experience, as opinions about morals and presumed violent nature are not something easily escapable. But ex-combatants active in postwar rebel networks live with this predicament. They live with the negative aspects of not hiding their ex-combatant identity because they appear to value the benefits of their postwar rebel network higher. So why are most of them men? Could it be so that women are simply not let in? Are women not seen fit to work alongside men on the informal security assignments, which postwar rebel networks are often recruited for? Given the fact that women took part in active combat in such high numbers during the wars, this does not seem likely. I would suggest that the ex-combatant identity in itself, because of gender perceptions, could be a heavier burden for women than for men, causing female ex-combatants to downplay their wartime past by not attaching themselves to postwar rebel networks, despite the benefits these connections might have.

To understand what an ex-combatant identity would imply for women in postwar Liberia and why such an identity could have different consequences for women than for men, an important starting point is to understand how female combatants are perceived *during* war and, in this specific context, conflict. This is not, however, a straightforward task. Although the attention to women and girls who actively participate in armed conflicts in Africa has increased significantly in recent decades, women, despite extensive research and documentation, are largely absent from mainstream studies and in most policy programming. Female fighters, if mentioned at all, are often seen as an anomaly, as it is often implied that women and girls instead are predominately "victims," while male fighters are uniformly described as "combatants" or, alternatively, "perpetrators."[16] Women's multifaceted and complex roles in fighting forces, especially those of combatants, rarely receive the attention they ought to, considering how common this phenomenon is. Why, then, are women's active roles, especially as fighters, often ignored? Part of the explanation can be found in prevalent gender stereotypes and notions of what women and men are, and ought to be, and do, in wars. Generalized images of masculinity and femininity, portraying men as aggressive and women as peaceful, and men as active and women as passive, are often associated with war. This polarization is, however, far from unproblematic. Not only is the image of the aggressive male a stereotype, but, more important, the notion of conflict and aggression as something inherently male is an effective way to conceal how women are affected by, and actively participate in, violent conflicts and wars as combatants.[17]

In the same way as gender stereotypes in mainstream thinking of war effectively conceal women's multifaceted roles in violent conflict, and especially those of frontline fighters, the same stereotypes of women as merely passive and peaceful could cause the women who actually are recognized as combatants and rebel soldiers to be regarded as completely deviant. When peace arrives, female ex-combatants are often looked on with suspicion and fear for having been perpetrators of violence but also for having violated established gender roles.[18] Accordingly, women violate taboos to a much higher degree than male combatants ever could, just by being combatants. As pointed out by Susan McKay and Dyan Mazurana, analyzing the situation for girl ex-combatants in northern Uganda, Mozambique, and Sierra Leone, having been a girl in a fighting force was found to be an acute source of shame. The feeling of shame is a complex and powerful phenomenon, poorly understood and acknowledged at the cultural level, and its gendered dimensions are often even less recognized.[19] In short, having been a combatant can be a source of shame for both men and women. Yet, because of gender norms, this shame is bound to affect men and women differently, and female ex-combatants are at risk of being stigmatized to an even higher degree than male ex-combatants.

All societies have different gender norms, and female former rebels are faced with different challenges and realities when it comes to issues of postwar shame and stigmatization, depending on the specific local context. When it comes to Liberia, a lot more has been written from the perspectives of male ex-combatants than on the situation of female combatants during and after war; therefore we cannot easily draw conclusions as to why so few women can be found in postwar rebel networks in Liberia. There are some important policy reports with specific focus on women and girls within fighting forces, but many often emphasize those who did not participate directly in actual combat during the war. There is also important research concentrated on female combatants' experiences with the Liberian DDRR process and its shortcomings when it came to gender mainstreaming and gender sensitivity in particular.[20]

In-depth research on female combatants also relevant for an understanding of female fighters in Liberia can be found in the case of neighboring Sierra Leone. And even though generalizations often are problematic, the situation for these women and girls can give us important clues to understanding the lives and experiences of Liberian female fighters, as the wars in the countries were so closely connected. Chris Coulter's research from 2006 and 2009 on what happened to rebel women during and after war in Sierra Leone provides comprehensive analyses on female combatants. Sierra Leonean women themselves articulate their experiences of war, specifically in relation to how they were seen after the war by their families and communities and the international community. Coulter found that female rebels in Sierra Leone were often regarded by the civilian population as monsters, barbarians, and more cold-blooded than male rebels. She relates such interpretations of women engaged in active combat to the notion of militarized masculinity and the stereotype of a male soldier, arguing that it was costly for Sierra Leonean women who deviated from acceptable feminine behavior and who opposed female stereotypes in times of war and conflict.[21]

My own research, although conducted on a smaller scale, among young female ex-combatants in Sierra Leone two years after peace officially was declared, supports this picture. The young women I met felt deeply stigmatized because of their past as violent rebel soldiers in a way their male comrades never experienced. For them to be viewed as ex-combatants was extremely shameful, and many did what they could to hide their past.[22] When it came to the official postconflict reconstruction initiatives in Sierra Leone, women and girls were often excluded from DDR programs because they, incorrectly, were not seen as "real" soldiers. Megan Mackenzie similarly found fear of stigmatization to be one of the reasons female ex-combatants themselves decided not to participate in the official reintegration process. Their association with programs for former rebels would imply being continually identified with the conflict. This was not an option for many women, who feared for their safety if they were seen publicly as ex-combatants.[23] Female fighters were also found to hide away from the DDRR process in the Liberian case, partly because they feared social exclusion if they revealed their ex-combatant status.[24] As seen from the experiences of my informants, living publicly with one's ex-combatant identity, like individuals within postwar rebel networks do, does not come without its problems. There are numerous disadvantages to being identified as an ex-combatant in postwar Liberia. The men within the postwar rebel networks I have followed have chosen this path despite its difficulties. For female ex-combatants it is likely that the same decision, to cling onto the ex-combatant identity, would have been a too high a price to pay.

In the remainder of this chapter I discuss how the ex-combatant identities of informants handled the expectations and prejudice held toward them by the surrounding community.

A Violent Ex-combatant in West Point or a Hardworking Liberian Citizen?

I struggled to keep up with Alex that day. He was walking briskly, and Will and I had to hurry along the narrow alleyways between the small zinc houses and sheds not to lose sight of him. We had to squeeze ourselves between women cooking for their families and children playing in the small open spaces and chasing one another between the houses. I apologized for being in the way and for walking where women were preparing food, having their meals, or taking a rest. Most people just gave me friendly smiles back and continued with their business. A few looked a bit surprised to see a stranger there, but most did not bother at all. I tried to focus on where Alex was going so he wouldn't have to wait for us on every corner, but I had not seen Will in a long time, and we got caught up in our conversation, so Alex patiently had to wait. Alex turned left and right along narrow paths between the cramped houses. I turned to Will and joked about whether Alex actually knew where he was going. Will laughed and admitted that he had no idea where we were either. But Alex knew his way around here. He used to live here for some years just after the war. For me West Point was still a maze. I had been in this community only a few times since I first started to visit Monrovia a few years earlier. Situated on a peninsula jutting out into the Atlantic Ocean, this township of the Liberian capital is not a place one often just passes by without any particular errand. But, as I was doing research on postwar rebel networks, it was in fact a bit strange that my research had not brought me to this township more often in the past, judging from its reputation as being inhabited by a large number of ex-combatants. But my informants had been residing elsewhere.

Alex and Will, two young men who used to spend their nights as vigilantes when I first got to know them a few years back, had introduced me to a friend of theirs who lived in West Point. I still could not find the way to Abraham's house on my own, so I was happy to have Alex and Will keeping me company. Will and I talked about West Point's unenviable reputation. The rumors of this notorious neighborhood would not pass anyone by unnoticed. West Point is desperately poor with few employment opportunities. It is heavily overcrowded, and the water and sanitation situation is catastrophic. People face tremendous challenges in this township. Still, there is something about how West Point and its inhabitants are being portrayed that I found very disturbing. Online articles and reportage on West Point describe the township as a society completely lost to anarchy, crime, and violence, with inhabitants portrayed mainly as drug-abusing ex-combatants making their money from drugs, prostitution, and armed robbery.

A few years ago a Swedish newspaper decided to portray Liberia and West Point in the same kind of manner. In an article describing Liberia as "hell on earth," "where murder, rape drugs and AIDS are everyone's everyday life," the newspaper drew attention, and posted a link, to what the filmmakers themselves called a "documentary." But *The VICE Guide to Liberia* was far from nuanced documentation of Liberia and West Point. Instead of trying to understand postwar Liberia and the situation of ex-combatants and others living in West Point and other impoverished areas, the TV team ran around Liberia in search of sensational news on "cannibal warlords," teenage prostitutes, and drug-abusing children. The film was appalling. My colleagues, Mats Utas and Ilmari Käihkö, and I decided to write a response. In the article we argue that the media generally present Africa and African conflict-related issues in an extremely stereotypical way. We suggest that the so-called documentary is a "worst case" example of this.[25] The film team runs from one scene to another, acting like their very lives are in danger. What they actually are fleeing from is less clear. Provoking, rather than interviewing, prostitutes and drug-affected residents, they seem to have no understanding of the chaos they themselves are creating with their cameras, intrusive ways, and lack of respect as they hunt for sensational stories in West Point late at night. Without knowledge of cultural codes or context, the reporters nervously laugh in front of the camera, proud to have dared to do reportage like this. Their combination of fear and excitement is evident. They had found what they wanted to portray, a neighborhood in total anarchy, chaos without any logic.

Even though he is used to it, Abraham always gets a bit annoyed when the negative image of West Point is brought up. He finds it unfair. Yes, West Point is poor, and crime is a problem, but we're not all bad people here, he often argues. Abraham is an ex-combatant.[26] And he is a resident of West Point. From time to time he makes a bit of extra money working as an informal security provider. His latest assignment was for the Congress of Democratic Change party, as he was mobilized during the elections, like so many other ex-combatants. Alex had been the one employing him. And, just like Alex, he had worked for Tubman during his campaigning for the previous elections already in 2005. But Abraham is also a father of six. He is married and makes his living from petty trading. That day Abraham, Alex, Will, and I spent the morning outside Abraham's little zinc house. The house next door was so close to Abraham's that I could touch it if I just leaned forward and reached out my arm. Some of the children passing by laughed a little when they saw me. One little boy got so frightened when he looked at me that he cried in panic and refused to walk by. I do not look Liberian, and it scared him. But other than that, my visit did not cause too much attention. Abraham's wife and daughters were preparing food nearby, and his younger children were playing and running errands for their mother. Sometimes they came closer to listen in on our discussions, but they quickly got bored and ran off to play again. I could not help but think of the images of the *VICE Guide to Liberia* documentary. Everyday life is so far removed from the violent chaos the filmmakers wanted to portray.

We talked about security, about crime and violence and the perception of West Point. Abraham is not particularly afraid in his neighborhood. He has lived there for a long time, and he knows his neighbors. But he is careful. He lives in a house with no windows. Will laughed at that: he could not believe why anyone would want to live in a house like that! But Abraham was persistent. With no windows there can be no unexpected visits in the night. And theft at night is still an issue. But break-ins and theft are obviously not phenomena isolated to West Point. Crime happens everywhere, Abraham often points out. In fact, my informants somewhat ironically argue that parts of West Point are safer than many other areas of Monrovia, not despite its poverty but because of it. "You know, the criminals, they live here, so of course they don't want to commit the crimes in their own community: that would cause them too many problems!" Abraham and Alex argue. And it somehow makes sense. Here housing is affordable, even for those who have the least, making it likely that people engaged in theft because of the lack of other economic opportunities would live here. And why risk being caught in one's own community?

Perceptions of Crime, Security, and "Anarchic" Neighborhoods

Nevertheless, crime is a problem in West Point, and theft seems to be what people are most worried about. Yet there is, if not an acceptance, then at least an understanding of those who engage in theft that I find interesting. People in West Point often saw theft as something young men and women were driven to from a lack of legal ways to make a living. Some of my informants even talked about theft as a form of business. The inhabitants did what they could to protect themselves against theft, but most Liberians I knew had been affected, at least on a small scale. Money being stolen from someone's bag during an unobservant moment or a mobile phone being snatched from someone's pocket was not unusual. But in West Point, as in many other parts of Monrovia, what was stolen could most often be bought back, and that was what the business side of theft was all about. People in the area knew where to turn if they found that some of their belongings had been stolen. Those engaged in this type of criminal activity often worked in networks, linked to an area leader. So when things were stolen, people turned to the leader, who often had received the item shortly after it had been taken. It was not unlikely that the person who had been affected could then buy the item back for a small amount of money. A young woman I knew told me about her grandfather, who had the misfortune of having one hundred U.S. dollars (a large amount of money for a poor Liberian) stolen from his pocket. Luckily enough, he later the same day successfully negotiated to buy back the same money for five U.S. dollars from the gang leader to whom the money had been brought. More often these negotiations took place over stolen mobile phones or other material items. But as seen from this example, even stolen money could return to the owner for a reasonable sum following this system. People were obviously enraged when they realized they had been stolen from, and no one liked to have to negotiate and buy their own belongings back. Yet even those affected appeared to have an understanding of theft as unavoidable in the absence of employment opportunities. In this respect West Point was far from a community lost to anarchy, as it is so often portrayed. Although this did not always apply, even theft could be seen to follow codes of morality, a system of social order, and a logic people could understand.

Sasha Newell finds a similar logic, or what he calls a "moral economy of theft," in a poor neighborhood in Abidjan, Côte d'Ivoire. Newell shows that theft was ruled by relationships of exchange and obligation and that social relationships were prioritized over financial gain. The Treichville community, where Newell conducted his research on lower-class urban youth—their sources of income, social formations, relationship to the state and other authorities, and so on—was structured around a moral economy of theft. The social interpretations of a crime are forms of exchange, which define social relations. Within this antisocial activity of expropriation lies a moral system built on social networks on which the thief depends for survival. Theft in this community, and probably elsewhere, is thereby part of the social organization itself.[27]

The Treichville community largely depends economically on criminal activity. A criminal network holds the center of the local economy and supplies the principal commodities of informal exchange through theft. The activities of this network complement a second group, the larger majority of people who in varying degrees are involved with the informal economy through illicit dealings, called *bizness*, by Ivoirians. *Bizness* can encompass activities such as selling stolen goods as intermediaries for the criminal network or relatively harmless activities like selling minutes on a mobile phone under a false account. But regardless of what kind of *bizness* activity people are involved in, they depend ultimately on the criminal network for the supply of stolen goods as well as protection from the police and from other thieves. Yet the same people involved in these criminal activities angrily defend themselves against theft. Thieves caught in the act of stealing can be killed by violent mobs. Herein lies a paradox, Newell notes, that within a society where the majority of the population is involved, at least indirectly, in criminal activities, residents maintain a system of justice regulating this very behavior, and crime is still considered as something bad. It is therefore more useful to look at crimes as particular events, each of which people interpret according to the social relationships involved.[28]

The collective interpretation of a crime, Newell finds, is dependent on the relationship of the criminal and the victim, but more importantly on the social networks to which both parties belong. Morality is relative to social belonging, which implies that thieves are not treated equally, as not all thieves are equally estranged. Newell found that the majority of thefts seemed to take place within the community itself. People could resort to theft from their closest friends. Yet this was often done with relative impunity, since it would be a graver act of betrayal to endanger the life of one's friend by denouncing the person as a thief than the actual theft itself.[29]

There are many similarities between the community described by Newell and that of West Point, as illustrated by my informants in many stories on crime and of those regarded as criminals—and ex-combatants are often assumed to belong to this category, both in West Point and elsewhere in Liberia, but at the same time they are also as accepted community members. But one of the most important lessons to draw from Newell's example and that of West Point is that societies assumed to be anarchic owing to poverty, criminality, and inhabitants with a violent past such as ex-combatants instead are likely to be governed by a complex social order that is far from chaotic. Furthermore, neighborhood security and people's perceptions of how safe a neighborhood really is do not necessarily correspond, even though they are most likely to affect each other. For instance, in his discussion on security and violence in Nkomazi, South Africa, Steffen Jensen distinguishes between two forms of security. On the one hand, there is the material side of security, in other words, the extent to which the population is the victim of crime and violence, which can be analyzed by surveys and statistics. The other side of security, however, is discursive and consists in how people talk about security. Concerns about crime can rise without having anything to do with the actual reported crime levels, illustrating how security and security threats are defined by power relations and people's perceptions. As Jensen argues, the relation between physical violence and security discourses is complex. Nkomazi is an area where police are less than effective and where the inhabitants are often left to deal with violence and criminals themselves. Various formations claim to be representing the community and protecting it against crime. A moral community is produced and established by eradicating the area of crime—and those identified to belong to the moral community may shift dramatically depending on which individuals or groups currently manage to curb crime. Violence plays a complex role in the constitution of moral communities, Jensen notes; it must be prevented for the moral community to materialize on the one hand, while it is paradoxically the very means used in the realization of the moral community on the other hand.[30]

Two important lessons applicable to the case of West Point can be drawn from Jensen's South African example. First, the actual security situation in West Point cannot be judged based merely on the perceptions of inhabitants, other Liberians, and the international community. Thus, how people perceive security and the actual crime levels do not necessarily correspond. For example, a research report conducted on security and environment in West Point from 2012 concluded that West Point's reputation as a "criminal safe haven" and "home to bad people" greatly contrasted with the experiences of the research team, who found that the stigmatization did not seem to respond to any empirical evidence.[31] This point might be obvious, but it is striking how often West Point is portrayed as a particularly insecure area without the statements being based on more than people's perceptions. Yet one should not underestimate the significance of reputation. If a neighborhood and its inhabitants are constantly stigmatized as particularly violent, this is likely to have important consequences. The feeling of being insecure in West Point, whether this feeling is based on real facts or not, surely affects people's lives in the area, as they risk both living in fear for crime and violence and being stigmatized themselves as violent, crime-prone, unpredictable citizens.

A second point relevant for the situation in West Point that can be drawn from Jensen's analysis is how violence always must be understood in its own specific context. Violence, carried out by informal security groups such as vigilantes, can be an integral part of a community's response to crime in the absence of functioning formal security providers.[32] Such violence, when it does occur, can therefore not simply be reduced to an evidence of the anarchic state of the neighborhood but could in fact bear evidence of the opposite as merely a different kind of social order.

VIEWING WEST POINT AND ITS INHABITANTS IN A DIFFERENT LIGHT

I had only just begun to get to know West Point and some of its inhabitants. No one can deny how desperately poor the township is, how hard people struggle just to get by on a daily basis, and how crime and the lack of social services constantly affect people's lives. West Point is a complex society, with inhabitants from all kinds of backgrounds in a variety of life situations. Some were fighters during the wars, but many were not. Still, the Liberian civil wars not too long ago cast a shadow over the lives of the residents in this community, as they do over so many other citizens of Liberia. West Point is many things, yet it is far from its stereotypical image as a place of mere chaos, anarchy, and violence. Chaos is something we tend to see when we do not understand how things work. Chaos is what we think we witness when we forget to take the time to listen to people's stories and let fear and excitement lead us in our hunt for sensational war stories. There is no lack of social order in West Point, but it does follow a different logic. Even theft, which at a first glance could be seen to indicate chaos and disorder, often follows a comprehensible pattern. The high number of ex-combatant residents has contributed to the unenviable reputation of West Point. And, yes, ex-combatants do take part in the networks involved in theft and robberies in the area. But many of the ex-combatants were also part of the informal security networks of the area, vigilante groups that protected the township against crime when the state and formal security apparatus had failed to do so. It is this complexity we so often fail to see and describe. Abraham is a man with a violent past. He is a poor resident of West Point. He is a man who lives in a small zinc house with seven other people, with no windows, running water, or electricity. But Abraham is also a man who devotes his life to his family, who struggles hard to pay his daughters' school fees, who has high hopes and dreams that his youngest son might become a politician one day, and who is annoyed with his oldest son for having so much that he himself never had growing up—such as two pairs of shoes, a decent house, and the opportunity to complete his schooling—without appreciating it. This too is everyday life in West Point, for ex-combatants and others.

WEST POINT AND THE EBOLA EPIDEMIC

The empirical findings on life in West Point was gathered before the tragic outbreak of Ebola in West Africa in 2014. Liberia, together with Sierra Leone, were in the very epicenter of this Ebola epidemic. West Point was also deeply affected, both in terms of the high numbers of people infected and how the neighborhood and its inhabitants have been portrayed in the media as well as treated by the national government. In a desperate bid to stop the spread of the deadly disease, the Liberian government placed West Point under quarantine. The quarantine came to have serious consequences. First of all, it did not stop people from moving in and out of the township, despite the heavily armed military presence guarding the entrances. The large-scale quarantine was unmanageable, and bribes were also used to move in and out. Second, the quarantine immediately led to the eruption of violent clashes, as inhabitants of West Point felt seriously threatened by the government's actions. Rumors of Ebola-infected patients from other parts of Liberia being transferred to West Point flourished. Prices on food and basic goods doubled, causing living conditions for the already poor inhabitants to deteriorate further. The quarantine only lasted little more than a week, but in reports West Point was once again reduced to nothing more than an anarchic neighborhood of violent inhabitants refusing to cooperate in the efforts to control the epidemic. Less was said about the inhabitants' rational suspicion of the government's action and lack of information on why these actions were taken.

As Susan Shepler pointed out during the Ebola crisis and the most intensive period of media coverage of Liberia, a main part of the news was on the "heroic health workers and the ignorant locals"—an ignorance Shepler strongly disputed. The crisis only revealed Liberians' general sense of mistrust of the state. People do not just ignore public health warnings because they doubt they would get the acquired assistance when needed; they actually believe that the state is out to get them. More precisely, as Shepler puts it, they believe that "big men" are using the apparatus of the state to enrich themselves at the expense of ordinary people, sometimes even costing them their lives. One rumor had it that the health ministry had a chemical spray they could use against people to increase the numbers of Ebola-infected people and deaths and thereby receive more international donations for the government. As Shepler concludes, the rumors cannot be seen as ignorance but must instead be understood in the light of how the state has acted in the past, in a "vampiric" fashion, feeding off the misery of the people. People are thereby responding not out of ignorance but out of experience.[33] What regardless can be concluded once again, this time from how the Ebola crisis in West Point particularly was treated locally as well as portrayed in international media, is that the will to understand the intentions and living conditions of inhabitants of such a notorious neighborhood in general weigh much less than the news value West Point continues to have if described as violent, incomprehensible, and anarchic.

Surviving Peace Despite or Because of the Ex-combatant Identity

The end of war seldom means the end of hardship for those affected. Peace does not automatically bring about new opportunities when it comes to livelihood options or even a safe and secure environment. That means that those who have survived war will also have to struggle to survive peace. This is true for civilians and ex-combatants alike. But postwar struggles may look very different for those who have been active combatants and for those who have not. A combatant past may be a heavy burden to carry for many reasons, due to psychological traumas from war, feelings of guilt, or the risks of facing stigmatization, for example. But a combatant past, and the connections it may have brought with it, could also be an advantage in a war-torn society. In the sections to come Malcom's and Jacob's struggles as ex-combatants in Liberia are discussed to further illuminate this complexity.

MALCOLM, WANTING OUT, BUT NEEDING TO BE IN

"Are you sure you don't want to sit inside?" Malcolm asked, looking a bit worried when we took a seat on a wooden bench outside his house. The sun was broiling over Vai Town and Monrovia, and Malcolm had electricity then, so he offered to turn on the fan in the little room of not quite ten square meters, which was his home for the time being. I assured him that the shade would do just fine, knowing it would be rather difficult to have a discussion with Malcolm and his neighbors inside his small home. Malcolm has done his best to decorate his home with his limited means. He had painted the concrete walls in a bright blue color and covered them with posters, mostly of hip-hop artists. There was a mattress on the floor under a mosquito net, a chair, and some shelves with his belongings. The room had a window facing the courtyard, where families residing in the building prepared their food, but wooden boards covered it from the inside, and a big padlock was used to secure the wooden door at night or when Malcolm was out. At that time Malcolm lived in this room for free. A few years ago there had been a lot of break-ins in this and the neighboring buildings, and that was how Malcolm came to move in. Malcolm had been renting another room from the same landlord in a nearby building at the time, but the landlord knew Malcolm's background as a rebel and that he still was involved in the security business, and he offered Malcolm to stay in the room for free as long as he kept a vigilant eye on the buildings of the courtyard. It had worked. The break-ins had decreased and Malcolm had somewhere to stay. Here he felt secure. Break-ins still occurred from time to time, and even Malcolm himself had been affected, "But what can you do?" Malcolm reasoned. He, like his neighbors, did his best to protect himself against crime, and his past as a combatant at least had an intimidating effect on criminals, he thought.

But Malcolm was tired of the whole "security business," he told me: he wanted out. He was forty years old, and he had been living with the consequences of putting his life at risk for more than half his lifetime. In 1990, at the age of seventeen, Malcolm had joined the National Patriotic Front of Liberia. He eventually became a commander with more and more responsibilities. Following Taylor's election victory in 1997, the Taylor administration created the Special Security Unit, initially intended for direct protection of the president and his family. Malcolm received six months' training before being transferred from Taylor's rebel force to the new official Liberian security unit. In 1999, after an additional training period of nine months, Malcolm came to join the Anti-Terrorist Unit, the notorious paramilitary force led by the son of Taylor—Chuckie Taylor—consisting of many experienced fighters from the National Patriotic Front of Liberia. Within the Anti-Terrorist Unit, Malcolm came to fight LURD during the second Liberian civil war until the peace agreement had been signed in 2003. Using his network from the war, Malcolm managed to get a position within Winston Tubman's security force prior to the presidential elections in 2005. He was hired again for the 2011 elections as a one of the informal security commanders. But if Malcolm had had any hopes of gaining an official employment, it died with Ellen Johnson Sirleaf's victory at the polls.

Today Malcolm survives day by day by taking on minor informal security assignments. He can be called in to organize security for a football match, a music concert, a beauty contest, or some other event in Monrovia. When he is put in charge as the security organizer, he uses his postwar rebel network to gather ex-combatants for the assignment. But Malcolm is tired of this way of living; he is tired of the whole security business, he says. It is too hard and too risky to do on a permanent basis. After fourteen years in war, people grow tired of living the way they do when they live by the gun, he tells me. There are two things, he says, that occupy your mind when you live like that. "If you live by the gun, you constantly think about people wanting to kill you. Even when you sleep. You live with your gun, and you are suspicious of everyone." "The second thing you think every day," he continues, "is that you will always return home. You never think of dying. You think that everybody around you can die. But you will never. You will return home. You have to develop that mind-set to survive." But he says he cannot do it anymore. He is tired of it. Life as an ex-combatant also implies living with the memories of a violent past, memories of the violence he has seen, the violence he has suffered, and the violence he has caused. Malcolm lives with these thoughts every day. He says that he is not suffering from nightmares or anxiety from guilt. The war was a time when people did what they had to. But when I once asked him if he did what he did because he felt he was forced, Malcolm shook his head. He does not see it in that way. He says, "You don't force a man to do some of the things I did. I was a commander, and no one had to force me. But things were different back then. It was a different time."

Malcolm's ex-combatant identity has given him the opportunity to survive after the war through private security work. While it is not the same as risking his life—or the lives of others—at war, it is still a dangerous line of work. Malcolm does not want to live his life like that anymore. And he does not want to survive by thinking the very same thoughts that got him through all those years of war. But this is the only opportunity an ex-combatant like him can get, he says. What secures his livelihood are his postwar rebel networks—his Anti-Terrorist Unit network that meets from time to time and

other constellations—as well as his ex-combatant identity and people knowing what he did and who he was, whether he wants it or not.[34]

JACOB, "THEY KNOW MY NAME, AND THEY FEAR ME"

If there ever was a winning and a losing side when the war finally came to an end
in 2003, Jacob was definitely among the losers. Jacob had been forced to change
sides after years in prison following the Camp Johnson incident in 1998. Charles
Taylor, the new Liberian president, had offered him the chance to take his side
in the war against LURD. For Jacob this meant he would be at war against not
only people he had fought and lived with for years but also his closest family and
friends. But Jacob had seen no other way than to accept Taylor's offer. But when
peace came, not only was the leader he had been forced to follow driven into
exile, leaving his men with no benefits, but Jacob was also locked out from his
most important network, the postwar rebel network that came to take control
over a significant part of the Liberian rubber industry through the occupation
of Guthrie Rubber Plantation. Jacob's ex-combatant identity has both offered
opportunities and been a heavy burden, as it has for all of my informants. But
for Jacob this identity has perhaps been even more complex to live with than for
many other ex-combatants. Many people knew of his past and viewed him with
suspicion, even by members of his own postwar rebel network.

Jacob lives in a small house in Gardnersville, a Monrovian suburb, with
his two young daughters and his mother. The only reason Jacob has been able
to build a house of his own was the fact that Taylor gave him money, as he was
made to turn on his former allies. Building a house was the very first thing
Jacob did after having been forced to accept Taylor's offer. Jacob had tears
in his eyes the first time he told me about his house. Jacob knew that Taylor
could turn on him at any second, that he could kill him and take his money
back as he saw fit. But after years in war, followed by years in prison, Jacob
needed something to remain after he was gone. If he was killed tomorrow,
Jacob thought, a house could be something to leave behind for his family,
somewhat like a symbol or proof even that he once had lived and had thought
of them. Giving his mother the money to start arranging for the house was
therefore the very first thing Jacob did.

The first years following the war were frustrating for Jacob. While his
closest friends and family were making lucrative deals on their illegal plantation occupation, Jacob was never fully trusted with the plantation business.
The plantation commanders, his best friend, and his cousin gave him small
amounts of money from time to time and helped him to get temporary informal security assignments through their contacts, but the plantation business was closed to him. Making a living has been a daily struggle for Jacob,
and, like other ex-combatants who cannot or have chosen not to hide their

wartime past, he has survived by taking on the various informal or private se-curity assignments he has been able to get. But Jacob's ex-combatant identity has more often than not kept him away from security assignments. Over the years Jacob has applied for several different governmental security jobs, but his applications are not even assessed, he says. He is an ex-combatant, and he will never be fully accepted back in society.

Jacob's achievements in war—how he managed to become a commander close to the rebel leader George Boley; a police commander following the first war; and then finally one of Taylor's presidential mansion commanders—have made him someone easily recognized, at least within the formal and infor-mal Liberian security arena. "They know my name, and they fear me," Jacob once told me. He had become notorious during his time as a rebel, especially during those years based in Monrovia as one of George Boley's main com-manders. He became fearless, he says. He almost lost the ability to be afraid, he recalls, because he simply could not afford to think in that way. "I will die one day, but a lot of people will have to die by my hand before that happens," he used to think to himself. Jacob became known and feared in Monrovia. He developed a reputation, which he has not escaped. Furthermore, Jacob was once charged with treason. Even though this was during the Taylor years, following the Camp Johnson incident, he will never get rid of this stigma, and this, he says, will lock him out of any future formal security job. Yet even though it is hard for Jacob, like many other ex-combatants, to find employ-ment in the formal security arena, the private and the informal arena is where Jacob can use his ex-combatant identity to his advantage. Through his cousin and former commander, Jacob was recently employed by a Chinese road-construction company. He is now the head of the company's small security team, a team he was trusted to handpick himself, and for this he used his ex-combatant network. He feels proud and happy that he has managed to secure jobs for other ex-combatants and that his reputation as a former rebel commander here is something he can use to his advantage. In this arena his skills in security from the war are valued, and he can be treated with respect, despite his ex-combatant identity or even because of it. But Jacob dreams of a different life that could offer more for an ex-combatant than the informal security arena. He is trying to save money to study and get a university degree. Only then, he thinks, can he build a better life for him and his daughters.[35]

Liberian Ex-combatants and the Return to War

"Where is the war?" Kieran Mitton asks in his article on the postwar situation of ex-combatants in Sierra Leone, while setting out to explain the country's lasting peace. And it is indeed a very relevant question. As Mitton notes, ever since the war came to an end in 2002, there have been frequent warnings in the United Nations, NGOS, and academic reports of the Sierra Leonean ex-combatants returning to war. It has been suggested that desperate political and socioeconomic prewar conditions persist, undermining ex-combatants' investment in peace. Yet, despite the warnings, Sierra Leone has experienced relatively low levels of violence since the war came to an end. Supported by this fact, Mitton argues that the risks of ex-combatants returning to arms have been exaggerated. Nevertheless, economic and political conditions continue to reconnect ex-combatants with peacetime violence. It is therefore unavoidable to question whether the warnings over the destructive potential of ex-combatants are misplaced or whether it is just a matter of time before Sierra Leone returns to war. As Mitton finds in the Sierra Leonean case, the frustration with the slow pace of development among former fighters and unemployed youths is real and may very well lead to desperate measures, such as turning to violence to vent grievances or to make a better living. Yet the nature of the risk is often misrepresented. For one thing, linking youth's frustration to renewed conflict is often predicated on misleading and simplistic readings of the causes of civil war. One of the many important aspects that Mitton raises is that the assumptions of a return to civil war to a significant extent rest on the implicit notion that ex-combatants are especially prone to violence, which in fact is certainly not the case for all former fighters. Even those among his informants who openly expressed a desire to return to fighting after demobilization have now undergone a difficult process of adjustment that became essential to survive peace and have accepted that the war truly is over. Many of the interviewed former fighters were, in fact, strongly opposed to renewed warfare.[36]

Much of this logic is true also in the Liberian case, where similar warnings have been raised frequently since the end of war. It is almost expected that the Liberian ex-combatants will return to war as soon as the opportunity arises and, furthermore, that being violent is a virtually inseparable part of the ex-combatant identity, which automatically will lead to a return to arms. Perhaps such assumptions are not so surprising after all, especially not in the case of former fighters within postwar rebel networks. These ex-combatants remained mobilized or at least preserved, rather than abandoned, their wartime links as well as chains of command from their time as rebels. And as we have seen, these networks have also been used not only because of their skills in the field of security but also because of their potential for violence. Still, even though ex-combatants in general, and postwar rebel networks in particular, have the preconditions to be used in renewed warfare, it is much too simplistic to assume that the ex-combatants within such networks would readily resort to violence, even when there are few other opportunities, when frustration is high and political and socioeconomic conditions are desperate. Yet, as McMullin has pointed out, the assumption that ex-combatant dissatisfaction

alone can return a country to war through violent protests or criminal ban-
ditry still underpins DDR programs, despite the fact that this claim disregards
the deep skepticism that most Liberian ex-combatants have about the future
efficacy of war.[37]

To understand why ex-combatants are not ready for violence and warfare as easily as assumed one needs to look not only at the structures and
capabilities of postwar rebel networks but also at the individual stories of the
ex-combatants within these networks and how they themselves use the different aspects of the ex-combatant identity, including being perceived as violent.
Malcolm's story, for instance, shows how vital his postwar rebel network is, especially when it comes to job opportunities. Malcolm is dependent on his ex-
combatant identity because it is through this identity, and this identity alone,
that he finds assignments within the informal security sector. Having been a
commander has perhaps also given him some benefits he might not have been
given as a foot solider, as he from time to time is called on to manage and
organize ex-combatants for security assignments. But Malcolm wants out. He
is tired of a life in the field of security where his violent potential is one of his
most necessary qualities. But this is the field open to him. This is where he has
the best chances for employment, and so he continues, even past the age of
forty and longing to leave the violence behind him.

Jacob also dreams of a life as something more than violent labor. He wants
to study to give his daughters a better future and leave the temporary security assignments he gets from time to time. But like Malcolm and other ex-
combatants, he has an ambivalent feeling toward his ex-combatant identity and
his past as a commander. He has a reputation from the war: he was notorious
and known to be fearless. This, he thinks, is what prevents him from finding
other forms of employment than those within the informal security arena. At
the same time, paradoxically, it is the combination of his ex-combatant identity, his postwar rebel network, and probably also his very reputation from the
war that secures the assignments he makes a living from. It is striking that the
one thing all my informants agree on and what they often have told me over
the years is that they do not want to see another war and that they would never
want to fight again, despite the fact that they all make their living by clinging
to their postwar rebel network, taking on informal security assignments, and
often using their violent potential or reputation as such while struggling with
poverty and limited opportunities.

What becomes clear by following the lives of individual ex-combatants is
that they themselves feel that they have more to lose than to gain from a new
war. That Michael would never want to see another war may not be unexpected. He has managed to establish himself in the Liberian society with formal employment and a university education. But that a man like Abraham,
who lives under strained circumstances in West Point, has the same point of

view might be more difficult to understand if one takes as a point of departure the way ex-combatants are often portrayed. Ex-combatants who keep their wartime networks are mobilized for informal security assignments, function as vigilantes, or simply do not hide their past and are clearly expected to be easily recruited for yet another war, according to the stereotypical perception of them as having little to lose, given their current situation. But Abraham, Jacob, Malcolm, Michael, and many others do not see it in this way. Abraham, for instance, feels that he can give so much more to his family than he ever got. His life in West Point does not look like much to the world, and, at first glance, or with a stereotypical perception of former rebels in mind, Abraham may appear to be a man who would easily and willingly give up his current life for the opportunities that life as a rebel could offer. But a deeper look at him, and so many other ex-combatants, reveals that this is far from the truth. Postwar rebel networks have all the skills to be used in renewed warfare, but many ex-combatants would not readily return to arms. War never gave them a better life, and they are certain, even though everyday life is a struggle, that another war would not give them a better future either. They use their ex-combatant identity, networks, and skills learned from war not because they are waiting for a new opportunity to fight but simply because this identity is their most important asset in trying to survive peace. New generations will come that, because of desperate living conditions, for example, might see war as their best option. We have seen in the West African wars and elsewhere that it is possible to build a militarized capacity quickly under the right circumstances. That the already existing networks of ex-combatants in Liberia and the region, who already have seen what the war brought—and did not bring—with it, should be the biggest threats toward lasting peace is not as likely from this perspective.

Conclusion

Malcolm kept his personal photos in a small paper box tucked away in his room for safekeeping. As they are for most people, his photos were precious to him. He did not have many. He, like most Liberians, did not own a camera and had photos taken only on special occasions. Wanting to show me a glimpse of his life, as showing photos implies for most of us, Malcolm took his paper box out into the courtyard one day when we were talking. There were photos of his loved ones: his family members and close friends. He showed me pictures of him and his father, other relatives, and a few of himself at different ages. I was happy to see Malcolm's photos. He showed me yet another piece of himself by letting me see the people that mattered to him. There was nothing out of the ordinary about them, as there rarely is with family photos, but they still represented an important part of who Malcolm was. One of the photos stood out to me. "Where is this from," I asked; "Who are they?" I had found a photo of two men dressed up in suits, waving to a crowd of people from an open SUV. Serious-looking men hung on the sides of the car, all dressed in black sunglasses with rolled-up sleeves to expose their toned arm muscles. "What," Malcolm laughed. "Don't you recognize me, don't you recognize us?!" After a closer look I obviously did. The men around the car were my informants during the 2011 election campaign, protecting Winston Tubman and George Weah, who greeted the crowd from the car. Then it struck me: apart from a picture of the men carrying guns in actual rebel combat on the streets of Monrovia, the photo came as close as it could to the stereotypical image of who Malcolm and the rest of my informants were believed to be and what they were expected to do. And, yes, the ex-combatant identity was one of Malcolm's and my other informants' identities. And, yes, it was a crucial one for them in postwar Liberia. Yet it was not the only one. It was but one of many. The ex-combatant identity in itself is also far more complex than the stereotypical image would have us believe.

We should remember that the ex-combatants we have met in this chapter, and in this book, are among those most intimately connected to their combatant past. They are those who could be considered to be the most hardened former fighters because of their continued activities and preserved networks. Many of the ex-combatants followed in this book have a background as rebel commanders. Yet even these men are far from the war-hungry, ready-to-fight-again militarized men the stereotypical images of them would suggest. To fully understand who the ex-combatants are, what they are capable of, and the security risks they constitute in Liberia and elsewhere today, we need to look at the ex-combatant identity from a more nuanced perspective than is most often shown in media, reports, and political statements. To do so we need to look at individual stories. When looking at ex-combatants as a group, we cannot easily escape the stereotypical perceptions attached to the ex-combatant identity. Because of media reporting and one-dimensional portrayals of wars and insecurity in Africa in general, we know them merely as violent, angry, evil, and irrational young men ready to go to war as soon as the opportunity is given. But when we look at individual stories, like those of Abraham, Malcolm, Jacob, and others, we are forced to see a bigger picture. As Malcolm's box of photos revealed, he—like all other ex-combatants—are so much more than a mere product of war. Seeing them only as such, we have no way of truly understanding ex-combatants' part in postwar life in Liberia or what their continued informal security activities imply, and will continue to imply, in the future.

CONCLUSION

Repurposed Rebels

FROM PERPETRATORS TO PROTECTORS

This book places itself within a growing body of literature on postwar Liberia, but more specifically on postwar ex-combatants in Liberia and beyond. The disarmament, demobilization, and reintegration (DDR) literature, both academic and policy oriented, has been particularly occupied with the complexity of the challenges that ex-combatants, and the society they are returning to after war, are faced with. But as the failures to successfully break down former rebel networks and reintegrate ex-combatants into civil society have been many, the focus in recent years has been on how to improve the practice of DDR for better and more long-lasting results. Special attention has especially been devoted to the complexity of one of the three components in particular: reintegration. While disarmament and demobilization have been considered to be more short-term processes involving mainly technical challenges, reintegration has been identified as perhaps the most vital, and difficult component when it comes to turning combatants into civilians. The research here has taken a different approach. As a first theme in this concluding chapter, I therefore discuss what I call the "Reintegration Paradox." I argue that demobilization of former rebel groups is much more than a technical procedure and is much more complicated than is often assumed. As this book has shown, rebel networks in practice can easily remain mobilized long after their initial rebel group has been dissolved, while individual members of these postwar rebel networks may in fact be much more reintegrated into civil society than is often understood. Second, I discuss the "Demobilization Dilemma" that arises from this paradox. Findings are summarized in relation to a wider discussion on why failures or successes to demobilize ex-combatants have had less to do with the practice of DDR than is generally recognized. I argue instead that the fundamental question should be whether there in fact exists a will, or even a need, for former rebel networks to stay active and mobilized, even though there are no wars to be fought in postconflict societies.

In this book I have shed light on the relevance of postwar rebel networks in Liberia. But, as we shall discover in the next theme of this chapter, which I call "Postwar Rebel Networks in Liberia and Beyond," this is not only a Liberian phenomenon. In this section I examine my findings through a wider discussion on ex-combatant networks in Liberia and other African countries. Here I call attention to the fact that postwar rebel networks have not been acknowledged to the extent that they should be. I suggest that this is because such networks are seldom examined unless they are involved in renewed warfare. With the case studies of this book reaching beyond ex-combatants as recycled regional warriors, I suggest how its findings can contribute to a more nuanced and complex understanding of postwar rebel networks in Liberia and beyond. But even though the phenomenon of existing postwar rebel networks has not been acknowledged to the extent I believe that it deserves, recent years have provided us with interesting findings on the topic on the African continent. In this section I wish to present such research and examine how my findings relate to this ongoing debate. We discover similarities as well as differences, and it leads me into a summarizing discussion of what risks networks of ex-combatants actually constitute after war. Are they simply the real, and most acute, threat to peace they are often described as, or is the danger with lingering rebel structures a more complex issue?

In the final theme of this concluding chapter, called "From Perpetrators to Security Providers," I engage in a deeper discussion of the ability to transform that ex-combatants and networks of ex-combatants have proved to possess. I summarize the discussion of why the move from warrior to security provider is one that the ex-combatants may find natural to make in a postconflict country like Liberia, where instability and insecurity are still everyday realities for many citizens. Here we once again come back to the importance of the ex-combatant identity. In a concluding discussion we further examine what this identity means for former rebels in postwar rebel networks. We return to the discussion of whether one can escape such an identity and in that case if it is even desirable. That leads us on to the question of how it can be possible that a life with an ex-combatant identity can be compatible with that of being a postwar informal security provider. It is my hope that such a discussion contributes to the understanding of who the ex-combatants are today and what relevance postwar rebel networks have and what roles they play in contemporary Liberia, but also how that in turn affects the security political climate of the country.

The Reintegration Paradox

DDR is a central component of nearly all large-scale peace operations today, whether run by the United Nations or other regional organizations.[1] According to the United Nations Disarmament, Demobilisation and Reintegration Resource Centre, DDR aims to deal with the postconflict security problem that arises when ex-combatants are left without livelihoods or support networks other than their former comrades, during the vital transition period from conflict to peace and development. This is done through a process of removing weapons from the hands of combatants, taking the combatants out of military structures, and helping them to integrate socially and economically into society.[2] Especially when it comes to Africa, comprehensive and effective DDR initiatives are often seen as a fundamental precondition for peace, stability, and human development in emerging postconflict societies. The challenges of DDR in Africa have been noted. But the first two components of DDR, disarmament and demobilization, are most of the time not seen as the main difficulties. These components have been seen to pose primarily technical challenges. Above all, combatants must be registered, arms must be collected, and cantonment sites for the demobilized must be built. It is believed that with proper planning the disarmament and demobilization steps can be effectively managed and implemented. Reintegration, on the other hand, is acknowledged as a far more complex and lengthy process, in which backsliding is common.[3]

While reintegration is a complex issue, the complexity of demobilization needs to be addressed to a much greater extent than it is today. It is of course, to a certain extent, a matter of definition and how we understand the concept of demobilization as such. According to the United Nations, demobilization is the formal and controlled discharge of active combatants from armed forces and groups. It is also seen as a multifaceted process that marks the change of status of a combatant from military to civilian.[4] But demobilization is also understood as the separation of combatants from their command and control structures or even as the actual elimination of military structures and units.[5] A too narrow definition of demobilization can never be fruitful. Demobilization must imply more than when a rebel group, for instance, officially ceases to exist and when its members officially register for demobilization. If we instead understand demobilization to also include the abandonment of command and control structures, we find that rebel structures easily continue to exist even after the DDR process. The ex-combatants remain mobilized even though they may not be armed or militarized. They may not be part of a rebel group, and they may not be mobilized for warfare, but their command structures remain beyond peace agreements. In that light a broader perspective on demobilization offers a better chance of understanding what happens, or does not happen, to rebel structures after the war.

Furthermore, when it comes to demobilization, it is of vital importance that we also discuss why we believe that postwar rebel networks should be broken at all costs. As the findings of this book suggest, there are good reasons for several actors to preserve, rather than to break, these structures. Hugo de Vries and Nikkie Wiegink have reached similar conclusions when it comes to common assumptions in the demobilization and reintegration of ex-combatants. As they have argued, the focus on breaking up ex-combatants' command and control structures under all circumstances takes insufficient account of several important factors. One factor they point out is that the collective experience of combat can create a bond between people that may transcend their former connections to families and communities. Other factors include security issues and economic reasons for sticking together with fellow ex-combatants, in the hope of protection in fragile societies where renewed violence is a constant risk and to conduct a common struggle for livelihoods where opportunities are scarce. De Vries and Wiegink also state that patronage dynamics may lie behind ex-combatants' reasons for staying together. Economic, social, and political benefits are provided for within networks of reciprocal relations. These relations may work horizontally between fellow ex-combatants or vertically between ex-combatants and their commanders to distribute benefits within the network such as jobs, loans, or other basic necessities.[6] These findings fit well with those of this book. For my informants the postwar rebel networks have become vital. They have provided economic as well as social safety nets. Therefore, I strongly agree with the authors as they suggest that an unreasonably strong emphasis has been put on the focus of dissolving ex-combatant networks to reintegrate ex-combatants. These structures may not be a more acute threat to renewed violence than individual ex-combatants, and they provide opportunities for ex-combatants' that postwar societies may be too weak to offer.

Continued mobilization in the form of postwar rebel networks has to a large extent been kept in the shadows and seldom been acknowledged, precisely because demobilization has been seen mainly as a mere technical component before the real challenge of reintegration can begin. Contrary to the general view within the DDR literature that often identifies problems with reintegration, not disarmament and demobilization, ex-combatants, in many cases, should be seen instead as more or less reintegrated but not demobilized. Looking more closely at the individuals we have followed in this book, we see that they, in many ways, are ordinary members of their communities. They are indeed faced with an everyday struggle for livelihood, and they battle poverty and unemployment, but so do their fellow community members with a civilian background. In this sense they could be seen as reintegrated— or remarginalized, to borrow a term from Utas—because they face the same difficulties and marginalization as ordinary Liberians without a combatant past. But they do have an advantage most civilians lack: their postwar rebel network, which from time to time can provide them with temporary informal security jobs and occasional income.[7] Accordingly, the increased focus on the complexity of reintegration of ex-combatants in recent years is not a problem as such but has rather drawn attention away from the equally complex issue of demobilization. And without understanding why continued mobilization of rebel networks is a natural outcome, no fruitful discussion on reintegration can come about either.

This book has demonstrated that a central aspect of the complexity of demobilization relates to the fact that postwar rebel networks may serve as a source of reintegration into civilian livelihoods after conflicts. Herein lies a reintegration paradox, namely that the preservation of wartime command structures—contrary to the received logic of DDR initiatives in general—provides some ex-combatants with a better chance at postwar reintegration. This paradox compels us to start looking at both the ex-combatant identity and reintegration in a new light instead of treating the ex-combatant identity as a mere factor for stigmatization or the ability to conduct violence, which therefore needs to be washed away to recreate productive and peaceful civilians in a reintegration process. We may need to come to terms with the fact that this very identity might be the ex-combatants' best chance for reintegration. This identity, along with their postwar rebel networks, may be the best option for many ex-combatants for finding a place and a role in postconflict societies. Postconflict rehabilitation initiatives, including DDR, therefore need to seriously and carefully consider whether it is in the best interest of ex-combatants and the postconflict societies at large that postwar rebel networks are broken in the way that reintegration initiatives traditionally have done. Consequently, this paradox complicates distinctions between military and civilian structures and unsettles the predominant focus on demobilization as a technical procedure. But it also challenges basic underlying aims and purposes with the processes of demobilization and reintegration. To put it sharply, these ex-combatants have succeeded in reintegrating themselves because they have not been demobilized.

The Demobilization Dilemma

The second problem with the concept of DDR connected to demobilization relates to the will and need for rebel structures to linger. I have given several examples of what the ex-combatants themselves, as well as actors in power and ordinary citizens, may have to gain with the existence of postwar rebel networks. While it can be an important, and sometimes the only, way for ex-combatants to secure employment, postwar rebel networks can be a means for elite actors to secure power, make financial gains, or show force. At the same time for ordinary citizens postwar rebel networks can function as an alternative, or sometimes more reliable, security institution for everyday protection in the form of vigilantes or other types of informal security-providing networks. In societies where such a need or will to preserve rebel networks exists, DDR initiatives, no matter how well they are carried out, have very little to do with the actual relevance and existence of postwar rebel networks beyond the formal end of hostilities. Such issues, like the potential need and will for the continued presence of rebel structures after the war, should be carefully examined before substantial resources are invested in the DDR process. We need to acknowledge and address the demobilization dilemma and the reintegration paradox and thereby challenge common assumptions of postwar rebel networks as mere security threats, to have a better chance of understanding postwar realities and to make better investments in peace and security in countries emerging from war.

Future research in examining what it actually means to be reintegrated as an ex-combatant is of vital importance. Here ex-combatants' own perceptions of what it means to be reintegrated and how they perceive both advantages and disadvantages associated with the ex-combatant identity should be studied. Predominant assumptions, suggesting that this identity needs to be abandoned for ex-combatants to find a place in a postwar society where they are not in risk of automatically being used for renewed warfare or violence or as an object for stigmatization, need to be challenged. We also need to seriously consider in what way and under what circumstances the preservation of postwar rebel networks in fact can facilitate reintegration as well as contribute to the strengthening of security, not merely how and when such networks can be used to create instability.

Postwar Rebel Networks in Liberia and Beyond

Postwar rebel networks have not been acknowledged to the extent they should be. One reason for this is that postwar rebel networks become visible only if followed over a lengthy period. By examining the situation of ex-combatants and their actions only on isolated occasions after the war, we miss the dynamics and mechanisms tying individual ex-combatants together in times of peace, long after war has come to an end. I have tried to do the opposite. I have followed many of my informants over a relatively long period. I have returned to the same field and individuals over a number of years, and it is only through this longitudinal perspective that I have been able to see why these networks have remained relevant and how they have been adapted to function in a context of continued insecurity and instability in times of peace.

The need to examine postwar rebel networks even in the absence of war leads me to another reason such networks have often remained in the shadows: because ex-combatants' continued state of mobilization is not necessarily a visible phenomenon *unless* they engage in renewed warfare.[8] We have seen several examples of attention paid to such developments, when ex-combatants, after the declaration of the end of one conflict, later reappear in another, not least in the West African region. For instance, in 2005 Human Rights Watch reported that a "migrant population of young fighters" was gliding back and forth across the West African borders to join new conflicts after having participated in the DDR process in Sierra Leone or Liberia. After interviews with former combatants from fifteen armed forces, Human Rights Watch noted that the ex-combatants argued that, given the dire economic conditions in the region, going to war was their best option for economic survival. A military intelligence source with extensive experience in West Africa was interviewed and quoted by Human Rights Watch about these postwar rebel networks as saying, "These guys form a part of a regional militia I call insurgent diaspora. They float in and out of wars and operate as they wish. They have no one to tell them when, where and how to behave. They've been incorporated into militias and armies all over the place—Sierra Leone, Côte d'Ivoire—and are really the most dangerous tool any government or rebel army can have."[9]

I also show how networks of ex-combatants moved over West Africa borders as recycled warriors in times of conflict and political instability in the region. While I do agree that these postwar rebel networks strongly contributed to the continued violence and warfare in the region, I have also shown how well organized recruitment and remobilization often is. Ex-combatants of postwar rebel networks clearly had someone to tell them when, where, and how to behave. This did not make them less of a threat to regional stability, but rather the opposite. When it comes to understanding how and why networks of ex-combatants were recruited for renewed warfare, I have especially relied on research by Danny Hoffman. His research on Sierra Leonean and Liberian ex-combatants as violent labor that, in a well-structured and coordinated manner, could be assembled and redeployed in new violent settings is an important and detailed contribution describing this specific use of postwar rebel networks. Findings from Hoffman's work have not only contributed to explaining the logic behind why networks of ex-combatants have been used in renewed warfare but have also given us important details of how this has been done. It has also presented further evidence against notions of the reengagement of ex-combatants in new warfare as unorganized and chaotic, which corresponds well with my own findings.[10]

Closely related to the discussion on ex-combatants engaged in renewed warfare is Anders Themnér's comparative research on why some ex-combatants return to organized violence while others do not. Looking at ex-combatant communities in the Democratic Republic of the Congo and in Sierra Leone, Themnér notes that a considerable number of former fighters resorted to organized violence after the declaration of peace. Themnér found that the most important determinants of ex-combatant violence are whether the former fighters have a strong social network binding them together and whether they have access to entrepreneurs of violence and intermediaries, so-called remobilizers, who promise selective incentives such as cash and loot and use feelings of affinity, trust, and fear to convince ex-combatants to resort to arms. Remarginalization, on the other hand, offers the least insight into why only some ex-combatants return to organized violence, since this is the reality for most ex-combatants.[11] My own research, in contrast to that of Themnér, does not focus mainly on ex-combatants in relation to renewed warfare, although this is an important aspect. Here my findings from Liberia, however, correspond well with those of Themnér in the cases of the Democratic Republic of the Congo and Sierra Leone when it comes to the importance of individuals through and around whom the ex-combatants may be mobilized. In chapter 2 we see how Michael, as an influential former rebel general, functioned as one among other key mobilizers when it came to recruiting for the Liberians United for Reconciliation and Democracy in the region before the second wave of warfare in Liberia. That Michael was already part of a strong postwar rebel network, which had not vanished with the end of the first war in Liberia, was a vital aspect of his success as a remobilizer, which works well with Themnér's argument about the need for strong social networks as a precondition for remobilization.

Another important contribution to research on postwar rebel networks and their reengagement in renewed warfare has come from Maya Mynster Christensen, who has followed former military and militia soldiers in Sierra Leone in the context of transition from war to peace. Christensen explores the process of mobilization that these ex-militias and wartime networks are engaged in today, following the end of war, and how they gradually transform into new constellations of soldiering. Using the concept of "shadow soldiering" to highlight the blurred lines of division between the visible and the invisible and the entanglement of what is considered legal and illegal, private and public, state and nonstate, and civil and military, Christensen shows how ex-militias in Sierra Leone morph into security contractors in Iraq or are mobilized into militarized networks in other parts of West Africa. Christensen examines processes of mobilization of militarized networks in Sierra Leone that are less visible and take place in the shadows. She makes an important point when she argues that shadow soldiering is not a marginal phenomenon, taking place in situations of armed conflict and open warfare. It is also a peacetime phenomenon that is becoming increasingly central in the context of security outsourcing and militarization in a global economy. Acknowledging that networks of ex-militias can be engaged for both violent and nonviolent purposes, Christensen focuses on violent forms of laboring in which male ex-militias engage, particularly their mobilization into militarized networks. By doing so Christensen illuminates how the postwar networks have transformed into political task forces and presidential guards, have become regional mercenaries, and have been engaged in international security contracting for private and military companies in Iraq.[12]

An important similarity to the Liberian postwar rebel networks in this book is that the networks of ex-militias that Christensen follows merge in a similar manner from one constellation of shadow soldiering to another over time in their struggle for survival, sometimes bringing them closer to their aspirations, while at other times a step further away.[13] Taking sides and letting oneself be mobilized for an informal security group during an election in Liberia has either fortunate or disastrous consequences for ex-combatants in a winner-takes-all context, as postwar settings tend to be. In the examples of postwar mobilization that Christensen presents, ex-militias have emerged mainly to be used in zones of renewed warfare. My own research provides only one example of postwar rebel networks used for this purpose (with the exception of the case study of the mobilization of ex-militias during the general elections in Sierra Leone). Instead, I have focused mainly on the mobilization of informal security groups from postwar rebel networks in times of peace. By doing so I hope to contribute to the understanding of the less visible continued mobilization of wartime networks that is still security related but not connected to renewed warfare, which remains an underresearched area that clearly would benefit from future in-depth research.

Postwar rebel networks must be understood as a peacetime phenomenon to a higher extent than they are today. What my case studies show is that the need, and the will, to keep such networks mobilized does not automatically vanish with the end of war. In other words, the continued existence of postwar rebel networks is not primarily a token of forces seeking to sustain war or start renewed warfare. Postwar rebel networks are powerful tools for warfare that can be, and are, from time to time used for such purposes. But as this book has provided examples of, individuals within postwar rebel networks are not necessarily part of them because they are interested in taking up arms once again. This might be an important alternative for them, but we should not assume that this is naturally their first choice. Ex-combatants linger in these networks because they provide them with their most likely opportunity for livelihood, as such networks might open doors for temporary employment such as informal security assignments. It would not make sense for ex-combatants in a severely marginalized postwar setting to abandon their perhaps most important network when there are so few other opportunities. For this reason postwar rebel networks cannot be understood simply as a threat to peace. They can be dangerous tools for actors seeking to conduct warfare and violent operations, but they can also be the very structures that keep ex-combatants away from conflict and provide some sort of stability following the end of war.

A similar conclusion has been drawn by Mats Utas, Anders Themnér, and Emy Lindberg in the Liberian case, as they argue that collaboration between governing elites and ex-commanders and their informal networks can in fact be central to the promotion of peace and stability. By using commanders as brokers for socioeconomic services, elites can reach ex-combatants they would otherwise have difficulty accessing to distribute support such as money, food, scholarships, and employment but also information and political influence. In return elites can secure loyalty that consequently will lead to stability, which is key in a successful postwar environment. Such collaboration can help the reintegration of ex-combatants into society, while at the same time it is an efficient way for postwar elites to create stability and control in the absence of strong state institutions. Where the DDR process has failed, this mutual dependence could be perceived as an alternative domestic solution to postwar insecurity.[14] Postwar rebel networks are, nevertheless, being used because of their potential to use violence. Yet they are not necessarily used for violent *purposes*, which is an important distinction to make that is often forgotten when postwar rebel networks or ex-combatants are discussed exclusively in relation to renewed warfare or the risk of such. It is my hope that the research herein has contributed to a more nuanced understanding of ex-combatants and postwar rebel networks and how this phenomenon relates to the risk of postwar instability, violence, or renewed warfare.

From Perpetrators to Security Providers

I have set out to answer the question of how and why networks of former rebels remain relevant in contemporary Liberia, many years after war has come to an end. I have tried to do so by shedding light on the current security situation, where I have shown how the formal state security organizations have failed to provide Liberian citizens with everyday protection. Ordinary citizens have had a history of searching for such protection elsewhere instead. In such an environment the informal security arena has become of vital importance for individuals looking for actors providing security. But this arena has become a natural platform for postwar rebel networks. From these networks informal security groups have emerged. For ordinary Liberian citizens, they have been useful mainly when they have emerged as vigilantes, providing protection in local communities in the absence of efficient police forces. But the existence of postwar rebel networks is not only, nor primarily, a result of the security needs of ordinary Liberian citizens looking for everyday protection. Actors at the highest level of the political and economic elite, contrary to official rhetoric, also have great interests in keeping postwar rebel networks mobilized. In chapter 2 we see how the political elite not only in Liberia but in the wider West African region sought to use postwar rebel networks in renewed warfare against political enemies. And this is how we are most used to seeing ex-combatants who have preserved their wartime networks: as recycled regional warriors.

But postwar rebel networks are not just of interest to elite actors when needed for warfare. Postwar rebel networks have clearly been found useful as informal security providers. Networks of ex-combatants are capable not only of creating chaos and causing violence; when given the task, postwar rebel networks can be efficient security providers. But the use of postwar rebel networks has at least two purposes seen from the elite actors' perspective. They are good at providing security, but they can also clearly have an intimidating effect on others, which can sometimes be used to advantage. In chapter 3 we see how the networks of ex-combatants remained active at the Guthrie Rubber Plantation after the government takeover. They did so not because the new management and the Liberian government failed to evict them but because the very same actors saw the lingering rebel structures at the plantation as a clear advantage. The ex-combatants were well organized, they had clear chains of command, and by using their wartime skills they were efficient security providers. Furthermore, the ex-combatants' violent past, particularly that of key former commanders, made them highly intimidating, not only toward potential rubber thieves but also toward other plantation workers. At a time when the new management often failed to pay their workers at the plantation, the management used the ex-combatants to protect their lands against intruders, and notorious former rebel commanders could also be seen "encouraging" workers to carry out their tasks despite not having been paid. The ex-combatants' violent potential thereby proved to be a very useful tool in the hands of the elite. With time, working conditions improved at the plantation, and the incentive to use the ex-combatants as intimidators against the plantation's own workers moderated. Simultaneously, the postwar rebel network at the plantation began to make their journey from informal to formal security providers. They were promised official status, ID cards, and uniforms. For the postwar rebel network this was the public recognition they had been waiting for. This was proof that they had made the journey from rebels to security providers. This was the evidence that they had officially transformed from perpetrators to protectors.

Also in chapter 4 we have seen evidence of the elite using postwar rebel networks as late as in 2011, eight years after the war was declared over, and this time for political purposes. Presidential candidate Winston Tubman's mobilization of postwar rebel networks as informal security providers and personal bodyguards during the 2011 Liberian elections sheds light on several important reasons for the continued relevance of postwar rebel networks in contemporary Liberia. As Tubman's personal informal security force, the ex-combatants first of all functioned as efficient security providers, but it was perhaps just as important for Tubman to use such a network as a public display of force. With the "repurposed rebels" on his side, now "tamed" as security providers, Tubman could demonstrate his power to also control the roughest elements in Liberia—that is, those who had once created such violence and chaos in the country. Providing the ex-combatants with employment, if only just during the preelection and election phase, could also have been a way to secure voters among the ex-combatant communities and their dependents. Similar tactics were used by the incumbent president, Ellen Johnson Sirleaf. Her reaching out to commanders within postwar rebel networks was a strategic choice to mobilize votes and to ensure that she also remained in control of these potential tools of violence. Providing at least a few of them, particularly key individuals, with security positions after her election victory has been a way to continue to secure her indirect rule over such networks. Postwar rebel networks, from which new informal constellations of ex-combatants can easily rise, thereby continue to be relevant tools that elite actors, even at the highest level of power, can use for different, often hidden, purposes in postwar Liberia.

But what does the journey from rebel to security provider imply for the ex-combatants themselves? In this book I have asked whether taking on temporary informal security jobs is what the ex-combatants desire and whether an identity as a security provider is even compatible with that of an ex-combatant. What I have found is that ex-combatants attach themselves to postwar rebel networks because through such structures, and sometimes only through these structures, they have a chance to survive after wars. By preserving the links to former commanders and former combatants, they have an opportunity to secure at least temporary employment. This has naturally been in the informal security sector, with the skills the ex-combatants achieved in times of war. What I have found is that ex-combatants remain within postwar rebel networks, contrary to what often is argued, not for sentimental reasons, in other words, not because the ex-combatant identity in itself is something they are proud of and wish to preserve. Neither is it because the ex-combatants are primarily seeking yet another war to fight. Ex-combatants are part of these structures because of their potential to provide a livelihood. The postwar rebel networks can provide a social and economic safety net where few other opportunities are available. The postwar identity as an ex-combatant thereby becomes important for the individuals within such networks, and it entails advantages as well as disadvantages. Negative perceptions are clearly attached to the ex-combatant identity, perceptions that are not easily escaped. Ex-combatants are seen as violent and unpredictable. And for some the stigmatization has been too much to bear, and hiding their combatant past has been the only way of coping. But for my informants, the ex-combatant identity, despite the difficulties ensuing from being categorized as such, has been the factor that has granted them access to work opportunities.

Working with informal security may not be what most ex-combatants dream of, but with a background as a rebel it is within this field they seem to have the most realistic opportunities for making a living. The ex-combatant identity is important because in a marginalized postwar society people need to play with what they have. For these individuals a mere civilian identity, even though this would imply less risk of stigmatization, would not be beneficial from a livelihood perspective. The ex-combatant identity is, therefore, for better or for worse, the very element that may provide individuals in postwar rebel networks with a role in civil society and enable a transformation in which they have the potential to evolve from perpetrators to protectors.

NOTES

Introduction. Liberia

1. To protect the identity of my informants, pseudonyms are used throughout this book.

2. See Adebajo 2002b for an analysis of the failed peace agreements.

3. The most commonly used acronym for this process is DDR, understood as disarmament, demobilization, and reintegration. In the Liberian process, however, an additional *R* for rehabilitation is included. In this book I use the abbreviation DDRR when I refer to the specific Liberian case and DDR when referring to the process in general.

4. UNMIL Today 2009.

5. Richards 2005, 14.

6. Nordstrom 2004, 141.

7. For a detailed overview of the evolution of the DDR process, involved actors, objectives, and practice on the African continent from the mid-1990s, see, for example, Knight 2008.

8. The comprehensive peace agreement signed in Accra, in August 2003, represented, besides the government of Liberia and the political parties, the rebel groups: the Liberians United for Reconciliation and Democracy and the Movement for Democracy in Liberia. The postwar rebel networks I refer to here include ex-combatants from these rebel groups or other Liberian rebel movements active in the first or second civil war between 1989 and 2003. More than one hundred thousand combatants were disarmed in the subsequent DDRR process.

9. See, for example, McMullin 2013a and Kilroy 2015 for Liberian case studies on the issue. There is also a substantial body of policy-oriented literature, as well as manuals, on DDR and the practice of reintegrating ex-combatants in particular, from sources such as the World Bank, the United Nations, NGOs, and policy institutes.

10. Knight 2008, 26.

11. Munive 2016.

12. Jennings 2007, 213.

13. Bowd and Özerdem 2013.

14. I return to the issue of reintegration in the last chapter of this book, suggesting that we may need to look at the meaning of the concept in a more comprehensive way than we traditionally have, to understand postwar rebel networks in relation to their overall communities.

15. Reno 2010, 134, 135.

16. Pugel 2007.

17. Rebel groups in civil wars sometimes change status. If victorious they can, for instance, transform into government forces, as was the case with the National Patriotic Front of Liberia when Charles Taylor came to power.

18. Meagher 2005, 219, 218, 230.

19. Lourenco-Lindell 2002, 22.

20. Braathen, Bøås, and Sæther 2000, 3–4.

21. See, for example, Global Witness 2005.

22. Hoffman 2007a, 417.

23. See Jörgel and Utas 2007 for a detailed account on why most actors within formal institutions would want to keep links to actors in the informal arena hidden, as they know the importance of the official image, especially in relation to Western donors.

24. Fujii 2009, 149–150.

25. Wood 2006, 373.

26. In-depth interviews and informal conversations with Alex were conducted several times during fieldwork in February, March, and October 2009, May 2010, September and October 2011, April 2012, and February and March 2013.

27. In-depth interviews and informal conversations with Michael were conducted several times during fieldwork in September and October 2011, April 2012, and February and March 2013, and with Simon during October 2009, May 2010, September and October 2011, and April 2012.

28. In-depth interviews and informal conversations with Jacob were conducted several times during fieldwork in February and March 2013.

29. In-depth interviews and informal conversations with Malcolm were conducted several times during fieldwork in September and October 2011, April 2012, and February and March 2013.

30. In-depth interviews and informal conversations with Alpha were conducted several times during fieldwork in October 2009, September and October 2011, and April 2012.

31. In-depth interviews and informal conversations with Abraham were conducted several times during fieldwork in February and March 2013.

32. Norman 2009, 73.

33. Fujii 2009, 150.

34. Nordstrom 1997, 79–80.

35. Bernard 2006, 210, 211, 213.

36. Robben 2012, 177.

37. Fujii 2009, 151.

38. Coulter 2006, 45.

39. Persson 2005.

Chapter 1. Informal Security Provision

1. Abrahamsen and Williams 2007, 131–132.
2. Higate 2017, 2.
3. Chabal and Daloz 1999, xvii.
4. Dunn 2013, 50–51, 55, 62.
5. Clapham 1996, 6.
6. Chabal and Daloz 1999, 1.
7. Ibid., 21–22.
8. Lund 2006, 686.
9. Reno 1998, 3.
10. Ebo 2007, 54.
11. Albrecht 2017, 52.
12. Baker 2008, 6, 19.
13. Ebo 2007, 56.
14. Berdal 2012, 314–315.
15. Hill, Temin, and Pacholek 2007, 38.
16. Nordstrom 1997, 12–13.
17. Baker 2008, 45.
18. Chabal and Daloz 1999, 77–78.
19. Baker and Scheye 2007, 512–513.
20. Baker 2008, 27.
21. Berdal 2012, 317.
22. Nordstrom 2004, 144.
23. United Nations Mission.
24. International Crisis Group 2009.
25. Kantor and Persson 2011, 285.
26. Podder 2013.
27. See, for example, Ebo 2005 and Bøås and Stig 2010.
28. Utas 2008, 7.
29. Clapham 1982, 3, 6–7.
30. Utas 2008, 8–9.
31. Truth and Reconciliation Commission 2009.
32. Ebo 2005.
33. Buur and Jensen 2004, 139–140.
34. Nina 2000.
35. Pratten and Sen 2007, 6.
36. Buur and Jensen 2004, 144–145.
37. Pratten 2008, 5.
38. Heald 2005, 265–266.
39. Pratten and Sen 2007, 2.
40. Kirsch and Grätz 2010, 1.
41. Abrahams 1987, 180.
42. Chabal and Daloz 1999, 79.
43. Lund 2006, 688.
44. Abrahams 2007, 423.

45. Hoffman 2007b, 642–643.

46. Utas and Jörgel 2008, 488, 491, 502–503.

47. The cases investigated by International Crisis Group are Sierra Leone, Uganda's Teso region, South Sudan's former Western Equatoria State, and Nigeria's northeast.

48. International Crisis Group 2017.

49. Kirsch and Grätz 2010, 4.

50. Pratten and Sen 2007, 13.

51. National Commission on Disarmament 2005.

52. For a more detailed discussion on the Liberian civil wars, see, for example, Adebajo 2002c, Ellis 2007, Moran 2006, Reno 1998, and Sawyer 2005.

53. As Bøås points out, a social conflict began already when the first settlers, freed slaves from the United States, arrived in Liberia between 1822 and 1861. The group that came to be known as the Americo-Liberians declared Liberia a republic in 1847, and what Bøås describes as both a one-party and apartheid state was created as the indigenous Liberians were strongly discriminated against. In this sense, as Bøås puts it, Liberia has been at "war" with itself from the beginning of its existence as an independent state. See Bøås 2005.

54. Reno 1998.

55. Berkeley 2001, 32.

56. Ellis 2007, 56.

57. Utas 2009, 268–269.

58. Ibid., 270.

59. Utas, 2005, 142–143.

60. Ibid., 150–151.

61. Hoffman 2007a, 417, 402.

62. Bøås and Hatløy 2008, 45, 50.

63. See, for example, Landmine Action 2006 and Global Witness 2005.

64. Republic of Liberia 2008, 56.

65. Global Witness 2005, 6, 12.

66. Abrahams 1987, 196.

67. Bledsoe 1990, 75.

Chapter 2. Regional Wars and Recycled Rebels

1. This chapter was written based on several interviews and conversations with Michael, Simon, and Jacob during periods of fieldwork in Liberia between 2009 and 2013. My first meeting with Simon was in 2009, while my first meeting with Michael was in 2011. But Michael is the one of my three informants mentioned in this chapter with whom I have had the most frequent contact during the years. Jacob and I met for the first time in 2013.

2. The Mano River region refers to the West African countries of Liberia, Sierra Leone, and Guinea. The actual Mano River originates in the Guinea highlands and forms a border between Liberia and Sierra Leone. In the International Association for Economic Cooperation the Mano River Union Côte d'Ivoire is also included.

3. Ellis 2007, 55–56.

4. Sawyer 2005, 18–19.

5. Adebajo 2002c, 20, 26.

6. Ibid., 20, 30.

7. Ellis 1998, 157.

8. Adebajo 2002a, 47.

9. Charles Dent was later to become a top commander in the emerging rebel group the Liberians United for Reconciliation and Democracy and chief of staff. Dent was killed in battle in 2001, however, and the top military position was passed to Prince Seo. For more details on LURD leadership and chains of command, see, for example, Brabazon 2003.

10. For more details on the peace treaty, see United Nations Security Council 1995.

11. Adebajo 2002c, 183.

12. Harris 2012, 153–154, 157.

13. For more information on the Camp Johnson Road fighting in 1998, see, for example, International Crisis Group 2002, 8; and Adebajo 2002c, 233.

14. Moran 2006, 123.

15. International Crisis Group 2002, 8.

16. Lidow 2016, 108.

17. See, for example, UN Office for Coordination 2002.

18. Peters 2011, 64–65, 76–77.

19. Hoffman 2011, 34.

20. Ibid., 174–175.

21. For more information on the January 6, 1999, rebel invasion and how the Civil Defence Forces was mobilized in support of the Sierra Leonean government, see Hoffman 2011, 47. Utas and Jörgel 2008 have described how the Kabbah government also strategically used former antagonists such as the West Side Boys rebels to fight the Armed Forces Revolutionary Council / Revolutionary United Front attack. But less is known and written about how Liberian fighters such as Michael and Simon were used by the Sierra Leonean authorities during this part of the war.

22. See, for example, Adebajo 2002a, 69.

23. BBC News 2001.

24. See, for example, International Crisis Group 2003, 11; and BBC News 2000.

25. The exact details of how Aisha Conneh came to win her influential and powerful position by President Conté's side we may never know. But many other statements, often less detailed, in general correspond with the account reported to me by Michael. A 2004 International Crisis Group report, for example, states that Aisha Conneh, by using her fortune-telling skills, forecasted a coup attempt against Conté in 1996, enabling her to replace Conté's previous soothsayer; see page 10.

26. Reno 2007, 69–70.

27. International Crisis Group 2003, 11, 12.

28. This information given to me by Michael also corresponds with findings made by Käihkö in his research on the evolvement of Liberians United for Reconciliation and Democracy, as a statement from an interviewed top-level commander from the rebel movement confirms that arrested Liberians were released by the Sierra Leonean government and at least given tacit support following a request by Guinean officials. See Käihkö 2015, 255.

29. Lidow 2016, 145.

30. Brabazon 2003, 6, 9–10.

31. Käihkö 2015.
32. Berdal 1996, 5
33. Themnér 2011, 1–2.
34. Berdal 1996, 5.
35. Themnér 2011, 7.
36. Hoffman 2011, 27.
37. Reno 2007, 70, 75.
38. Bøås and Dunn 2007, 30.

Chapter 3. From Rebels to Security Providers

1. United Nations Mission 2006, 78.
2. Global Witness 2006, 10.
3. Joint Government of Liberia 2006, 1, 9.
4. Tamagnini 2009.
5. Ibid., 18.
6. This chapter has been written partly based on several interviews and conversations that I have had mainly with Michael in Monrovia, during September and October 2011 and April 2012.
7. International Crisis Group 2011, 1.
8. Global Witness 2006, 10.
9. Tamagnini 2009, 17.
10. I have chosen not to present the three main commanders of the monitors by name. But one of the two main deputies, is hereafter referred to as "Alpha."
11. This section has been written partly based on several conversations that I had mainly with Alpha in Bong County, Liberia, during October 2009 and September 2011.
12. The twin brother of Alpha was a general in the National Patriotic Front of Liberia, which included Taylor's Gbaranga executive mansion commander, Cassius Jacobs. In fear of internal competition, Taylor ordered his execution in 1994.
13. Conversation with a former Plantation Protection Department member, Monrovia, October 2009.
14. Interview with Boakai Sirleaf, Guthrie Rubber Plantation, October 2009.
15. This section is based on fieldwork in and around the plantation area and interviews and personal communication with Alpha and other plantation workers, in Bong County, Liberia, in September 2011.
16. Personal communication with a Sime Darby Security force member, Bong County, Liberia, September 2011.
17. Berdal and Zaum 2013, 4–5.
18. Reno 1998, 79–80.
19. Nordstrom 2004, 211.
20. Jörgel and Utas 2007, 70–71.

Chapter 4. Nothing Left for the Losers in Winner-Takes-All Elections

1. To protect the identities of my informants, Michael's real name or current employer is not presented in this chapter.
2. United Nations Disarmament, n.d.

3. For a more detailed discussion on the challenges and insecurities during postconflict elections, see, for example, Lyons 2005, Obi 2007, and Harris 2012.

4. This chapter was written based on several interviews and personal conversations, predominately with Alex and Michael, during periods of fieldwork between 2009 and 2013.

5. Reilly 2013, 33.

6. See, for example, Mehler 2007, Laakso 2007, and Höglund 2010.

7. Moran 2006, 1, 6.

8. Harris and Lewis 2013, 81.

9. Lyons 1998, 232.

10. Lyons 2005, 131.

11. Reno 2011, 20.

12. Reilly 2013, 43.

13. Harris 2012, 161.

14. Ibid.

15. Sawyer 2008, 199.

16. Adolphus Dolo was also known as "General Peanut Butter" during the war.

17. Sawyer 2008, 195.

18. For more details and information on Liberian vigilantes, see Kantor and Persson 2011.

19. Personal communication with a community member where the vigilante group had been active in Sinkor, Monrovia, April 2012.

20. "Gone into politics" is a common expression among my informants to explain their partaking primarily as informal security providers during the 2011 elections.

21. See, for example, BBC News 2005.

22. For a detailed analysis of the 2005 Liberian elections, see, for example, Harris 2012.

23. Even though few ex-combatants have had the ability to study at the university, some of the more influential former commanders appear to have had degrees in criminal justice sponsored by politicians or other influential actors. Why the trend has been to obtain a degree in criminal justice specifically among more successful ex-combatants I can only speculate. This could be seen as a way to make use of previously acquired knowledge in security, a field many of them know well from years in battle, and an attempt to secure a future position on the formal side of the Liberian security system, when many other sectors are closed to them.

24. This section is based mainly on personal communication and interviews with Michael in September and October 2011 and April 2012. But much of the information in the chapter is also based on several interviews and meetings with ex-combatants and workers at Guthrie, Bomi County, between the years of 2010 and 2012.

25. National Election Commission 2011b.

26. See, for example, BBC News 2011 and Utas 2012.

27. National Election Commission 2011a.

28. Christensen and Utas 2008, 521–522, 523, 528.

29. Conteh and Harris 2014, 67.

30. Hoffman 2011, 192.

31. Laakso 2007, 228.

32. Lyons 2005, 41.

33. Jennings 2008, 6.

34. Munive 2010, 323, 330, 333.

35. McMullin 2013b.

36. Mitton 2009, 173.

37. Bøås and Utas 2014.

Chapter 5. Once a Rebel, Always a Rebel?

1. Ever since international efforts to end prolonged conflicts after the Cold War began to include more focused initiatives to deal with the situation of ex-combatants, a growing body of literature has been devoted to challenges faced by them or the societies they are expected to be reintegrated into. Policy-oriented analyses of such challenges have over the years come from different United Nations organizations, humanitarian NGOs, and policy institutes. Academic research on the topic can be found mainly within the fields of political sciences and anthropology. These analyses of the situation of ex-combatants often have a particular focus on DDR programs. But less is known about the challenges faced by ex-combatants after and beyond such programs and international peace-building initiatives.

2. Hardgrove 2017, 103.

3. Ngozi Adichie 2009.

4. Atkinson 1996.

5. Ibid.

6. Ellis 2007, 17–18.

7. Ibid., 18.

8. Richards 1996, xv–xvii.

9. This book does not provide a specific analysis of the complex and diverging reasons behind the combatants' decision to take part in the war. But these individual decisions were, of course, not taken in a vacuum but relate to the overall root social, economic, and security causes of the war. For a deeper discussion on the motives and strategies behind the type of violence used in the West African wars, see, for example, Keen 2008 for an analysis on why the violence often intended to be profoundly humiliating; Utas and Jörgel 2008 for an analysis on the use of extreme violence and unorthodox appearance as military tools; and Mitton 2013 for an analysis on the violence as irrational but inspired and utilized for rational ends.

10. McMullin 2013b.

11. Bolten 2012.

12. Maringira 2013.

13. Bjarnesen 2014.

14. The crucial role of women in war is easily forgotten when conflict analyses lack a gender perspective. The groundbreaking researcher Cynthia Enloe has inspired scholars in the field of political science and beyond to always simply ask, "Where are the women?" in the study of politics and war. She was one of the first to look for women in the real landscape of international politics; see Enloe 1989. Inspired by this way of thinking, in this chapter I investigate the apparent lack of women in postwar rebel networks in Liberia.

15. See, for example, Sherif 2008, 26.

16. Coulter, Persson, and Utas 2012, 63.

17. Coulter, Persson, and Utas 2008, 5.

18. Ibid., 35.

19. McKay and Mazurana 2004, 44.

20. See, for example, Jennings 2009 and Baisini 2013.

21. Coulter 2006, 2009, 14.

22. Persson 2005.

23. MacKenzie 2012, 90–91.

24. Specht 2006, 88.

25. *Aftonbladet* 2010; Vice 2010; Utas, Persson, and Käihkö 2010.

26. This section is based on fieldwork in the Monrovian neighborhood West Point and personal communication with Abraham during February and March 2013.

27. Newell 2006, 181.

28. Ibid., 184.

29. Ibid., 186–187, 189–190.

30. Jensen 2007, 105–106.

31. Early Warning Early Response 2012, 4.

32. Findings within the 2012 Early Warning Early Response Working Group research report support this point, as community members of West Point in their surveys were overwhelmingly positive toward the area's vigilante and community defense groups because they were seen to be plugging gaps in the formal security system; see page 31.

33. Shepler 2014.

34. This section has been written based on several conversations with Malcolm in Monrovia, particularly during February and March 2013 but also in September and October 2011 and April 2012.

35. This section has been written based on several conversations with Jacob in Monrovia, during February and March 2013.

36. Mitton 2013, 321, 323, 325.

37. McMullin 2013b, 395.

Conclusion. Repurposed Rebels

1. Berdal and Ucko 2009, 2.

2. United Nations Disarmament, n.d.

3. Nzekani Zena 2013.

4. United Nations General Assembly 2006.

5. See, for example, Nezam and Alexandre 2009 and Rufer 2005, 10.

6. De Vries and Wiegink 2011, 41–43.

7. Utas has argued that remarginalization rather than reintegration appeared to be the norm for a large portion of ex-combatants after the war. Since many of the Liberian rebels initially came from the already marginalized and dissatisfied urban youth, remarginalization and not reintegration was the natural outcome. See Utas 2005, 150.

8. An important exception is Reno's 2010 research on the transformation of West African militia networks into commercial organizations and community-based NGOs,

for example. Here Reno shows how networks of former fighters can find economic niches in which to turn wartime bonds to commercial advantages. But the transformation of wartime networks, as presented in the research for this book, has been limited mainly to security-related activities. The situation at the Guthrie Rubber Plantation nonetheless differs in this aspect, as the postwar rebel networks activities there initially could be seen as a commercial organization in the sense Reno describes them.

9. Human Rights Watch 2005, 11.

10. See Hoffman 2011.

11. Themnér 2011, 161–162.

12. Christensen 2013, 5.

13. Ibid., 9.

14. Utas, Themnér, and Lindberg 2014.

REFERENCES

Abrahams, Ray. 1987. "Sungusungu: Village Vigilante Groups in Tanzania." *African Affairs* 86, no. 343: 179–196.

———. 2007. "Some Thoughts on the Comparative Study of Vigilantism." In Ed. Pratten and Sen 2007, 419–442.

Abrahamsen, Rita, and Michael C. Williams. 2007. "Introduction: The Privatisation and Globalisation of Security in Africa." *International Relations* 21, no. 2: 131–141.

Adebajo, Adekeye. 2002a. *Building Peace in West Africa: Liberia, Sierra Leone and Guinea-Bissau.* Boulder, Colo.: Rienner.

———. 2002b. "Liberia: A Warlord's Peace." In *Ending Civil Wars: The Implementation of Peace Agreements*, edited by Stephen John Stedman, Donald Rothchild, and Elizabeth M. Cousens, 599–630. Boulder, Colo.: Rienner.

———. 2002c. *Liberia's Civil War: Nigeria, ECOMOG and Regional Security in West Africa.* Boulder, Colo.: Rienner.

Aftonbladet. 2010. "Frihetens land: Helvetet på jorden [The land of freedom: Hell on earth]." March 23. https://www.aftonbladet.se/nyheter/a/a2vlBd/frihetens-land--helvetet-pa-jorden.

Albrecht, Peter. 2017. "Private Security beyond the Private Sector: Community Policing and Secret Societies in Sierra Leone." In Higate 2017, 52–69.

Atkinson, Philippa. 1996. "The Liberian Civil War: Images and Reality." *Contemporary Politics* 2, no. 1: 79–88.

Baisini, Helen S. A. 2013. "Gendering Mainstreaming Unraveled: The Case of *DDRR* in Liberia." *International Interactions* 39, no. 4: 535–557.

Baker, Bruce. 2008. *Multi-choice Policing in Africa.* Uppsala, Sweden: Nordic Africa Institute.

Baker, Bruce, and Eric Scheye. 2007. "Multi-layered Justice and Security Delivery in Post-conflict and Fragile States." *Conflict, Security and Development* 7, no. 4: 503–508.

Basedau, Matthias, Gero Erdmann, and Andreas Mehler, eds. 2007. *Votes, Money and Violence: Political Parties and Elections in Sub-Saharan Africa.* Uppsala, Sweden: Nordic Africa Institute.

BBC News. 2000. "Guinea Rebel Attacks Increase Tensions." September 18. http://news
.bbc.co.uk/2/hi/africa/930191.stm.
———. 2001. "The Guinea Conflict Explained." February 13. http://news.bbc.co.uk/2/hi
/africa/1167811.stm.
———. 2005. "Liberian Poll: The Main Contenders." October 5. http://news.bbc.co.uk/2
/hi/africa/4309302.stm.
———. 2011. "Liberia Election: CDC Monrovia Protest Turns Deadly." November 7.
http://www.bbc.co.uk/news/world-africa-15624471.
Berdal, Mats. 1996. *Disarmament and Demobilisation after Civil Wars: Arms, Soldiers
and the Termination of Armed Conflicts*. Adelphi Papers 303. Oxford: Oxford University Press.
———. 2012. "Reflections on Post-war Violence and Peacebuilding." In *The Peace in
Between: Post-war Violence and Peacebuilding*, edited by in Astri Suhrke and Mats
Berdal, 309–326. New York: Routledge.
Berdal, Mats, and David H. Ucko, eds. 2009. *Reintegrating Armed Groups after Conflict:
Politics, Violence and Transition*. New York: Routledge.
Berdal, Mats, and Dominik Zaum. 2013. *Political Economy of Statebuilding: Power after
Peace*. New York: Routledge.
Berkeley, Bill. 2001. *The Graves Are Not Yet Full: Race, Tribe and Power in the Heart of
Africa*. New York: Basic Books.
Bernard, H. Russell. 2006. *Research Methods in Anthropology: Qualitative and Quantitative Approaches*. 4th ed. Lanham, Md.: AltaMira.
Bjarnesen, Jesper. 2014. "Social Branding in Urban Burkina Faso." *Nordic Journal of
African Studies* 23, no. 2: 83–99.
Bledsoe, Caroline. 1990. "'No Success without Struggle': Social Mobility and Hardship
for Foster Children in Sierra Leone." *Man, n.s.*, 25, no. 1: 70–88.
Bøås, Morten. 2005. "The Liberian Civil War: New War/Old War?" *Global Security* 19,
no. 1: 73–88.
Bøås, Morten, and Kevin C. Dunn. 2007. *African Guerrillas: Raging against the
Machine*. Boulder, Colo.: Rienner.
Bøås, Morten, and Anne Hatløy. 2008. "Getting In, Getting Out: Militia Membership
and Prospects for Re-integration in Post-war Liberia." *Modern African Studies* 46,
no. 1: 35–55.
Bøås, Morten, and Karianne Stig. 2010. "Security Sector Reform in Liberia: An Uneven
Partnership without Local Ownership." *Journal of Intervention and Statebuilding* 4,
no. 3: 285–303.
Bøås, Morten, and Mats Utas. 2014. "The Political Landscape of Postwar Liberia:
Reflections on National Reconciliation and Elections." *Africa Today* 60, no. 4: 47–65.
Bolten, Catherine. 2012. "'We Have Been Sensitized': Ex-combatants, Marginalization,
and Youth in Postwar Sierra Leone." *American Anthropologist* 114, no. 3: 496–508.
Bowd, Richard, and Alpaslan Özerdem. 2013. "How to Assess Social Reintegration of
Ex-combatants." *Journal of Intervention and Statebuilding* 7, no. 4: 453–475.
Braathen, Einar, Morten Bøås, and Gjermund Sæther. 2000. "*Ethnicity Kills? The Politics of War, Peace and Ethnicity in Sub-Saharan Africa*." New York: Macmillan.
Brabazon, James. 2003. "Liberia: Liberians United for Reconciliation and Democracy (LURD)." Briefing Paper 1. Royal Institute of International Affairs: Africa

Programme, February. https://www.chathamhouse.org/sites/default/files/public/Research/Africa/brabazon_bp.pdf.

Buur, Lars, and Steffen Jensen. 2004. "Vigilantism and the Policing of Everyday Life in South Africa." *Africa* 78, no. 1: 139–152.

Chabal, Patrick, and Jean-Pascal Daloz. 1999. *Africa Works: Disorder as Political Instrument*. Bloomington: Indiana University Press.

Christensen, Maya Mynster. 2013. "Shadow Soldering: Mobilisation, Militarisation and the Politics of Global Security in Sierra Leone." PhD dissertation, University of Copenhagen.

Christensen, Maya Mynster, and Mats Utas. 2008. "Mercenaries of Democracy: The 'Politricks' of Remobilized Combatants in the 2007 General Elections, Sierra Leone." *African Affairs* 107, no. 429: 515–539.

Clapham, Christopher. 1982. *Private Patronage and Public Power: Political Clientelism in the Modern State*. New York: Palgrave Macmillan.

———. 1996. *Africa and the International System: The Politics of State Survival*. Cambridge: Cambridge University Press.

Conteh, Felix M., and David Harris. 2014. "Swings and Roundabouts: The Vagaries of Democratic Consolidation and 'Electoral Rituals' in Sierra Leone." *Critical African Studies* 6 no. 1: 57–70.

Coulter, Chris. 2006. "Being a Bush Wife: Women's Lives through War and Peace in Northern Sierra Leone." PhD dissertation, Uppsala University.

———. 2009. *Bush Wives and Girl Soldiers: Women's Lives through War and Peace in Sierra Leone*. Ithaca, N.Y.: Cornell University Press.

Coulter, Chris, Mariam Persson, and Mats Utas. 2008. *Young Female Fighters in African Wars: Conflict and Its Consequences*. Uppsala Sweden: Nordic Africa Institute.

———. 2012. "Young Women in African Wars." In *Beyond "Gender and Stir": Reflections on Gender and SSR in the Aftermath of African Conflicts*, edited by Maria Eriksson Baaz and Mats Utas, 63–71. Uppsala, Sweden: Nordic Africa Institute.

De Vries, Hugo, and Nikkie Wiegink. 2011. "Breaking Up and Going Home? Contesting Two Assumptions in the Demobilization and Reintegration of Former Combatants." *International Peacekeeping* 18, no. 1: 38–51.

Dunn, Kevin C. 2013. "MadLib #32: The (Blank) African State: Rethinking the Sovereign State in International Relations Theory." In *Africa's Challenge to International Relations Theory*, edited by Kevin C. Dunn and Timothy M. Shaw, 46–63. New York: Palgrave Macmillan.

Early Warning Early Response Working Group. 2012. "Security, Environment and Opportunities in West Point: A Community Led Urban Early-Warning and Empowerment Project." https://lavotest.files.wordpress.com/2012/07/security-environment-and-opportunities-in-west-point-2012-pdf-1-89-mb.pdf.

Ebo, Adedeji. 2005. "Challenges and Opportunities of Security Sector Reform in Post-conflict Liberia." Occasional Paper 9. Geneva Centre for the Democratic Control of Armed Forces, December. https://www.files.ethz.ch/isn/15054/occasional_9.pdf.

———. 2007. "Non-state Actors, Peacebuilding and Security Governance in West Africa: Beyond Commercialisation." *Journal of Peacebuilding and Development* 3, no. 2: 53–69.

Ellis, Stephen. 1998. "Liberia's Warlord Insurgency." In *African Guerrillas*, edited by Christopher Clapham, 155–171. Melton, U.K.: Currey.

———. 2007. *The Mask of Anarchy: The Destruction of Liberia and the Religious Dimensions of an African Civil War*. 2nd ed. New York: New York University Press.

Enloe, Cynthia. 1989. *Bananas, Beaches and Bases: Making Feminist Sense of International Politics*. Berkeley: University of California Press.

Fujii, Lee Ann. 2009. "Interpreting Truth and Lies in the Stories of Conflict and Violence." In Sriram et al. 2009, 147–162.

Global Witness. 2005. "Timber, Taylor, Soldier, Spy: How Liberia's Uncontrolled Resource Exploitation, Charles Taylor's Manipulation and the Re-recruitment of Ex-combatants Are Threatening Regional Peace." June 15. https://www.globalwitness.org/en/archive/timber-taylor-soldier-spy/.

———. 2006. "Cautiously Optimistic: The Case for Maintaining Sanctions in Liberia." Global Witness, June. https://reliefweb.int/sites/reliefweb.int/files/resources/81E1FB35576BCC9F49257181000E7BB8-gb-lib-1jun.pdf.

Hardgrove, Abby. 2017. *Life after Guns: Reciprocity and Respect among Young Men in Liberia*. New York: Rutgers University Press.

Harris, David. 2012. *Civil War and Democracy in West Africa: Conflict Resolution, Elections and Justice in Sierra Leone and Liberia*. London: Tauris.

Harris, David, and Tereza Lewis. 2013. "Liberia in 2011: Still Ploughing Its Own Democratic Furrow?" *Commonwealth and Comparative Politics* 51, no. 1: 76–96.

Heald, Suzette. 2005. "State, Law, and Vigilantism in Northern Tanzania." *African Affairs* 105, no. 419: 256–283.

Higate, Paul, ed. 2017. *Private Security in Africa: From Global Assemblage to the Everyday*. London: Zed Books.

Hill, Richard, Jonathan Temin, and Lisa Pacholek. 2007. "Building Security Where There Is No Security." *Journal of Peacebuilding and Development* 3, no. 2: 38–52.

Hoffman, Danny. 2007a. "The City as Barracks: Freetown, Monrovia, and the Organization of Violence in Postcolonial African Cities." *Cultural Anthropology* 22, no. 3: 400–428.

———. 2007b. "The Meaning of a Militia: Understanding the Civil Defence Forces of Sierra Leone." *African Affairs* 106, no. 425: 639–662.

———. 2011. *The War Machines: Young Men and Violence in Sierra Leone and Liberia*. Durham: Duke University Press.

Höglund, Kristine. 2010. "Electoral Violence in Conflict-Ridden Societies: Concepts, Causes, and Consequences." *Terrorism and Political Violence* 21, no. 3: 412–427.

Human Rights Watch. 2005. "Youth, Poverty and Blood: The Lethal Legacy of West Africa's Regional Warriors." April 13. https://www.hrw.org/report/2005/04/13/youth-poverty-and-blood/lethal-legacy-west-africas-regional-warriors.

International Crisis Group. 2002. "Liberia: The Key to Ending Regional Instability." *Africa Report* 43. April 24. https://www.crisisgroup.org/africa/west-africa/liberia/liberia-key-ending-regional-instability.

———. 2003. "Tackling Liberia: The Eye of the Regional Storm." *Africa Report* 62. April 30. https://www.crisisgroup.org/africa/west-africa/liberia/tackling-liberia-eye-regional-storm.

———. 2004. "Rebuilding Liberia: Prospects and Perils." *Africa Report* 75 January 30. https://www.crisisgroup.org/africa/west-africa/liberia/rebuilding-liberia-prospects -and-perils.

———. 2009. "Liberia: Uneven Progress in the Security Sector Reform." *Africa Report* 148. January 13. https://www.crisisgroup.org/africa/west-africa/liberia/liberia -uneven-progress-security-sector-reform.

———. 2011. "Liberia: How Sustainable Is the Recovery." *Africa Report* 177. August 19. https://www.crisisgroup.org/africa/west-africa/liberia/liberia-how-sustainable -recovery.

———. 2017. "Double-Edged Sword, Vigilantes in African Counter-insurgencies." *Africa Report* 251. September 7. https://www.crisisgroup.org/africa/west-africa/sierra-leone /251-double-edged-sword-vigilantes-african-counter-insurgencies.

Jennings, Kathleen M. 2007. "The Struggle to Satisfy: DDR through the Eyes of Ex-combatants in Liberia." *International Peacekeeping* 14, no. 2: 204–218.

———. 2008. "Seeing DDR from Below: Challenges and Dilemmas Raised by the Experience of Ex-combatants in Liberia." Fafo-Report 2008:03. https://fafo.no/media /com_netsukii/20045.pdf.

———. 2009. "The Political Economy of DDR in Liberia: A Gendered Critique." Conflict, Security and Development 9, no. 4: 475–494.

Jensen, Steffen. 2007. "Security and Violence on the Frontier of the State." In *Violence and Non-violence in Africa*, edited by Paul Ahluwalia, Louise Bethlehem, and Ruth Ginio, 103–123. New York: Routledge.

Joint Government of Liberia, United Nations Rubber Plantations Task Force. 2006. "Report Presented to H. E. Mrs. Ellen Johnson Sirleaf, President of Liberia, 23 May 2006." http://www.laborrights.org/files/Rubber_TF_Report.pdf (site discontinued).

Jörgel, Magnus, and Mats Utas. 2007. *The Mano River Basin Area: Formal and Informal Security Providers in Liberia, Guinea and Sierra Leone*. Stockholm: Swedish Defence Research Agency. http://www.asclibrary.nl/docs/370/157/370157273.pdf.

Käihkö, Ilmari. 2015. "'Taylor Must Go': The Strategy of the Liberians United for Reconciliation and Democracy." *Small Wars and Insurgencies* 26, no. 2: 248–270.

Kantor, Ana, and Mariam Persson. 2011. "Liberian Vigilantes: Informal Security Provision on the Margins of Security Sector Reform." In *The Politics of Security Sector Reform: Challenges and Opportunities for the European Union's Global Role*, edited by Magnus Ekengren and Greg Simons, 273–304. Farnham, U.K.: Ashgate.

Kaplan, Robert. 1994. "The Coming Anarchy: How Scarcity, Crime, Overpopulation, Tribalism, and Disease Are Rapidly Destroying the Social Fabric of Our Planet." *Atlantic Monthly* 273, no. 2. https://www.theatlantic.com/magazine/archive/1994/02 /the-coming-anarchy/304670/.

Keen, David. 2008. *Complex Emergencies*. Cambridge, U.K.: Polity.

Kilroy, Walt. 2015. *Reintegration of Ex-combatants after Conflict: Participatory Approaches in Sierra Leone and Liberia*. New York: Palgrave Macmillan.

Kirsch, Thomas G., and Tilo Grätz, eds. 2010. *Domesticating Vigilantism in Africa*. Melton, U.K.: Currey.

Knight, W. Andy. 2008. "Disarmament, Demobilization, and Reintegration and Post-conflict Peacebuilding in Africa: An Overview." *African Security* 1, no. 1: 24–52.

Laakso, Liisa. 2007. "Insights into Electoral Violence in Africa." In Basedau, Erdmann, and Mehler 2007, 224–252.

Landmine Action. 2006. *Feasibility Study into the Rehabilitation and Reintegration of Unregistered Ex-combatants, Guthrie Rubber Plantation, Liberia*. London: Department for International Development. https://www.aoav.org.uk/wp-content /uploads/2013/06/Vulnerable-Youth-Feasibility-Study-September-December -2006.pdf.

Lidow, Nicholai Hart. 2016. *Violent Order: Understanding Rebel Governance through Liberia's Civil War*. Cambridge: Cambridge University Press.

Lourenco-Lindell, Ilda. 2002. *Walking the Tight Rope: Informal Livelihoods and Social Networks in a West-African City*. Stockholm: Almqvist and Wiksell International.

Lund, Christian. 2006. "Twilight Institutions: Public Authority and Local Politics in Africa." *Development and Change* 37, no. 4: 685–705.

Lyons, Terrence. 1998. "Liberia's Path from Anarchy to Elections." *Current History* 97, no. 619: 229–233.

———. 2005. *Demilitarizing Politics: Elections and the Uncertain Road to Peace*. Boulder, Colo.: Rienner.

MacKenzie, Megan H. 2012. *Female Soldiers in Sierra Leone: Sex, Security, and Post-conflict Development*. New York: New York University Press.

Maringira, Godfrey. 2013. *The Persistence of Military Identities among Ex-combatants in South Africa*. With Jasmina Brankovic. Cape Town: Centre for Study of Violence and Reconciliation/Centre for Humanities Research.

McKay, Susan, and Dyan Mazurana. 2004. *Where Are the Girls? Girls in Fighting Forces in Northern Uganda, Sierra Leone and Mozambique: Their Lives during and after War*. Montreal: Rights and Democracy.

McMullin, Jaremey. 2013a. *Ex-combatants and the Post-conflict State: Challenges of Reintegration*. New York: Palgrave Macmillan.

———. 2013b. "Integration or Separation? The Stigmatisation of Ex-combatants after War." *Review of International Studies* 39: 385–414.

Meagher, Kate. 2005. "Social Capital or Analytical Liability? Social Networks and African Informal Economies." *Global Networks* 5, no. 3: 217–238.

Mehler, Andreas. 2007. "Political Parties and Violence in Africa: Systematic Reflections against Empirical Background." In Basedau, Erdmann, and Mehler 2007, 194–223.

Mitton, Kieran. 2009. "Engaging with Disengagement: The Political Reintegration of Sierra Leone's Revolutionary United Front." In Berdal and Ucko 2009, 172–198.

———. 2013. "Where Is the War? Explaining Peace in Sierra Leone." *International Peacekeeping* 20, no. 3: 321–337.

Moran, Mary H. 2006. *Liberia: The Violence of Democracy*. Philadelphia: University of Pennsylvania Press.

Munive, Jairo. 2010. "The Army of 'Unemployed' Young People." *Nordic Journal of Youth Research* 18, no. 3: 321–338.

———. 2016. "Beyond Disarmament, Demobilization and Reintegration of Ex-combatants." Oxford Research Group, May 25. https://www.oxfordresearchgroup .org.uk/Blog/beyond-disarmament-demobilization-and-reintegration-of-ex -combatants.

National Commission on Disarmament, Demobilization, Rehabilitation and Reintegration. 2005. "DDRR Consolidated Report Phase 1, 2 and 3." January 16. https://reliefweb.int/sites/reliefweb.int/files/resources/Full_Report_1258.pdf.

National Election Commission. 2011a. "Bomi County." *Liberia: 2011 Presidential and Legislative Elections.* November 15. http://www.necliberia.org/results2011/county_3_1.html.

———. 2011b. "National Tally." *Liberia: 2011 Presidential and Legislative Elections,* November 15. http://www.necliberia.org/results2011/.

Newell, Sasha. 2006. "Estranged Belongings: A Moral Economy if Theft in Abidjan, Côte d'Ivoire." *Anthropological Theory* 6, no. 2: 179–203.

Nezam, Taies, and Marc Alexandre. 2009. "Disarmament, Demobilization and Reintegration." *Social Development Department, Conflict, Crime and Violence,* no. 119. February. http://siteresources.worldbank.org/EXTSOCIALDEVELOPMENT/Resources/244362-1164107274725/DDRFinal3-print.pdf.

Ngozi Adichie, Chimamanda. 2009. "The Danger of a Single Story." TED Talks, October 7. https://www.youtube.com/watch?v=D9Ihs241zeg.

Nina, Daniel. 2000. "Dirty Harry Is Back: Vigilantism in South Africa; The (Re)emergence of 'Good' and 'Bad' Community." *African Security Review* 9, no. 1: 18–28.

Nordstrom, Carolyn. 1997. *A Different Kind of War Story.* Philadelphia: University of Pennsylvania Press.

———. 2004. *Shadows of War: Violence, Power and International Profiteering in the Twenty-First Century.* Berkeley: University of California Press.

Norman, Julie. 2009. "Got Trust? The Challenge of Gaining Access in Conflict Zones." In Sriram et al. 2009, 71–90.

Nzekani Zena, Prosper. 2013. "The Lessons and Limits of DDR in Africa." *Africa Security Brief* 24. January. https://pdfs.semanticscholar.org/c770/f6837aec087fd62c660e6ae831a7b0293cc7.pdf.

Obi, Cyril. 2007. "Introduction: Elections and the Challenge of Post-conflict Democratisation in West Africa." *African Journal of International Affairs* 10, nos. 1–2: 1–12.

Persson, Mariam. 2005. *"In Their Eyes We'll Always be Rebels": A Minor Field Study of Female Ex-combatants in Sierra Leone.* Minor Field Study 50. Uppsala: Uppsala University, Development Studies.

Peters, Krijn. 2011. *War and the Crisis of Youth in Sierra Leone.* Cambridge: Cambridge University Press.

Podder, Sukanya. 2013. "Bridging the 'Conceptual-Contextual' Divide: Security Sector Reform in Liberia and UNMIL Transition." *Journal of Intervention and Statebuilding* 7, no. 3: 353–380.

Pratten, David. 2008. "The Politics of Protection: Perspectives on Vigilantism in Nigeria." *Africa* 78, no. 1: 1–15.

Pratten, David, and Atreyee Sen. 2007. *Global Vigilantes.* London: HURST.

Pugel, James. 2007. *What the Fighters Say: A Survey of Ex-combatants in Liberia.* United Nations Development Programme, February–March 2006. http://www.operationspaix.net/DATA/DOCUMENT/904~v~What_the_Fighters_Say__A_Survey_of_Ex-combatants_in_Liberia.pdf.

Reilly, Benjamin. 2013. "Elections and Post-conflict Political Development." In Berdal and Zaum 2013, 33–47.

Reno, William. 1998. *Warlord Politics and African States*. Boulder, Colo.: Rienner.

———. 2007. "Liberia: The LURDs of the New Church." In Bøås and Dunn 2007, 69–80.

———. 2010. "Transforming West African Militia Networks for Postwar Recovery." In *Troubled Regions and Failing States: The Clustering and Contagion of Armed Conflict*, edited by Kristian Berg, 127–149. Bingley, U.K.: Emerald.

———. 2011. *Warfare in Independent Africa: New Approaches to African History*. Cambridge: Cambridge University Press.

Republic of Liberia. 2008. *Liberia: Poverty Reduction Strategy*. IMF Country Report 08/219. International Monetary Fund. July. https://www.imf.org/external/pubs/ft/scr/2008/cr08219.pdf.

Richards, Paul. 1996. *Fighting for the Rain Forest: War, Youth and Resources in Sierra Leone*. Melton, U.K.: Currey.

———. 2005. *No Peace, No War: An Anthropology of Contemporary Armed Conflicts*. Athens: Ohio University Press.

Robben, Antonius. 2012. "The Politics of Truth and Emotion among Victims and Perpetrators of Violence." In *Ethnographic Fieldwork: An Anthropological Reader*, edited by Antonius Robben and Jeffery Sluka, 175–190. Hoboken, N.J.: Wiley-Blackwell.

Rufer, Reto. 2005. "Disarmament, Demobilisation and Reintegration (DDR): Conceptual Approaches, Specific Settings, Practical Experiences." Geneva Centre for the Democratic Control of Armed Forces (DCAF). https://dcaf.ch/sites/default/files/publications/documents/RUFER_final.pdf.

Sawyer, Amos. 2005. *Beyond Plunder: Towards Democratic Governance in Liberia*. Boulder, Colo.: Rienner.

———. 2008. "Emerging Patterns in Liberia's Post-conflict Politics: Observations from the 2005 Elections." *African Affairs* 107, no. 427: 177–199.

Shepler, Susan. 2014. "The Ebola Virus and the Vampire State." *Mats Utas*, July 21. https://matsutas.wordpress.com/2014/07/21/the-ebola-virus-and-the-vampire-state-by-susan-shepler/.

Sherif, Abu. 2008. "Reintegration of Female War-Affected and Ex-combatants in Liberia." *Accord: Conflict Trends* 3: 26–33.

Specht, Irma. 2006. *Red Shoes: Experiences of Girl-Combatants in Liberia*. Geneva: International Labour Office. https://www.ilo.org/wcmsp5/groups/public/---ed_emp/---emp_ent/---ifp_crisis/documents/publication/wcms_116435.pdf.

Sriram, Chandra Lekha, John C. King, Julie A. Mertus, Olga Martin-Ortega, and Johanna Herman, eds. 2009. *Surviving Field Research: Working in Violent and Difficult Situations*, New York: Routledge.

Tamagnini, Andrea. 2009. "End-of-Assignment Report." October 1. Monrovia: United Nations Mission in Liberia, United Nations Peacekeeping.

Themnér, Anders. 2011. *Violence in Post-conflict Societies: Remarginalization, Remobilizers and Relationships*. New York: Routledge.

Truth and Reconciliation Commission of Liberia. 2009. *Consolidated Final Report*. Ghana: Twidan Grafix.

United Nations Disarmament, Demobilization and Reintegration Resource Centre. 2014. *Operational Guide to the Integrated Disarmament, Demobilization and Reintegration Standards*. United Nations. https://www.unddr.org/uploads/documents /Operational%20Guide.pdf.

United Nations General Assembly. 2006. "Disarmament, Demobilization, and Reintegration: Report of the Secretary General." A/60/705. March 2. https://digitallibrary .un.org/record/571084.

United Nations Mission in Liberia. 2006. *Human Rights in Liberia's Rubber Plantations: Tapping into the Future*. May. https://www.refworld.org/docid/473dade10.html.

———. n.d. "Closure of UNMIL." Accessed on October 30, 2019. https://unmil .unmissions.org/background.

United Nations Security Council. 1995. "Abuja Agreement." S/1995/742. August 28. https://peacemaker.un.org/sites/peacemaker.un.org/files/LR_950819 _AbujaAgreement.pdf.

UNMIL Today. 2009. "DDR Wraps Up." *Unmil Today* 6, no. 2: 1. https://reliefweb.int/sites /reliefweb.int/files/resources/AF6933E315639B274925761F00199484-Full_Report.pdf.

UN Office for Coordination of Humanitarian Affairs. 2002. "Liberia: Liberia Humanitarian Situation Report March 2002." *ReliefWeb Report*. http://reielfweb.int/report /liberia/liberia-humanitarian-situation-report-mar-2002 (site discontinued).

Utas, Mats. 2005. "Building a Future? The Reintegration and Remarginalisation of Youth in Liberia." In Richards 2005, 137–154.

———. 2008. *Liberia beyond the Blueprints: Poverty Reduction Strategy Papers, Big Men and Informal Networks*. Uppsala, Sweden: Nordic Africa Institute.

———. 2009. "Malignant Organisms: Continuities of State-Run Violence in Rural Liberia." In *Crisis of the State: War and Social Upheaval*, edited by Bruce Kapferer and Bjorn Enge Bertelsen, 265–291. New York: Berghahn Books.

———. 2012. "Liberia Post-election: On CDC Popularity and Odd Election Results." *Mats Utas*. April 5. http://matsutas.wordpress.com/2012/04/05/liberia-post-election -on-cdc-popularity-and-odd-election-results/.

Utas, Mats, and Magnus Jörgel. 2008. "The West Side Boys: Military Navigation in the Sierra Lone Civil War." *Journal of Modern African Studies* 46, no. 3: 487–511.

Utas, Mats, Mariam Persson, and Ilmari Käihkö. 2010. "Varning för Aftonbladets Jackass journalistik i 'det mörkaste Afrika.'" *Newsmill*, March 31. http://www.newsmill .se/artikel/2010/03/31/forskare-varning-for-aftonbladets-jackass-journalistik-i-det -morkaste-afrika (site discontinued).

Utas, Mats, Anders Themnér, and Emy Lindberg. 2014. "Commanders for Good and Bad: Alternative Post-war Reconstruction and Ex-commanders in Liberia." *Policy Note* 6. https://uu.diva-portal.org/smash/get/diva2:850360/FULLTEXT01.pdf.

VICE. 2010. *The VICE Guide to Liberia*. June 3. https://www.youtube.com/watch?v= ZRuSSoiiFyo.

Wood, Elisabeth Jean. 2006. "The Ethical Challenges of Field Research in Conflict Zones." *Qualitative Sociology* 29: 373–386.

INDEX

Milton Keynes UK
Ingram Content Group UK Ltd.
UKHW010236120224
437546UK00011B/162